Business Week's
Guide to Personal Business

Business Week's
Guide to Personal Business

JOSEPH L. WILTSEE

Personal Business Editor of *Business Week*
Member of the Ohio Bar

McGRAW-HILL BOOK COMPANY

New York   St. Louis   San Francisco   Düsseldorf   London
Mexico   Panama   Sydney   Toronto

Sponsoring Editors   M. Joseph Dooher/Dale L. Dutton
Director of Production   Stephen J. Boldish
Designer   Naomi Auerbach
Editing Supervisor   Karen Kesti
Editing and Production Staff   Gretlyn Blau,
   Teresa F. Leaden, George E. Oechsner

BUSINESS WEEK'S GUIDE TO PERSONAL BUSINESS

Personal Business Planning:
A Neglected Operation

Many a man who should know better—whose business or professional income is, say, $25,000 to $50,000 or more—treats his own personal business like a third cousin who turns up in town in search of a loan. He brushes off his private affairs. He lets them go hang.

This gent is apt to have a precariously balanced checkbook, top-heavy insurance coverage, a non-saving monthly budget (if any), a non-existent college financing plan for his kids, and a hodge-podge investment portfolio that is clearly the result of innumerable uncertain decisions. He buys a share of stock here, sells it there (often on the strength of somebody's luncheon table tip), digs up doubtful tax-saving ideas over cocktails, and sells bonds inherited from his parents to pay off debts—you name it.

Like as not, his career moves are haphazard, and he is burdened by extra-curricular business activities that take up far too many evenings. He lacks enough time for his wife and teenagers, and finds it hard to unearth a free day for his annual physical exam, much less a needed hour *every day* for physical exercise. If he is over 50, he worries about his sex life which he suspects could be better (it *could* be, if he would learn to uncoil after a taxing day). He puts off such things as dentistry, hernia repairs, foreign films, quick trips to Mexico with his wife (to celebrate important anniversaries), and Saturday ball games with his kids. When his golf clubs get their monthly workout, usually it's a hypertensive 18 holes with the boss. Or with a customer. As for home chores, his wife chides him because he hires people to do everything from paint gutters and fix screens to trim backyard trees and shrubs. In truth, he would *like* to put on old pants and do these chores, and raise tomato plants, too.

At times, feelings of guilt get him down. When this happens, he takes the whole family to an overpriced resort for a long weekend but finds the routine a strain because he can't really afford the expense (true) or the time (he thinks). While away on such weekend junkets, he discovers that thoughts of Monday morning creep into his mind, without fail. This begins on Saturday along about 2 P.M. In fact, Monday morning invades his thoughts *most* weekends, no matter where he is.

He works for a competitive company or in a similar uptight situation where the pressure to survive as a manager is greater than it need be. The pressure, though, *isn't* as great as he imagines. He blows hot as a pistol for the company all day and keeps on firing like a capgun in his off hours. He burns up a week's worth of energy in the course of two days at the office, but spends barely two days a year (if that much) in attending to his own personal finances. He lets them happen.

Too much is never too much. He takes two weeks' vacation each summer instead of a possible four and even splits the two weeks to quickly duck back into the office to do some work (or fret over some work) that could and *should* be done by others. No wonder he has a third martini when two should do!

He is on a corporate ladder, and this is true even if he works for a college or hospital as a middle-line administrator. He is riding an escalator that may boost him to his level of expectations. It just may. In the process, though, it may leave him high but rather dry. With it all, he is decent and sincere and his abilities, though strained, are somewhat above average. His solace — and he clings to it for dear life — is the fact that he makes good money. The trouble is, he fails to cling to any of the money. At least, this is one of his problems and the one most emphasized in these pages.

To compress this type of profile into a few lines is hard because the case is classic. And if the profile appears to be strained and unhappy, so be it. ("He" — whoever he is — is a bit strained and unhappy, too.) Be that as it may, the whole picture sizes up parts and pieces of the lives of many men these days, even if the shading is a little on the harsh side.

The fact is that the habit of mismanaging or *non*-managing personal affairs is prevalent among people who are intelligent, hard-working, and successful. No man should feel alone in this, though it is a question of degree. It comes in bunches and, like the tax form 1040 in April, is everywhere. It can be estimated that neglect of personal finances, especially — to one extent or another — is a well-established fact of life among a good 50% of all "junior" executives. This means any college grad who is in business, aggressive, and the owner of at least two $25 shirt-and-tie combinations. And the habit *sticks* through the years as the junior man works his way up the line and one day makes the grade as a top-rank manager.

Take a simple case. There is a good argument for periodically updating one's will, assuming a will has been written in the first place. An old will should be taken out of its box and dusted off in a lawyer's office every now and again (some say every five years). This is in view of any number of changing circumstances that can make a will obsolete — but the reviewing can be done quickly and cheaply ($25 to $50 is par). It holds true for young married couples who have little property, but have children. But this relatively simple chore is widely neglected and probably causes half of all serious estate foulups that in turn cause so much grief and added expense for families. As with a written will, a higher-income businessman or professional needs to review periodically all his front-line personal business affairs. He needs to revise and rework his plans, financial and otherwise, to gain even an approach to maximum performance.

Obvious? Not really—if you judge by the year-in, year-out experience of top advisers who make a living unwinding the knots in peoples' private affairs. And though it may sound dull and laborious, the needed reviewing and updating *can* be done in a businesslike and workable way. It needn't become a fetish nor a total bore—after all, there is some pleasure in knowing that you are plastering your walls with something besides confetti, graffiti and receipted bills.

A man can become emotional and make a minor (or major) misery of his personal affairs planning—if he stews, frets, and worries in place of taking any action. But it's also possible to do the job with a minimum amount of strain and a remarkably small investment in terms of time and money.

Just how prevalent is the neglect of personal affairs planning? And what are the elements that go so neglected? If all Americans in the $25,000-and-up income brackets could be surveyed, the results would be shocking.

The following figures are estimates—but highly realistic estimates—based on over 1,000 interviews with (1) family lawyers, (2) accountants who regularly do family tax work, (3) bank trust department and investment advisory officers, (4) insurance consultants (non-sales), (5) stockbrokers and independent investment counselors, and (6) established real estate brokers and consultants:

A solid 25% of all businessmen and professionals in the $25,000-and-up range have no written wills at all. (An estate planning adviser at a leading New York bank thinks the figure is more like 35%, or even higher.) These are cases of rank procrastination, *not* ignorance or misinformation. Among the 75% who do have wills, only a small number—a third, at most—update their wills periodically. Says a Cincinnati lawyer whose clients include some of the town's most affluent families: "It usually takes a death or a divorce to get a man to bring in his will for checking, though there are many reasons for updating." A family lawyer in Buffalo, New York, notes that changes in state law alone frequently disrupt wills long outstanding. "We try to notify people for whom we've written wills, but sometimes you can't locate them—and sometimes they just won't bother, anyway."

Only about 10% of all $25,000-plus corporate executives have smartly designed estate plans that coordinate their company fringe benefits (pensions, profit sharing payoffs, deferred pay, insurance payoffs) with other property such as their houses and stock portfolios that will one day pass to their families under their wills. This gap in coordination is probably the most glaring mistake in the whole area of estate planning by executives. "It's a foolish and costly blunder—and it's *so* widespread," says New York City attorney and estate consultant Robert Brosterman.

As to basic estate planning, roughly 40% of the $25,000-plus group should be making at least some effort to cut down on the estate taxes that one day will have to be paid by their families. That is, 40% in this group have enough income now—and sufficient expectations in terms of more income or probable inheritance—to warrant giving some serious thought to the idea of saving estate taxes. This 40% should be taking advantage of devices that are—as of today—clearly built into the law. But of the 40% only a small number, a third, say (to be liberal), have made any effort whatsoever to cope with the tax, with or without the help of a family lawyer or other adviser. Shamefully ignored, for instance, is the fact that a lifetime gift plan—an easy-to-work, systematic program for giving property to the children *with safeguards*—is a highly profitable way for many families to sidestep the estate tax. (With, say, three children, a man and his wife can turn over—free from estate tax—$240,000 over a span of 10 years; and they can do it without incurring any gift tax along the way.)

Go a step ahead. Of those who do attempt estate tax saving, only about 50%, at most, make use of the smartest idea on the books for affluent families: the *trust.* It's true that the 1969 tax reform law dimmed some of the brighter facets of the trust. But still there are enough advantages remaining to lure a prosperous man into an adviser's office. *You can go further.* Of the small percentage of people who use some version of the trust, only a small percentage, in turn, use the "living trust" which is the type that carries with it the biggest benefits—in most cases, at least. The concept is simple: The property goes to the trustee (family member, lawyer, banker) today while the donor—the businessman or professional—is still alive. The property is managed as an investment, for income purposes and growth of principal, until the donor dies. It then is automatically distributed to the heirs of the donor—or is retained in trust for their benefit—according to the precise wishes of the donor as spelled out in the trust agreement. This distribution is made free of the complications of a formal written will—and this means free of the slow and often expensive probate procedure, the routine that family lawyers are accused of coddling and cherishing so persistently.

So, for long-range "estate planning", it comes to this: Of the $25,000-plus people who need it, just a fraction—maybe 10% maximum—get it, at least in any meaningful, organized way. And note: Only a third, at most, of those who should have estate planning actually ever get around to bring any sort of professional adviser *before* the husband becomes an entry on the obituary page. After that, it's too late.

Year-to-year personal business management suffers, too. Here the estimates of neglectfulness are equally as drab:

A maximum of 60% of those in the $25,000-plus range hire income tax men of any sort, from attorney-CPAs down to run-of-the-mill accountants. And no more than half of the 60% employ either lawyers or CPAs. So a majority of people in higher income brackets either handle their yearly tax work themselves or get something less than the best advice on the market.

About 40% of all $25,000-plus people who routinely invest in the stock market get their portfolio advice from brokers' registered "reps"—and go to no other source. A second 40% go a step ahead. They rely on registered reps, but in addition read various market "letters", and articles on investments in specialized magazines, financial publications, and books. Some do a reasonable job; others kill their time and money.

Only the remaining 20% go beyond this point, and seek out reliable investment information through study, investigation, and the use of advisers other than brokers. This means that just 20% of $25,000-plus income earners who invest in the market do what amounts to a smart job of probing and double-checking before they lay out their cash.

About 20% of the group, at most, take the trouble to seek some form of independent advice on life insurance. This means at least comparing policies offered by two or more competing insurance companies and discussing them with some skilled person other than the life insurance salesmen involved. The other 80% go along hook-line-and-sinker with the sales pitches, and buy on the basis of company reputation alone. And this is an outlay of bread-and-butter money that deserves some investigation and, hopefully, just a bit of ordinary buyer's skepticism.

No more than 10% of the $25,000-plus group hire independent real estate appraisers before buying standing houses in the $40,000-and-up range. The vast majority, again, buy without any real amount of investigation and are safeguarded mostly by the prudence of banks and other mortgage lenders. And this is another area where the salesmanship is as pitch-laden as you can find anyplace.

As for checking the references of contractors and home remodelers before they are hired—this can be put down at 10% maximum, too, among people in the $25,000-plus brackets.

Only about 40% of the income group—with teen-agers in junior and senior high school—carry out any sort of reasonable college financing scheme. This includes everything from smart short-term trust arrangements to the simplest form of bank savings plan. The other 60% simply let college funds develop out of last-minute desperation—and one way or another this generally means some form of borrowing at high cost.

The annual physical exam? Despite all the justified propaganda in favor of the yearly health check, and the fact that many large and medium-sized companies offer their executives this service gratis, only around 30 to 40% of businessmen and professionals in the $25,000-plus income range take the trouble to have thorough exams each year. Here is a rule of thumb offered by a leading physician who specializes in the annual physical: "Of every 100 men over age 40 who have executive-level incomes," he says, "one-third have exams every year, one-third every three to five years, and one-third get the 'physical' only when hospitalized or warned by their physicians. For them, it is sometimes too late."

Why do so many businessmen, executives, and professionals persistently neglect their important personal affairs? Several answers can be ticked off, some apparent and some not:

One reason is the overpowering volume of "advice" and hucksterism that surrounds everyone these days. A man goes to his office in the morning and finds the mail packed with market tip sheets and invitations to everything from wine-tasting events (strictly commercial) to sauna equipment showings. He scans the tip sheets, throws the rest in his waste basket, and hopes that his broker won't phone at 10:45—but he does. At lunch, a friend offers him a choice: (1) a way to make money on raw land, or (2) a way to lose money on a prefab summer cottage at the shore. At 3:00, his friendly insurance man phones for the fifth time in two weeks asking for an appointment, and at 4:00 a girl comes in offering a part-time secretarial service for businessmen who work late. At home in the evening, he finds his second pile of junk mail for the day, with offers covering everything from cars with built-in radar and $100 non-skid tires to revealing books on how to keep middleage sex life from collapsing. He sees more new-style hair pieces advertised in the evening paper, and more ads in the financial press selling one-shot personal finance services to VIPs.

Before bed he turns off the TV in the middle of a commercial and realizes that he is engulfed by sellers, pushers, and hucksters. He is surrounded by people who want to tell him how to run his life, but whose main interest appears to be—indeed *is*—in planning their own financial security.

The quality of so-called professional advice is weak, too. Much of it has a built-in smugness that covers up abilities that are wafer thin. If you run through the list of "advisers"—from brokers to art consultants to lawyers—you will find a surprising lack of solid reliability all along the line. And the second-raters appear to be in a state of aggressive multiplication, year to year. The ill-qualified "pro" has become a glut on the market.

No group of self-styled professionals is immune. Lawyers start out with the needed equipment—the tools of their trade. But if a man started 20 or 30 years back and has since been asleep, his preachments might be reduced to 50% hot air and 50% cut-and-dried palaver. His work may be routine stuff, at best, no matter how honest a man he happens to be. Even the law changes with time, and unhappily the lawyer who is behind the times is no rare bird.

Or, take independent investment counselors. They lay claim to professional status. But what does this mean if the field lacks meaningful licensing standards? It means little. Real estate brokers too frequently sell houses by playing on peoples' fears and false hopes; and the brokers all too often know more about how to apply slick soft-sell psychology than how to apply an honest sales pitch to an honest product. Job consultants frequently charge fees of from $1,000 to as high as $3,000—for nothing more than artful hand-holding.

Travel agents "sell" trips the way Nathan's sells hot dogs at Times Square, but frequently the product isn't nearly so savory or beneficial. There is the travel agent—and he isn't rare—who wouldn't know the difference between the Ajax hotel in Cincinnati and the Savoy in London if both lobbies fell on his head. Yet this gent will market expensive "package" travel to Europe, complete with reams of picked-up brochure advice on lodgings, restaurants, and sight-seeing. In the process, his whole sales spiel will carefully bypass the fact that *his* last trip abroad was before the airlines had jets.

So it goes, down the line of "professional" advisers, from honest-but-tired bank trust officers to gabby car salesmen to building contractors who lose little money on cracked lumber. In such a setting, the victimized man in the middle is apt to do just what might be expected. That is, he will turn off *all* advisers, good and bad—or as many as possible—and handle his own affairs in his own way. But turning a deaf ear frequently leads to procrastination and neglect.

Then there is the question of job demand. It may be stating the obvious, but most businessmen, especially corporate executives —and some fast-moving professionals—operate under considerable career pressure. And despite what junior executives think of the men on top, this pressure is something that doesn't let up a bit as a man climbs higher on the ladder. The truth? The truth is that the first-rate manager in business, especially, isn't under stress by pure chance or misfortune. He *asks* for it. He *needs* it to make the grade at his work. He even needs it to be happy. And if he doesn't *need* it—yes, he is a square peg in the wrong office.

Many men can, of course, adjust to even the tightest office grind without letting it cut too sharply into their personal lives. They are able to carry on at least a minimum or reasonable routine of personal affairs planning. But many others are forced to let their affairs slide.

There also is a marriage pattern that trips up quite a few executive and professional types. It stems from early housekeeping days. A lot of young junior executives, for instance, intent on forging ahead in business, get into the easy habit of turning over all of their bill-paying chores to their wives. Many eventually turn over their paychecks, too. And finally, for some, the whole domestic dollar routine winds up in feminine hands. This often breaks the back of a man's natural yen to labor with his own finances, tax returns, and other dollar-and-doughnut chores. After a while such a man gets psychologically out of tune with the whole idea of self-management. His wife will see that the bills get paid, but she's hardly planning-minded.

But psychology aside, there is another very practical reason why a man may sidestep his own affairs. It's the false notion that really top-grade planning takes high-powered advice, and that this type of counseling—if available at all—costs a considerable outlay of cash each year. It's something that is reserved for the $50,000 or $100,000 man. This is nonsense.

The basics of long-range estate and financial planning, and year-to-year dollar planning, for the most part can be gleaned by reading and digesting a few chapters in a book. A Washington, D.C., tax lawyer and CPA says this: "There is no mysterious package of magic that will cut your taxes, conserve your income, create your estate plan, streamline your insurance, shave your expenses, and put eggs in your beer. Rich people get that way just by adding together a number of small points that make good common sense—and they add them up one at a time." The small points, he notes, can be summed up in a few pages that cost no more than a fifth of bourbon.

Moreover, the cost of *executing* a personal affairs "plan" is no heavy burden. For example, a man in the $25,000 to $35,000 income range might figure that $5 a week or $250 a year, on average, will pay for the management of his personal business. Mainly this means money spent for lawyers, tax men, and such occasional helpers as real estate appraisers. The cost of a needed publication or two surely might be tossed in for good measure.

The 1040 man alone—if he knows his way around taxes—will likely save such a client at least 50% of the $250 laid out for the year, and he may come up with far greater savings. And do it legitimately! This is not to mention long-range advice on tax planning which might one day save the family a small fortune.

In terms of time, one hour a week will usually do the job. This is of course, about 55 minutes more than the average man spends on his personal affairs planning and managing. So it comes to $250 a year—subject to a tax offset—and 50 hours a year. This is quite a bargain, even if the total proposition *is* oversimplified!

Thus the truth is that the fast-stepping junior executive, with shining morning face and bulging briefcase—rushing off to the office in anticipation of big money some day—can easily pick up the sharpest ideas for personal betterment on the market. And he can do it without sacrificing the purchase of a new bikini for his bride or playpen for his two-year-old. Surely, if the junior exec can garner such beneficial wisdom so easily, so can the higher bracket man who has been around for another 15 or 20 years.

To clear a point: It isn't only the $25,000 man who tends to sidestep his own financial and related planning. The habit hits $50,000-and-up people, too. There's many a senior executive who persistently fails to do this basic job. Often he is a man who has stepped up into higher income rapidly, without too much pausing for breath. It is a case of having the income and not knowing quite how to handle it.

In a word, it takes a bit of practice to *own* money and property —just as it does to earn it.

Contents

PART ONE

Dollars

ONE

Investments: How Not
to Lose Your Shirt

It's one thing to self-insure and act as your own investment adviser with just a small sum riding in the stock market. It's another thing to try this risky business when you have all your shirt and sock money tied up in securities. One rule of thumb says that a businessman or professional with $25,000 or $50,000 or more invested in a mixed securities portfolio needs to spend an hour a day acting as his own portfolio supervisor—if he expects to take full advantage of all chances that the stock market offers. This holds true if a portfolio is what it should be: a package plan for maximum benefit. So goes the rule of thumb.

The hour-a-day rule is overblown, of course. A conservative

3

investor might get by with an hour a week. But ask yourself: Have you an hour a week to spend sweating over your investments, let alone an hour a day? And even if you have the time— do you know just what kind of sweating to do? Do you know enough about Wall Street? Many professional advisers don't know enough, and you'll save many a dollar if you merely keep this basic fact in mind.

So it's smart to review the sources of investment advice. And there is no better place to start than at the door of the brokerage house. Behind this door lurks a lot of possible benefit—and a lot of possible trouble. But keep a balanced view.

Don't cuss your broker for everything

One of the top sports these days is cuss-your-broker. "There are plenty of investors who, when they do well, go to lunch and boast about their own acumen," says one Wall Street pro. "But when they do badly, they go to the broker's office and raise hell."

But before bragging—or raising hell—an investor would be wise to set aside an hour or so for a probing review of his stockbroker relations. This is smart procedure even if you use your broker only occasionally for advice and information. And it makes lots of sense if you're fearful of your portfolio's performance in the coming year.

A key point to remember: It's not always the broker who's neglectful of the account—just as often it can be the investor. There are, of course, careless and incompetent registered representatives. Says the head of a large carriage-trade brokerage: "Every office has its 'churner'—the registered rep who will try to stir up buys and sells just for bigger commissions. It's the manager's job to spot him."

But some investors contribute to the "churning" of their own accounts. Do you? Those most likely to demand unneeded action, and suffer as a consequence, are investors who (1) persist in jumping from broker to broker and (2) those who have little experience in the market. For these, one point is essential: Take time to get a clear view of your investment objectives.

But relations with brokers can turn sour even for those who believe they have a clear notion of their aims in the market. Some who have been in the market for years will fail to tell their brokers of changing goals for investment—caused perhaps by a death, marriage, or inheritance.

Others can easily confuse their brokers. "A blue-chip man will get restive and want to take a flyer or two," says one brokerage house manager. "After a while the rep won't know where his client wants to go." For this breed, one piece of advice is: Set aside 10 or 15% of your account for flyers—and make sure your broker clearly understands this.

More damning of brokers arises because the market's rumor mills have been grinding faster than ever in the last few years. "Rumors are running double what they were 10 years ago." says a broker. "People seem more tip-prone than ever. They'll ask a rep for information on a stock—and then ignore it." Some investors even fail to cash in on a tip smartly. A typical case: jumping on a hot stock, then holding too long. One way to avoid this mistake is to phone your broker the day after the buy is made, instead of the week after.

Note: In a general review of your broker relations, let your registered rep know what you're reading in the way of market information. Some market and investment letters remain a menace despite efforts by the SEC to curb their publishers. If you lack this kind of confidence in your broker—then maybe you need a new man.

As an investor, you have a basic responsibility that can't be delegated: knowing what's going on. This theme is pushed hard by informed Wall Street people. Says an ex-executive in a top brokerage house: "If you have, for example, $50,000 in a mixed portfolio, and can't spend a minimum amount of time studying the market—you shouldn't have an account with a broker." You should, he adds, have a good portfolio manager, or a mutual fund.

Some suggestions for the investor: (1) Read not just annual reports, but interim ones, plus company surveys by Standard & Poor's and Moody's; (2) meet with your registered rep at least monthly to fix instructions; (3) before taking an extended trip, give the broker your itinerary plus any needed "open order" (to buy or sell at a price); (4) acquaint your wife with your plans.

Besides executing orders efficiently, a good broker will keep you informed—and look on this as a vital part of his job. He'll phone you (even overseas) if you are a good customer and an event occurs that may shake one of your companies. "He should do this *without* instructions," says a brokerage executive.

As to churning (which you yourself can spot by comparing your dollar performance over, say, six months with what you would have done with no trades), some brokerage executives, in effect, say *caveat emptor*. Some also admit that firms often find it hard to police their own men.

If a general review puts you to seeking a new broker, remember that picking the firm isn't hard; you're safe with a well-established house. The real problem is picking your registered rep. The manager, or partner, will suggest a man—but nobody can screen him for you. *Suggestion:* When finally you find a registered rep you like (a man who suits your ideas and who appears to have just a minimum of churn in his blood), be *sure* of him by placing just small transactions with him—and tell him candidly that you are going to do this. If he proves out over a span of, say, six months, up your ante and give him more and bigger business.

Apart from churning, some registered reps fail to take advantage of the research facilities of their own firms. They tend to go off in directions of their own. Guard against this—unless you find a rep who's a genius.

**Latching onto the wholly
"independent" man**

Suppose that you've given up on brokers as a source of information and advice, and have decided to use your registered rep as an order-taker and nothing more. A logical step is to seek an "independent" investment counselor—meaning a firm that has no ties to banks, brokerages, or such, and that operates (hopefully) on a totally objective basis. This can be a smart step. It can also be a hard one.

There are over 200 SEC-registered independents around the country that sell only advice and often portfolio management—plus at least 300 more that are so small that they aren't required to register. It's a wide-open field in which professional competence varies like the hues of a rainbow.

True, you don't look for size alone. Some one-man shops are A-1, and this type of operation might suit your investment objectives. But in your search—at least as a first step—you might prudently let size and established reputation in the field set your course.

In any case, make finding a counselor a project. Why not take, say, six months, and maybe place your money at a safe 6% in the meantime? And the question may be, when you've found your independent adviser—will you follow his advice? Some people pay for it, then resist it. Complete investigation of the adviser helps avoid the problem. With more confidence in your man, you feel more like listening to what he says.

You might follow this procedure: Go first to a leading national firm such as Scudder, Stevens & Clark, Loomis-Sayles, Stein Roe & Farnham, Brundage, Story & Rose, Naess & Thomas, or T. Rowe Price. The idea, of course, is to shop at these addresses to see how they evaluate your investment needs. If you've never gone this route before, you're likely to find the array of services and facilities impressive.

Note: Some of these firms operate no-load (no sales commission) mutual funds. But the fact that a firm handling individual accounts also has a large pool account needn't pose a conflict-of-interest question.

You may, of course, find the berth you want with one of the bigger houses. If not, then take the second step: Check a list of several smaller regional firms in your area. You can get a partial listing by writing to the Investment Counsel Association of

America, 49 Park Avenue, New York, N.Y. To locate others—
including the little known but sometimes brilliant one-man
operation—talk with your banker, broker, and lawyer. If you
press the point, and make it amply clear that you want a small
independent instead of a more conventional source—you'll find
him.

In dealing with any counseling firm, first get across your
personal objectives. The counseling of the leading firms falls
into a fairly standard pattern. You can get just about whatever
you require. If you want income, they'll plan it; if you want
growth, they'll plan that. But with a small firm, you run into
investment viewpoints that vary as widely as men's suits—from
solid conservative to unbridled flamboyance. So you have to
put more stress on the *firm's qualities,* and this may well take
considerable searching around.

It's a case of making sure that the firm's competence—and
mode of operation—will satisfy your individual demands as an
investor. A shaky or deflated stock market makes your search
harder, of course—it's easy for a counselor to ride high in a bull
market. But not so if even the blue chips are down.

Getting a firm idea of any counselor's basic approach to investment may not be easy. The danger is that you'll wind up
talking generalities. But you can avoid this by pinning down
some hard questions and answers. Find out, especially, what
positions were taken in the market at certain critical points—
for example, during the early 1966 market peak, and, of course,
during the big drop that began early in 1970. It's a question of
getting answers, and making some comparisons.

There is pure counseling, where you merely buy advice, but
the trend today is to full portfolio management—where the
adviser deals with the broker and handles all transactions,
sometimes under a limited power of attorney from the client.
Standard account minimums at the large national firms range
from $200,000 to $300,000, much less at smaller regional firms.
The customary annual fee (though this is subject to variation)
is ½ of 1% of portfolio market value. A new trend: $50,000 mini-
mum accounts, with a ¾ of 1% annual fee.

Look to banks for help with stocks

You might also take a look at what the big-city banks are offering these days in the way of investment services. You may be surprised. In operating their "investment advisory" or "portfolio management" departments, the leading, progressive banks have left the old widow-and-orphan philosophy of "safe" investment far behind. Pretty far, anyway.

The fixed-income approach is still part of the banks' package. But also available is advice on all-common-stock portfolios. And there is much that lies between. It's true, of course—and doubtless, always will be—that if you're a speculator, you may as well forget about going to a bank. Indeed, the banks steer clear of clients who want to duck in and out of the market fast. The quick killing based on "inside" tips isn't in the banker's bailiwick. It is also true that typically even a top bank's advisory personnel hasn't the glamour profile that can be found elsewhere.

But the *progressive* banks are now a lot more interested in meeting the competition. This means tailoring advice to suit the individual. Ten or fifteen years ago, even the progressives tended to recommend portfolios of common stocks that spread over the broadest possible spectrum of the economy. The idea was safety in numbers, through diversification. But in recent years, there has been a change. The forward-thinking banks have been leading clients into faster-moving stock groups.

Today they want to serve not only the conservative man, but also the man who sets his sights on outperforming the market averages. *And note:* On balance the top banks' performance for clients has been steadily improving—though, of course, the big 1970 slump hit the bank advisers along with everybody else.

The banks, of course, claim their investment advice is best, and it's true that the big-city "name" banks maintain sizable research staffs, and have wide commercial connections in the U.S. and abroad. At a smaller regional bank, however, you will be on narrower ground. This is a point to check carefully. Some regional banks do a superior job, of course; others just ladle out second-hand information and advice on investments.

So much for philosophy. The fee you pay for a bank's investment advisory service will depend somewhat on where you keep your account. In New York and other major cities, the cost is about ½ of 1% on the first $500,000. In smaller cities in the Midwest and South the fees run about 20% less.

As to minimum account size, some New York banks require $200,000 or more. But this varies greatly. A leading Cincinnati bank—typical of the Midwest—has a $50,000 minimum. Some banks take even smaller amounts, but may charge more for the service—say, ¾ of 1% instead of ½ of 1%.

Investment advisory service at a bank includes "custody," or routine portfolio handling. However, you can get this service alone, just for convenience.

A rising number of well-heeled Wall Street clients have been hiring banks to do their portfolio housekeeping chores. Chase Manhattan, U.S. Trust Co., and other top banks report the trend. What's more, some brokers have even been sending occasional clients to the banks—because sometimes they would as soon avoid the paperwork.

The bank's trust department will hold your stocks and bonds, collect dividends and interest, and keep you informed of stock rights, tender offers, and mergers that affect your holdings. It will collect stock-dividend and stock-split shares and the proceeds of matured and called bonds.

The bank handles securities that you buy or sell, and it pays or collects accordingly. Finally, it sends you a monthly or quarterly statement, and some banks—for an added fee—send a year-end statement complete enough to file with your 1040 form in April.

You can even get "family financial accounting" if your portfolio is large enough. This means that the bank keeps all cash accounts for you, pays your bills, and so on. This service can make sense, say, for a man who is retired and travels widely.

Despite all these chores that the bank handles, "custody" is strictly a non-advisory service. You continue normal relations with your broker. He still takes direct instructions, handles your orders, and gets his regular commissions. The bank doesn't enter into your investment decisions at all.

For these housekeeping tasks, the bank's fee is fairly low. The yearly charge generally comes to about 0.1% of the current market value of your portfolio—and the fee is tax deductible.

What about self-help? Suppose that you are determined to manage your own portfolio of securities and decide that, after all, you have that one hour a day—or one hour a week—to devote to sweating and straining over your investments. You intend to do some reading up on your own—and to keep up. You will then assemble the comments of brokers, bankers, consultants, friends, tipsters, etc., and will decide for yourself precisely where you will go in the stockmarket, and when and how.

Investing by plan—not patchwork

The decision that self-help will be your modus operandi means that several basic (and sometimes tedious) techniques must be followed. For instance, there is a procedure that sounds deathly dull and elementary: portfolio review. But it's a must, and it must be done periodically if you're to end up with anything close to maximum performance.

Look at your list of securities. If you're like most investors, you will find that you need updating more than you had realized. So get down to grubby fundamentals—and start by tracing your own investor profile. Do two things: First, analyze what you hold in the market in relation to your middle-range and long-range goals. If this means resetting sights on these goals, then you have some serious self-searching to do. Second, get a clear reading on any propensity you have for pushing too hard for quick, unrealistic short-term profits *or* listening too much to tips instead of solid research. Take three typical portfolio cases:

▪ The conservative-minded businessman: This middle-aged gent has been in the stockmarket for years. Through thick and thin he sticks with a list of blue-chip stocks that were movers perhaps 10 or 15 or 20 years ago. They're not just solid — they are stiff. Today they produce very little in the way of annual growth, though the income from them is livable. They are safe — and you can't say much more. It's just possible, too, that they may not continue to be safe in years to come.

What is frequently needed here are some issues that in the normal range of expectation will produce annual growth of, say, 10 or 15%. Such issues must be bought with middle-range and long-range objectives in mind — even if the short-range result seems uncertain. This may mean a painful and major shift in investments for this stockholder. Or it may mean a partial updating of his portfolio. At the very least, it means a rethinking of overly conservative investment attitudes.

- The would-be speculator: This family man isn't really a true speculator. He lacks the nerve and the horse-race psychology — but he likes to play at the game nonetheless and is inclined to overload his portfolio with too many $5 flyers. The flyers — mostly over-the-counter stocks — should take up, say, 5 or 10% of his holdings, not 30 or 40% or more. He may need a shift in investments, too — in the opposite direction. In any case, he needs some sensible self-examination and more information. The typical flyer, for instance, has about a 1% chance of continuing a high growth rate over a 10-year span, and less than a 25% chance of still being in business at all. The would-be speculator's answer, of course, is that he has no notion of holding his $5 buys for even one year, much less 10 years. The big trouble is that he keeps missing the runway with his flyers. The flyer that's great for two months, he holds for three; the one that goes like blazes for six months, he holds for a year. He needs to know what flying in the market is all about — or else settle down.

- The mutual fund candidate: Sometimes a man will be playing it very safe with such investments as, say, 1987–92 4¼% treasury bonds — maybe inherited from his dear departed rich uncle. He stays with the bonds largely out of fear of the stockmarket. This gent isn't a conservative investor. He's just not an investor at all. Since he obviously couldn't handle a conventional account himself—even with the aid of a broker or other adviser—he might be pegged as a mutual fund candidate. He requires some kind of specific plan of action that will take him out of the bonds—or at least part way out. He shouldn't be scared off by weak mutual fund performance (reflecting the state of the market) *or* by the fact that most funds charge an 8% load. This gent needs equity.

There are other portfolio types as well. The question is: Where do *you* fit in? What's your profile as an investor? Whether you go it alone, acting as your own investment manager—or work closely with an adviser—you need this answer. Says an old pro on Wall Street: "Once a man sees clearly his own 'profile,' he's in a position to formulate a plan based on his own true objectives—which is what most investors really need."

Reading up: The hardest part of self-help is getting started. One good way is to dig into three or four specialized books on investments. Some good ones are listed at the end of this chapter.

A yardstick for your own stock deals

Another "must"—once you're past the casual-investor stage—is to be able to chart your own performance in the market. Far too many people neglect this. They know only whether they're up or down, making or losing money, on paper. But they *don't* really know precisely how much, and many would miss the mark by a far cry if pressed for an answer.

If you feel that you need a working track record, there is a way to set up your own simple—but informative—personal performance index. It will help you know (1) exactly where you stand on paper, (2) whether your research—or advice—has been good, bad, or indifferent, and (3) whether your portfolio needs more work, time, and personal attention.

To set up an index, you first add the current market values of the various securities in your portfolio. Then you divide this total by an arbitrarily chosen divisor, say 100. This gives you a base index, a starting point.

Say your portfolio totals $100,000; if your divisor is 100, your base index becomes 1,000. A simple chart based on 1,000 units can be used to trace progress. If your 200 shares of XYZ Corporation go up $10 in a week, the new reading on your index is 1,020 ($102,000 divided by 100). That's a 2% gain—over and above your original $100,000 portfolio value.

The divisor (100) stays the same until you liquidate part of your holdings, or invest more money. When this happens, you adjust the original divisor. If you add $20,000 to your $100,000 portfolio, the new divisor (x) would be $100/x = \$100,000/120,000$. Or, by cross-multiplying, 120. So you divide your new total investment by 120 and this keeps your base index at 1,000. No matter how your total investment in the market may change, you retain the same base index from which to judge your performance.

The fun comes when you measure your market performance against some of the established indexes, such as the Dow-Jones average of industrial common stocks, or Standard & Poor's average based on 500 commons (the latter is more revealing since it's broadly based).

You'll get a more realistic comparison when you pit your personal index against those of top professional investors. To beat the Dow is one thing; to beat the best-performing mutual funds quite another. You can obtain figures on funds through your broker, or from *Fundscope* magazine (1900 Avenue of the Stars, Los Angeles, Calif.).

When you try comparing your investment performance with those of the professionals, you'll find that you can make firmer judgments about your own research and the sources of your advice and shape of your portfolio. But you'll also come up sharply against the question: Just what are you hoping to do in the market? The whole exercise will probably help you to keep your objectives fixed more firmly in mind.

Tax note: Keep accurate records of all buys and sells in the market. Among other things, they help in filing a clean tax form 1040, and even may keep you from selling something held 5½ months, just short of the capital gains starting point.

**Take it easy when selling for a
tax loss**

The techniques of investments fill volumes. Here is a capsule review of some of the more widely used methods, starting with year-end tax selling.

The tax selling idea, of course, is to take a paper loss by selling and then use it to offset capital gains taken earlier in the year. Or, conversely, you can take gains to offset earlier losses. Either way it's a tax saver. But either way it can also be a considerable abuse of assets. "It's usually foolish to tear into your portfolio for tax reasons alone," says a Wall Street adviser, "but many people do." So plan ahead before you make a year-end sale.

Let's say that you want to take a tax loss, but you're uncertain about what to do with the money from the sale. One option is to wait out the market. Say that you have realized $20,000 or more. You might go temporarily into U.S. Treasury bills. Or perhaps you'll buy short-term commercial paper (corporate notes).

Or take a reverse tack. Sometimes people know where to invest the money from a tax sale, but forget to plan for short-term cash needs—such as taxes. Perhaps you have used the total proceeds of your tax sale to buy a quality stock. You could get caught in a bind next April 15, assuming you still owe a big tax bill. This gets sticky if you have sold off your weak stocks for losses and have to sell a quality issue to pay Internal Revenue—especially if the quality stock happens to be low at the time. Holding back some cash from the tax-loss sale to put into Treasury bills or other short-term investments might be a smart pre-April tax ploy to keep in mind.

Some investors also get tripped up by the liberal carry-over rule. It lets you take a tax loss of any size, even if it can't be used currently—and carry it over indefinitely until it's used up. "It's too much of a lure for some people," says an old pro. "They dig too deeply into worthwhile stocks, hoping to come up with losses." This, he adds, is the height of getting carried away by tax motivations.

Excesses aside, though, you can rack up some profits with year-end tax sales. Given the proper time, here's what you can do: You can make a loss sale by December 31 to offset capital gains. You use the loss to offset up to $1,000 of ordinary income, and then carry the rest forward into future tax years. In the "reverse" offset, you can take paper profits by, say, December 23 (to adhere to a new five-day trading rule), and offset them against losses taken earlier in the year.

The reverse offset has lately become more popular. And note: When selling for a gain, you can buy back the same stock the same day if you want to—and not worry about the 31-day wash-sale rule that erases the tax deduction if you act in the meantime.

You can maintain your original position in a stock when making a loss sale if you do a bit of juggling.

One way is to "double up" in November—that is, buy a like number of shares of the same stock—then wait 31 days (to clear the strict wash-sale rule), and sell to take the loss before the end of the year.

Or, of course, you can take the loss by December 31, then wait 31 days to buy back. Doubling up before year's end is the surer method; people who resolve to wait the required time and buy back usually get itchy and end up buying something else, often not as good as the original stock.

A third popular method of juggling—promoted by many brokers—is to switch into a similar stock in the same industry, using a list of "paired" stocks furnished by the broker. Some pros, though, caution against getting needlessly locked into a single industry.

If you work it right, you can freeze a profit—or loss—and postpone the tax result until the following year. If you want to fix your paper profit in a stock but avoid paying the capital gains tax next April, you simply sell short (sell shares borrowed from a broker), and in January deliver your original shares in payment. The gain on the late-year short sale becomes next year's income.

Caution: There is a possible drawback in freezing your present level of profit. If the stock nosedives, your result is fine—but if it zooms, you miss out.

The pros point out that stocks that decline throughout the year may, by and large, be in even deeper depression in early December. So you might wisely plan on selling earlier—in November—and beat the doldrums in prices caused by late-rush tax-sellers.

1040 woes: investors' deductions

Speaking of taxes in relation to handling a portfolio, there's much confusion in the average stockholder's mind over the question of investment-related tax deductions. A 1970 federal court case, for instance, points up the frequently forgotten rule that if you spend money to inspect a *possible* investment—as opposed to one you already own—you cannot deduct the expense. In this case, the taxpayer tried to deduct his travel expenses. All he could do, it turns out, was to add these items to his *cost basis*—if and when he actually paid his money to make the investment.

It's understood that you can deduct the cost of a safe deposit box—but you can go further. Fees for investment advice are deductible, and this is true whether you pay for counseling alone or full portfolio management. State taxes on a stock sale are deductible—which some people miss.

Not only can you deduct the cost of travel to inspect investment property you own—assuming you have a valid business purpose—there are also some occasions when you can deduct for travel to an annual meeting of a company in which you own a sizable share. This, though, is a gray area; you should be able to prove that the trip was necessary—not just an outing.

A pitfall: IRS will clamp down fast if it discovers that you are deducting brokers' commissions or any expenses related to tax-exempt bonds.

For a good, straightforward review of most types of deductions see *J. K. Lasser's Your Income Tax,* by Bernard Greisman (Simon & Schuster).

Stock splits and dividends

Stock splits—and dividends paid in stock instead of in cash—are another tax-related portfolio problem. Each year a rash of new splits is announced, usually during the annual corporate-meeting "season" in early springtime.

First, note that the tax rules are exactly the same for splits and stock dividends. In both cases, generally, you pay no tax simply for picking up the added shares. And you needn't report the deal on your 1040. But there's one exception—and it's rare: If you have a choice of either cash or stock, you pay tax—even if you decide to take the shares.

When you *sell* split or dividend shares, you have to figure your cost basis to arrive at taxable profit. Here's how: When you pick up the same class of shares, say, common on common, simply divide your new total number of shares into the original cost of your old shares. This gives you the adjusted cost basis per share.

When you pick up a different class of stock, it's trickier. For example, say you originally paid $10,000 for 100 common. You now get 20 preferred as a tax-free dividend. Ex-dividend, the common is worth $150, the preferred $250. Thus, your 100 common are worth $15,000, and the 20 preferred $5,000—total $20,000. To get the cost basis, allocate in the same ratio: that is, 75% of cost, or $7,500, to the 100 common, and 25%, or $2,500, to the 20 preferred.

Note: When you sell split or dividend shares, you get capital gains—25% maximum in 1970, up to 35% maximum starting in 1972—if you held your original shares over six months.

The rewards—and risks—in "going short"

Turn away from taxes to other accepted techniques, and take a look at "going short"—a major item in the stockmarket in some of the darkest bearish moments of 1970. When the market is headed down, even a prudent investor doesn't have to wait it out in hopes of better times. With some care and daring, he can go short if he's convinced that the prices of certain stocks will in the future hit new lows.

You go short—successfully—by selling borrowed shares and paying your debt later when the price of the stock has declined. You bet against the stock and thrive on someone's misfortune. Some investors question the morality of such deals. But an active investor may miss good chances for profits if he religiously refrains from short sales.

Here is what happens when you go short in a stock: Say you are convinced that XYZ stock—now at $50—will take a slide in the next three or four months. You borrow 500 shares of XYZ from your broker and put up, say, 80% of the value, or $20,000. Your broker immediately sells the 500 shares at $50, thus establishing for you an *actual sale* at that price. You pay the broker his usual commission on the sale, plus interest (currently about 10%) on the margin he has provided.

Thus you get advantage of the sale at $50, and owe your broker 500 shares of XYZ. If your prediction materializes and XYZ drops to, say, $30 in the next three months, you buy 500 shares at $30 and use them to pay off your $50 debt. The broker earns another commission on the purchase. And your profit on the whole deal comes to $10,000, less commissions and margin interest.

It sounds simple. But unless you're lucky, or quite skilled, you can get into real trouble by going short. As a safeguard, you can limit your possible loss when you go short by placing a stop order with your broker to buy the covering shares at a fixed price.

One obvious caution: When you buy a stock in the usual way— banking that it will go up—you can lose no more than your investment. But with a short sale there's no limit to your possible loss if the stock goes sky-high. If it goes *up,* you must pay that much more for shares with which to pay off your debt.

Timing is the critical element in selling short. And here the stock market chartists can help. Before you try a short sale, carefully study a stock's price and volume performance over the past year or two. This should give you a clue to the probable start of a price decline in that stock.

Also important is the basis for the decline. To be reasonably safe for shorting, the decline should grow out of some serious pressure on the stock. You must be sure that the drop isn't just a temporary reaction to overpricing, and that the basic flaw relating to the company hasn't already been discounted by the market.

One reason to go short in a stock is to pick up what can become a sizable tax break. Generally you do this when you already own the stock and make a short sale "against the box"—that is, you cover the short sale with your own original shares instead of buying new shares to cover.

Most commonly, you do this with a stock on which you have already made a gain—and at a time when you figure your investment is due for a decline. You establish your gain the moment you sell short: it's the difference between the purchase price of the original stock and the price at which you sell short. If the stock slides even below your original price, you're that much better off.

One big advantage here: Though you establish your gain when you go short, you owe no taxes on it until you complete the transaction by covering the borrowed stock. This can let you shift tax liabilities from one year to another, and—depending on your situation—big savings can result.

When you go short against the box, your gain will be either long-term or short-term, depending on how long you had held the stock as of the date of your short sale. *But note:* When you cover a short sale in the usual manner—by buying more shares to pay off—your gain is always short-term regardless of how long you stayed short or how long you owned a similar block of shares.

Puts and calls: maneuvering in the market

When the market lunges and plunges a la 1970, some of Wall Street's more arcane arts—such as puts and calls—take on fresh appeal. Depending on how you play them, put-and-call options on a stock let you engage in out-and-out speculation, or hedge your bets to a fine degree. Some people even play around with puts and calls on a theoretical basis; they get their fun out of doing the mathematics and don't put up money. But there's no doubt that maneuvering in the market with puts and calls can give you big leverage with little cash outlay.

When you buy a put, you get an option to sell a stock at a specific price within a fixed time limit. A call is the reverse: You get an option to buy. Beyond that come some weird combinations of puts and calls to which Wall Streeters give such names as straddles, spreads, strips, and straps. Says Larry Botts, one of the Street's leading put-and-call specialists: "The shame is that few investors really know the ins and outs. They might find some fascinating chances, especially in a volatile market."

The basic idea is simple. If you think the price of a stock will decline, you buy a put option that lets you sell the stock later at its current price. If you think the stock is going up, you purchase a call to buy at the current price before the option's expiration date. Thus you can speculate to pick up capital gains, to protect paper profits—or to limit a loss on a position you hold.

Puts and calls always cover a round lot of 100 shares, though you aren't limited to any fixed number of lots. The time of the option runs 30, 60, or 90 days, or six months plus 10 days, and some run to a year.

One lure is that the option takes less capital than buying the stock itself, and it offers a limited risk. The price of the put or call varies; it depends on the stock's price, the time element, and demand among buyers for options. Usually you pay 8% to 15% of the current market price of a 100-share lot.

For instance, if you buy a call for 15% of a stock's price and the stock rises 30%, you double your money upon exercising the option. If the stock collapses, you can lose no more than you paid for the call. *Note:* You don't even have to exercise the option to make a profit. You can simply resell your put or call and maybe get a tax break in the bargain.

Say you own XYZ stock and are convinced that it's going

down. You go to your own broker—or directly to a put-and-call broker—and buy a put. XYZ sells at $100; you buy the put for 90 days for perhaps $800, covering 100 shares—or 8% of the market price. You are guaranteed a buyer at $100 a share regardless of how the stock moves within the next 90 days.

Assume XYZ drops to $60. You then buy 100 shares at that price and exercise your option to sell them at $100. This brings a gross profit of $40 per share, or $4,000. Subtract the $800 cost of the put plus about $100 in commissions, and you have a net profit on the deal of $3,100. On the other hand, if your guess goes wrong and XYZ goes up, you can lose only $800.

If instead you had made a straight short sale and you covered when XYZ hit, say, $120, your loss would be $2,000 plus commissions. And the loss on the short sale could be unlimited if you stalled while XYZ went higher and higher.

Suppose instead that you feel bullish—you're sure that XYZ stock will go up. You reverse signals and buy a call for $800. Say XYZ goes from $100 to $120 a share. You exercise the option, buying 100 shares at $10,000 and sell them on the market for $12,000—with a gross profit of $2,000 or net profit of about $1,100.

Straddles are double options that combine a put and call on the same stock at the same price. You don't know which way the stock is going but are pretty sure it will move. You hope that the action either way will be enough to outweigh the double cost of buying two options.

If you want a clear-cut, 160-page explanation, see John D. Cunnion's *How to Get Maximum Leverage from Puts and Calls.* It could be a highly profitable venture for anybody past the novice stage (Business Reports, Larchmont, N.Y.).

Margin buying: a lever for bigger profits

At this writing there isn't much of a spotlight on margin buying. But at some periods, the technique is a big money mover. This is the ploy, of course, that lets you buy listed shares with a limited investment (right now its 65% of total market value)—and borrow the rest from your stockbroker. It's an idea that needs the closest going-over, pro and con. Margin buying is effective — maybe up to the bonanza level—when the market is going up. It can be disaster in a severe downswing, such as the suicide squeeze that hit margin buyers in the crash of 1929.

The big plus is that you can pick up about a third more shares than you could for all cash, and thus have a chance for bigger profits. For example, a five-point rise in a $50 stock produces a 15% profit for a 65% margin, instead of the 10% that a cash account would gain. If the rise were 20 points, the margin account would gain over 60%, the cash account 40%. But margin leverage can work both ways. A drop in the price of a stock cuts down your equity faster than with a cash account.

When you buy on margin, you can put up either cash or securities. If you deposit securities, their market value must be over three times the cash equivalent. Thus you can make a $10,000 stock purchase on margin for $6,500 in cash, or about $20,000 worth of securities. Either way, the broker puts up the remaining part of the purchase price. And he charges you interest on this "debit balance" and keeps the stock as collateral.

The margin set by the Federal Reserve isn't the only requirement you face. Both the New York Stock Exchange (NYSE) and the American Exchange require that, if your stock falls in price far enough to cut your actual equity in your account below 25%, you must put up more margin. And in practice, brokers boost this requirement to 30%; some go as high as 40%. Under the 30% rule, if $10,000 in stock bought on 65% margin dropped much below $4,500, you would have to put up more margin.

When an account falls below the margin minimum, the broker sends out a "call" by phone, wire, or letter, asking for more equity—usually to be sent within four business days, but sometimes in a shorter time. You can put up cash, stocks owned outright, or you can sell some of your margined stock. Of course, if the stock goes up, none of these woes beset you.

If a drop in the market cuts your equity *below* 65% of current value, your margin account becomes "restricted." Nothing happens unless you trade on the account—but if you do trade, all new purchases must be at 65% margin, and, in addition, 65% of sales proceeds must be applied to margin until your account is brought up to the required 65% level. So only 35% of sales proceeds are released on a restricted account.

This rule holds, too, when an old account—started on a lower margin—becomes restricted because of a later boost in the margin rate.

Note: Same-day substitution—buying and selling on the same day stocks of equal value—is a way around the rule. You can still trade and improve your position without applying 65% of the proceeds to margin.

How to follow the market from faraway places

What about the stock portfolio and its state of health when the owner is traveling on a global swing? If you skip from Chicago to London to Tokyo a few times a year—as a regular part of your business routine—how can you keep tabs on your investments? Today this isn't as hard as it was a few years back. Since about 1960, brokerage houses have beefed up their overseas operations, and the new communications links put Rome or even Hong Kong almost as close to Wall Street as midtown Manhattan.

At some brokerage offices in such centers as Geneva, Paris, and London you can even get a quote on any Big Board stock within 60 seconds after the tape prints. What has happened is a vast expansion in use of the private wire. Thus, the domestic and foreign offices of Bache, for example, are now in a single network that centers in downtown New York. The same holds for Merrill Lynch, and in various degrees for other leading brokers, such as Harris Upham, Dean Witter, Kidder Peabody, F. I. du Pont, and Lehman Bros.

More and better communications have reduced reliance on such devices as the stop order and power of attorney—which, in effect, let your broker make decisions while you're away. Many brokers now believe that it's usually best for an investor

to keep direct control. In any case, the first point to remember—
if you do decide to keep on top of your account—is to leave a
detailed trip itinerary with your broker, so that he can contact
you for instructions.

Some brokers suggest that before an extended trip, you also
(1) leave any "active" securities with your broker, signing stock
powers (assignment certificates) so the shares can be conve-
niently sold if necessary; and (2) make arrangements to pay for
stocks to be bought during your trip. The broker may agree to
make payment if you leave other shares as collateral; or a "c.o.d."
can be left behind, instructing your bank to pay.

If you'll be traveling to remote locations, a special Reuters
service lets you prearrange delivery of investment news to
outposts in Africa, Asia, Latin America. Write to Comtelburo,
82 Beaver Street, New York, N.Y.

The typical overseas branch of a U.S. brokerage house is
smaller and less hectic than the average office here at home.
The atmosphere is also apt to be more discreet and formal.
There's ample service available, but not as much catering to
Americans (except top VIPs) as you might imagine. The reason
is that 90% of the business in these offices is with local people
who invest in Wall Street. Office hours, you'll find, are in tune
with New York. Thus, many European brokers stay open until
9 or 10 P.M., to catch the market closing here. Swing around the
globe to Hong Kong, and you can do business at night.

From wherever you are, you can phone or visit the nearest
branch of your own broker's firm, have them contact him in the
U.S., ask an opinion—and get a reply within an hour. You can
then flash instructions within minutes. But have your home
office notify the foreign branches you expect to use; that way,
they'll have your account number, etc., for easy identification.
If your broker has no branches abroad, you can use the "give-up"
order. For example, a customer of Courts & Co., of Atlanta, goes
to the Merrill Lynch office in Geneva, has a transaction made,
asking that it be credited or "given up" to Courts. Thus, the
Courts customer gets use of the Merrill Lynch facilities, with
the two firms splitting the commission. Often, of course, you can

use the information facilities of an American branch abroad, within reason—then privately phone or cable your broker.

The branch office abroad—if you have a credit balance with your broker at home—often will deliver cash if you appear in person. U.S. brokers will do this at such locations as Frankfurt, Rome, Geneva, and Beirut. Or, if it's locally unlawful, as in some countries, they'll arrange a wire money order.

A branch office will help you gather local business information, and may even furnish letters of introduction. But don't expect a branch in Paris to get you a reservation at the Hassler hotel in Rome, or to cable Madrid for bull-fight tickets. Requests of this sort—along with currency-exchange problems—are a nuisance to brokers, especially in the summertime tourist season.

You get branch service overseas at no extra charge, and can even phone your personal broker collect—*if* you have a solid account.

Hard cash: overseas

Speaking of travel and investments, remember that it's rarely practical to carry on a trip abroad more than a few thousand dollars in travelers checks. So, if your plans call for more spending money—*or* a sizable outlay for some type of investment—you might find it practical to get a traveler's letter of credit at your bank back home. For this, you pay a small service charge, usually no more than 1%.

The letter of credit works like a checking account wherever you go. What you do is cash drafts against the "letter" and carry in your pocket a booklet listing various banks in the U.S. and abroad that will honor the document.

A more personal letter from your local banker can also work wonders. The "banker's letter of introduction" becomes more useful as more U.S. banks open branches abroad. Today, some regional banks (Mellon National of Pittsburgh, City National of Detroit, for example) are overseas, as well as the big names (such as Bank of America, Chase Manhattan, First National

City). You'll see new additions to the regional bank listing abroad.

Besides affording introductions, a banker's letter—assuming it specifies a credit line—can be a way to cash sizable personal checks without delay at specified banks. Without the letter, you wait 24 to 36 hours for a cable reply from home. In any case, if you know you'll be needing cash when you leave, say, Zurich, and are heading for Beirut, you can cable your home bank (or its branch overseas) and have it wire a deposit in your name to your destination.

Note: If you'll be working in, say, Milan, for several months, your home bank can routinely set up a checking account at a local bank overseas. A limitation is that check-cashing privileges often will extend only to the particular branch of the foreign bank where the deposit is made, unless written instructions are sent to other branches. Still, a local account can help in many ways if you take up temporary residence.

Where to put cash that's not in stocks

If you have a sizable amount of cash on hand and feel uncertain about putting it across the line into stocks, you might be smart to wait out the market and put your money temporarily into short- and long-term debt securities.

Treasury bills, the closest thing to cash, at this writing are paying fine yields. For example, yield on a mid-1970 90-day issue was 7.5%, and on a 180-day bill, 7.60%. Commercial banks charge just $15 to $20 for the transaction on deals of less than $100,000. At certain times, investors shift funds from sources such as savings accounts in order to get the bills' higher interest.

Treasury bonds maturing in five years or more have good yields. Two recent top-yield issues were 5¾% February 1975 and 6% May 1975—both yielding about 8%. Among shorter-term treasury notes: 18 months at 8¼% interest, yielding about 7.70%; and 3½ years at 8⅛%, yielding 7.77%.

Debt instruments sold by federal agencies are almost as easily traded as Treasury bills, and they have lately had high yields, too: for example, a January, 1971, Federal Home Loan Bank issue yielding 8.30%. Some have terms of up to two years.

Tax-exempt municipal bonds are a prime choice—and the 1969 tax reform law didn't undermine their basic advantage. A 5.25% bond, for example, pays the equivalent of 9.55% to a man with a $25,000 taxable income who files a joint return, or 12.36% if income is $40,000. In some states, New York and Pennsylvania among them, you are freed of state levies as well as federal if you buy issues of those states. On the minus side: Only income from municipals is tax-exempt. If you sell later at a higher price, your capital gain is taxable.

Note: Generally, corporate bonds aren't suggested for the short term.

Some smaller banks put out negotiable certificates of deposit in denominations ranging from $2,500 to $100,000. The interest range has lately been 5% for less than a year, 5½% for one to two years, and 5¾% for over two years. Many city banks now pay up to 5¾% or 6% on $500 minimum deposits for over two years.

Savings and loan companies and commercial banks pay 7½% on one-year deposits of more than $100,000. Savings banks offer certificates of $500 to $50,000 that recently paid 5¼% for 90 days to a year, up to 6% for two years and longer.

Smart money goes into places that make big money fast. Like a vacant lot, for instance. Or commodity futures. Or buying art. You name it. In the past two years, the so-called smart-money people have jumped about in vast circles, mostly getting dizzy and losing their hatbands. Hot franchise stocks were "in" for a spell. (Go-go mutual funds had just bowed out.) Then came a spurt of interest in coins and stamps. Then came the dire stock-market plunge in the spring of 1970 and the smart-money crowd went into a tailspin trying to search out some fertile new pothole in which bright, crisp greenbacks could be grown.

If this sounds flip, then so do many of the smart-money ideas and attitudes that periodically sweep through the financial community. At the very least, these approaches require close scrutiny before a man should willingly put down even a dime of his savings. With these warnings tucked away, it is safe to review a few of the more popular smart-money ideas that come back again and again to capture investors and their pocketbooks. We'll start with a couple that are really far-out (almost in left field)—then proceed to a few that operate closer to common sense.

Breeding world: join the thoroughbreds

Consider a smart-money oldie: breeding throughbred race horses. This gives you more than an outside track to the glamour and excitement of the racing world. It can be lucrative, if handled right. And for people with high incomes, the tax benefits of animal breeding—whether horses, beef cattle, or show dogs—can underwrite some costs as well as shield some profits.

The tax theory works like this: Animals bought for breeding can be depreciated—five years for horses, seven for cattle, 10 for dogs. If you keep the offspring for more than 12 months—either for breeding, racing, or showing—and later sell them, the transaction is taxed under capital gains rules. Otherwise, the sale is subject to ordinary tax rates. Costs—ranging from insurance to stud fees to repairs on buildings—are deductible as business expenses, while equipment and improvements such as stables, fencing, harnesses can be depreciated.

You get these tax breaks, of course, *only if you're operating a business and not just a hobby.* You must prove to Internal Revenue that you're in it for profit and back up your case with detailed records.

All this presupposes sophisticated tax counsel, of course. It also helps if you have a healthy financial base—especially with race horses.

Shell out between $15,000 and $30,000, and you have bought a thoroughbred brood mare and former race horse. Price varies with the amount of "black type" in her record and pedigree that shows the number of high-stake race winners and runner-ups.

A brood mare (a racing filly ending her career at age five) can be bought privately or at breeders' sales near major racing centers. Occasionally you can pick up one at a bargain ($6,000 or $8,000) in a claiming race.

Whatever your approach, it takes a hefty initial investment. If blood lines are good, however, the horse should pay for herself in two to four years with foals of racing caliber. (Usually you'll buy a mare already in foal.) When the foal is a year old, you can put it up for auction. Bids will range anywhere between $5,000 and $25,000—depending on conformation, blood lines. But bids at the summer Saratoga and Keeneland sales often go higher—up to $175,000. Both supply many winners, so stakes are high.

Or you can keep the foal until age two and race it yourself. Here you're foregoing immediate profit and banking on the possibility of big future purses. In the interim, figure on a monthly outlay of $700 to $800 to keep the horse on an eight-month racing circuit. By comparison, upkeep on a brood mare runs $200 a month; the foal costs the same once it's weaned.

Of course, you'll be paying stud fees. Top champion stallions command upwards of $10,000. A low $1,000 fee would go for "unproved" stallions—those who have yet to sire an issue with a racing record.

Stallions sell for astronomical figures ($200,000 to $300,000), and are temperamental and expensive to feed. They're usually syndicated, with ownership divided among some 30 shareholders. But stallion syndication isn't cheap. Single shares to top-rank stallions sometimes sell at auction for upwards of $50,000 or $75,000. The reason for joining a syndicate is not so much the chance to share in the stud fees, but the opportunity to breed one's mare to a top stallion. But you get no money-back guarantee of a live foal, since you pay no stud fee.

"Breeder's awards" are extra benefits of breeding thoroughbred race horses. In states where racing is an important source of income—New York, Florida, California, New Jersey, Maryland—from 1 to 10% of the winning purse of a home-bred horse goes to the breeder (the mare's owner at the time she drops her foal). Thus, you may continue to receive a string of checks long after breeding a horse.

For information on thoroughbred breeding, write Horsemen's Benevolent & Protective Association (Aqueduct Racetrack, Ozone Park, N.Y.) and Thoroughbred Breeders Service Bureau (598 Madison Avenue, New York, N.Y.).

The Broadway "bomb" beat

If race horses are a smart money oldie, Broadway shows are strictly a *quickie*. Despite all the attention that's been given to backing legitimate plays and musicals, the whole Broadway scene deserves little serious attention. Investor attention, that is.

Before you indulge in the fun of staking out even a small claim as part owner of a show, take note: About 50 shows reach the Broadway stage each season, September through May. At least half of these, on average, are quick flops and total losses financially. Of the remainder, another 20 will enjoy some measure of artistic success—but will return little or nothing to investors. So—only five of the original 50 will come up with worthwhile profits. Even some of the big hits won't pay off much because oftentimes some sizable cuts are taken off "the top"—from box-office gross—by producers, stars, directors, even set designers. The outside investor is left holding a much-reduced bag of profits.

And note: Getting "in" on a likely looking hit put together by a leading producer isn't easy. Producers have their lists of long-time, loyal investors—at least, those do who have a respectable record of shows behind them. The David Merrick show that's being imported from London after a long run in the West End is way out of reach for most investors. The Hal Prince musical that looks hot, or the new Neil Simon comedy coming in to Broadway, is simply out of the question for most investors who aren't already on the inside of show business.

Moral: Any novice who puts cash into a Broadway show—or, heaven help him, into an *off*-Broadway show—should be willing to part with his money like a little trouper, unless he has an inside track to the Merricks and the Princes of show biz. Says a theater-lover who's regularly on the Manhattan scene and who has backed 11 Broadway offerings as a small investor: "What I always seem to wind up with is the third-rate venture that makes Clive Barnes mad [the *New York Times* critic]—and folds before I can invite my brother and his wife in from Pelham."

Art for art's sake—and a small profit

Assuming you know your way around, a more sensible smart money move is the well-executed purchase of a work of art. No matter the gyrations of the stock market, buying into the arts can still give you a solid growth situation.

A shrinkage in the supply of fine paintings and other art works has led to a sustained upsurge in values—a case of limited or fixed supply in the face of growing demand. In a recent survey by *International Art Market* (a fine small publication devoted to following auctions, prices, and such), the post-impressionists and moderns among the quality painters were given close attention. Painting by such artists as Utrillo, Vlaminck, and Picasso were shown to appreciate as much as 64% in a year's time. Boosts in value of 45 and 50% in a year were shown to be common.

And the boom in art covers everything from 200-year-old paperweights to Calder mobiles. In 1969 at an auction in New York, a piece of furniture—a Philadelphia Chippendale highboy —sold for $60,000. And it needn't be a "name" antique or art piece. Today the work of a relatively obscure contemporary painter that sold for, say, $1,500 in 1965 may sell for a good $3,000. Antique English silver has doubled in price in the last two years, and pre-1800 American silver—especially Paul Revere pieces—are up even more. You can go on and on.

Note: For a monthly survey of this market, *International Art Market* is quite valuable. Write to Interart, 115 Central Park West, New York, N.Y.

Some of the perils you face

Ideally, you buy a painting or a mobile or an ancient print at a favorable price, wait five years, and sell at a profit of, say, 500%. The trouble is that in this day of the slick artist—as well as the fine artist—you stand far too much chance of being gypped. There's no area of consumerism more rife with disappointment and tears than the art market. If only Ralph Nader knew the difference between a highboy and a lowboy, or a Picasso and a MacDougal Street Special!

Today—and this is frightening—the cheaters and forgers are even going in for mechanical reproduction methods. And the sad part is, these methods frequently are so skillful that even some professionals in the art world are fooled. Brentano's book stores in New York and a string of department stores around the country have even sold some "chromographically" reproduced paintings—so true to the originals that they were purposely reduced 10% in size and plainly stamped "authorized reproduction". Imagine what some of the forgers are doing within their garret rooms.

So the reputable art experts are worried. It was bad enough when hand forgery was the prime weapon. Now that science has entered the scene, there is no telling what will happen. Mechanical reproduction, they fear, may become a new menace among forgery techniques. Anyway, the top pros in the art field offer some guidelines:

▪ If you're buying original art, go to an established, reputable dealer after first checking him out through a local art museum. For further checking, contact the Art Dealers Association (575 Madison Avenue, New York, N.Y. 10022).

▪ If it's a sizable purchase, get a provenance ("pedigree") from the seller. This lists previous owners, and you can check with them. If you are refused a provenance, you might be smart not to buy.

Getting a painting authenticated is often difficult, sometimes impossible. Museums generally won't authenticate, though there are exceptions. The Boston Museum of Fine Arts will tell you if it's an obvious fake, or it may perform tests for a fee. Washington's National Gallery will authenticate a painting free (by appointment, 10 A.M. to noon, Wednesdays and Thursdays). The Smithsonian performs a similar service for American art only.

Major private galleries in New York and Chicago will sometimes authenticate a work for a long-established customer, or for a small fee (1% of your purchase price). The art history departments of some universities (Columbia, Harvard, Michigan) might also be willing to help you authenticate works of art.

In most states, laws against fraud are your sole protection should you discover you have been cheated. But such laws are often difficult to enforce. In New York, though, a new law says that your invoice is, in effect, a warranty *if* it names the artist. A similar law is being introduced in Illinois. In any case, be wary of fuzzy wording on invoices and in art catalogues. A statement that a painting carries an artist's name is generally no legal guarantee that he actually painted it.

New York auction houses—and auction houses in some other states—are legally responsible if the catalogue incorrectly attributes a painting to an artist, despite any disclaimer. Parke-Bernet, by far the biggest auction center in the country, has special house rules to protect you against any possible fraud.

For background reading, see *Economics of Taste,* by Gerald Reitlinger (Holt, Rinehart & Winston), *Corporations and the Arts,* by Richard Eells (Macmillan), and *Collecting Original Art,* by J. H. Loria (Harper). Richard Rush's *Art As An Investment* (Prentice-Hall) is an excellent basic work. These books, incidentally, can often be scanned at a public library.

Keeping on top of your own art boom

You may have invested in some art works in past years—paintings, sculpture, antiques, or such—and not know what they are worth today. In fact, if you're like many people, you have no idea at all as to the value of, say, a small freehand drawing by Picasso bought fifteen years ago when you and your wife saw

Paris in the spring. The point is, of course, that you may already have a goodly investment in art—and not really know where you stand.

As mentioned above, heavy demand and limited supply have in many cases driven art prices way up, often far beyond what the non-professional owner might imagine. So before you consider buying art, it would be wise to take inventory at home to see what you have and what it's worth. Among other surprises, you may find that your collection of arts and antiques is vastly underinsured.

Getting a precise measure on the value of your possessions is important if you have serious ideas about art investment, and it's vital if you're to be properly insured. Many insurance companies require an appraiser's certificate for items valued at more than $1,000.

If you have one valuable painting, get in touch with the dealer who sold it. He may reappraise it free, as a favor. For a collection, you may need separate appraisers for art works and for antiques. Many dealers and auction houses will do this work—or will refer you to a specialist.

There's no real uniformity in the rates appraisers will charge, nor in their standards of appraisal. The American Society of Appraisers, Washington, D.C., warns, however, that if you want an accurate appraisal you'll do best to look for a man who bases his fees on the time he spends or on the number of items he looks over. If he charges a percentage of appraised value, you may wind up with an inflated estimate.

For other leads, check the Appraisers Association of America (663 Fifth Avenue, New York, N.Y.). The Art Dealers Association (575 Madison Avenue, New York, N.Y.) will appraise charitable donations of fine arts for tax purposes.

After appraisal, figuring out insurance is simple enough. Rates vary from city to city, but typically you'll pay about $5 per $1,000 for "all-risk" coverage. Full protection against breakage of valuable glass items will run you an extra $1.50 per $1,000. If you have a personal articles floater (see Chapter 2, "Insurance") on your homeowners insurance policy, you would be wise to reappraise your art and antique collections when you renew the policy every three years.

If you decide to sell a painting or an antique, you can count on getting roughly 50% of its current market value direct from a dealer. An alternative: Sell on consignment. The dealer finds you a buyer, charges you 20 to 40% for his fee. (Of course, you may have to wait longer for your money.)

Selling at auction is more of a gamble, but may well bring a higher price for you. Commissions average about 15%. But before you start trading at auctions, bone up on the market. Besides the books noted above, *The Art Game*, by Robert Wraight (Simon & Schuster), is witty and realistic.

Commodity futures: the markets for fast action

If you have some risk capital to spare, another place where you can find fast action is in commodity futures contracts. Profits are big if you guess right, and losses are rapid if you pick the wrong numbers. Price swings in commodities can be fast and wide. There was a great deal of interest in this game before the 1970 decline in the stock market. The interest will perk up again, sooner or later. Bache & Co. (big in the commodity business for years) notes that sales of futures contracts were in a steady uptrend from 1965 through 1969.

One reason more speculators have been commodity-minded is that more commodities have gone on the trading block in the past few years. The list is now over 35 and covers everything from wheat to frozen orange juice to platinum, with forestry products—plywood and cut lumber—added late in 1969. The gamble may look tempting. But before you dive in, note the advice of an old pro: "You can couple information and timing and make a big killing. But it takes study and concentration. If you can't spare time for that—stay out."

The mechanics are simple. You deposit the required margin with your broker and give him an order to buy one or more commodity contracts. You might buy cotton futures traded on the New York Cotton Exchange, or steers traded on the Chicago Board of Trade. There are a dozen major exchanges. The contract is the minimum trading unit, like a share of stock. For cotton it is 50,000 lb., for cocoa 30,000 lb., for platinum 50 oz., and so on. Buying a futures contract means simply that you agree to accept delivery at a future date, usually within a year, at a specified price. The speculator's goal is to sell his contract at a profit before delivery date.

Besides a big profit potential, a sizable plus is the leverage you get. Usually you put up a margin deposit of only 10 to 20% of the total value of the contract. There's no interest due on the balance, but there is a proviso for added calls when a price drop eats up more than 25% of your deposit. Another plus: low commissions. They're well under 1% of the total dollar value of the contract. The rate for cocoa is $70 for a buy-and-sell transaction with the contract worth $12,000. With wheat, the two-way commission is $22, and the contract is worth $7,000.

A third possible advantage is that, in theory at least, there's no inside information to work against the individual. All statistics are public property, and news that affects commodities—such as weather changes, labor troubles, brushfire wars—is mostly open information.

But because prices are sensitive to everything from politics to plant diseases, a market can nosedive very suddenly. Take a simple deal: Say that you buy four 5,000-bu. soybean contracts at $2.50 a bu., calling for delivery two months later, in January. On each $12,500 contract your margin deposit comes to $600, or a total of $2,400. On December 1 you sell at $2.55 a bu.—a profit of 5¢ a bu., or $1,000 total. After an $88 commission, net profit is $912.

But suppose the market *drops* 5¢ a bu. You would have an added $600 margin call when the market was down only 3¢, bringing your total deposit to $3,000. On December 1, you sell at $2.45, losing $1,000 on your 20,000 bu. Here your cost is $1,000 plus $88 commission. You get back just $1,912 of your $3,000.

"Whether you go up or down 5¢ can depend on something as hard to predict as the weather," says one top broker. In commodities, everything can ride on the pinpoint accuracy of your information. So, it's hardly wise to be using money that's sacred. Some old hands suggest that you should start with at least $5,000 of venture capital, be willing to risk $3,000 immediately, and use the rest as a back-up fund for margin calls.

To discourage extremely wide price swings that quickly follow big news breaks affecting commodities, the commodity exchanges have set daily price fluctuation limits. Wheat and soybeans, for instance, can go up or down just 10¢ a bu. in one day, and pork bellies (bacon) 1½¢ a lb.

A second buffer is the widely used stop-loss order. Here you instruct your broker to sell automatically if the price of your holding drops below a specified level. Too many novices, say the pros, hold on too long during a downswing when a stop-loss order can eliminate unnecessary agony.

The smartest safeguard is to read up. A first-rate basic review is contained in Gerald Gold's *Modern Commodity Futures Trading* (Commodity Research Bureau, 140 Broadway, New York, N.Y. 10005).

Flying high with "convertibles"

Eager money (if not smart money) sometimes takes turns that are far removed from speculation in raw land, or soy beans, or arts and antiques. There has been less recent interest in convertible debentures, but they've had their flings and doubtless will once again. Convertibles—corporate bonds that can be converted into common stocks on certain fixed terms—have in the past had a lot of general appeal. Their big lure for the eager-money investor has been the fact that they always can be bought on margin.

At this writing, the margin rule is 50% as fixed by the Federal Reserve. This means that you can borrow up to 50% of the gross amount you pay for the debentures. Thus, when you convert them into common stock, you have bought yourself a position in the stock with a relatively small equity. If you should be fortunate enough to be in a rising stock market, you can boost your possible profit leverage considerably above the limit that's possible under a 65% margin rule covering direct stock purchases. Simply put, your leverage is 2-to-1, as against about 1½-to-1 with the 65% rule.

So the case for buying convertibles on margin is clear-cut. They're a somewhat cheaper way of buying into a common stock. But if you aren't willing to buy on margin, "converts" have an advantage only when: (1) the bond yield is greater than the stock dividend; (2) prospects for the related stock promise to boost the market price of the convertible; and (3) the bond's investment value is so well secured that in a downswing it will usually hold up better than its related stock.

If these conditions aren't fulfilled, you're better off buying either a straight bond or stock — depending on whether you want the safety of a bond or the growth potential of the stock.

Note: Don't be misled by the idea that the bond aspect of a convertible keeps a floor under its price while the convertible feature allows a maximum ride with the stock. It isn't necessarily so. It's seldom possible to play it both ways. Usually you must give up some bond quality — or yield — in return for the conversion sweetener. Also, the more attractive the conversion terms and stock prospects, the more likely the convertible is to drop off in a market downswing. If you want price protection in a bearish market, you have to pick a convertible strictly on its merits as a bond, independent of any appealing conversion privilege.

To figure a convertible's value as a bond, check Moody's and Standard & Poor's "investment-value" ratings. These show the current price the bond would sell for without any conversion feature. As a rule of thumb, when a convertible is selling for more than 25% to 30% over this investment value, it ceases to have a bond's price protection — and is pretty much at the mercy of the stock market's gyrations.

The price of a convertible, of course, hinges on the price of the stock. For example, XYZ Corp. has a $1,000 convertible that provides for conversion to 100 shares of XYZ common — at $10 a share. When the stock goes to $12, the convertible price moves to $1,200—in theory. But in practice, a convertible will often sell at a premium over its current conversion value—bid up either by bullish prospects for the stock or by margin buyers who can afford the premium on their low equity.

As for a bear market situation: generally, when stock prices are down, margin buyers get out—or stay out—of convertibles.

Go-go funds: Wall Street's fast game

The fast-appreciation mutual funds are mostly dead at this writing. But they'll have a comeback, along with investment in rare stamps and race horses. Anyway, in good times you might conclude that these maximum-performance mutual funds, which put your money into a high percentage of speculative issues, have two clear advantages:

- You can play the market for possible high stakes with a spread of perhaps 100 or more risks (better than going it alone with a few flyers).
- You can do it with the aid of a professional whose business it is to sift risky situations (better than "inside" tips that all too often fall flat).

There's truth to both propositions. But most top advisers with no ax to grind will tell you that the go-go funds—even when they're going good—need considerably closer inspection. "First redefine your definition of 'performance,'" says top New York consultant Leo Barnes. "It's actually rate of return, plus risk—not just return. Concentrate on this when you consider a go-go."

A go-go fund may get you high appreciation on the up side, but it can also move down just as fast. If you hold one while the market moves up and then down, you may well wind up with little or no more gain than you could have achieved with a more conservative growth mutual fund. That, at any rate, has been the experience of some buyers of go-go funds.

So the question is: Why buy the go-go when you might do just as well with the conservative fund—and at considerably less risk? The answer is that the go-go funds are designed more for traders than for people who like to sit 18 months or more on their investments. To get the big gains, you have to keep a sharp eye on your fund's performance and be ready to move fast.

A go-go fund, the pros agree, should be able to smartly out-pace the gains of solid, high-growth stocks if it's to deserve its title. If the high-growth group (like IBM, etc.) goes up in price 15% to 20% in a good year, then a go-go should be up in the *25% to 30% range.* The trouble is that even the smartest go-go fund managers will sooner or later face two pitfalls:

- The funds tend to favor many of the same fast-moving stocks. If one or more of the funds start selling the same stock, the price of that stock can nosedive—and all the go-go funds holding it are affected.

- Once a fund reaches a certain size—$200 million or so in assets—it usually can't find enough fast-moving, small com-panies to fill out its high-growth portfolio. The fund manager is forced to compromise by putting more money into less specula-tive issues.

The net result: The biggest gains for a go-go fund are likely to come when it is new, small, and still in its fast-growth stage. That is also when the risks are highest—and when you have to keep the closest watch.

Assuming good times and a healthy market, if you have $50,-000 to $100,000 riding in the market, how much of this might you consider putting into go-go funds? This, of course, depends on your objectives. But the pros say that, on the average, you're wise to think in terms of 10 to 20% of your portfolio, no more. Go-go funds fell like stones in water in the 1970 market slump, and haven't been tested over the long haul.

Besides your broker, *Fundscope* magazine has the statistics (Fundscope, 1900 Avenue of the Stars, Los Angeles, Calif.).

Basic funds: biggest package plan around

Smart-money moves aside, it may be sensible to look briefly at *basic* mutual funds—those that offer the standard investment approaches and packages. One point is certain: the funds have long since passed the stage where the small-budget man is the mutual fund man. He's still in funds, but the profile of the fund buyer today is far different from, say, five or ten years ago.

The Investment Company Institute reports that of well over 3 million people who own fund shares, a good 500,000 or more may be classed as businessmen, professionals, and administrators. A solid 250,000 fund share owners have holdings worth $25,000 or more. Anyway, if you've never taken a serious view of the funds, here are a few basic thoughts.

It's true that there are some disadvantages, or at least possible disadvantages, to the mutual fund idea—apart from their dire 1970 performance. Some critics point out that funds often over-trade—sometimes turning over 30% or more of their assets annually—thus adding heavily and maybe unnecessarily to commission costs. A few funds, according to the Stock Exchange Commission have been damaged by improper insider dealings and other abuses. And the unwary investor can be caught up by such practices as periodic capital gains distribution (which can add unnecessary taxes) and "guaranteed" income plans that may actually drain away the investor's capital.

But it's equally true of the mutuals that their advantages are often obscured by unfair comparisons. A look at some of these may make sense as a preliminary to any serious review of types of funds in relation to your own investment objectives.

In trying to select a fund for investment, it can be unfair to ask whether it tops the performance of leading market averages. A reasonable answer is, maybe not (and many funds, in fact, fall short)—but the fund's performance is probably better than the record you, as an individual, could achieve on your own.

Also, some funds (such as those with balanced stock-and-bond portfolios) aren't designed to top the averages—by their nature they move more slowly, both up and down.

Also, it's unfair to compare what it costs to buy, say, $10,000 in mutual fund shares and 200 shares of one stock selling at $50. The mutual fund buy might cost about $800 in commissions, and the single stock just $88. The really fair cost line-up is to compare the $800 with what a mix of, say, 25 different stocks worth $10,000 would cost to buy. Here the total buying cost would be roughly $275—and the total buying-and-selling cost, about $550. And note that the average fund, in fact, has not 25, but as many as 100 stocks in its portfolio (plus bonds).

The buy-and-sell cost for the mutual fund would stay at $800, since the funds don't charge for share redemption. This, incidentally, points to another plus in favor of the funds—they offer quick, easy liquidity at full current net asset value. And, of course, the funds give you professional management in addition to a highly diversified portfolio.

Picking a mutual fund from a field of several hundred can be (and probably should be) a painstaking chore. It takes a lot of table reading, and right away you can run into some deceptions. For example, some tables that compare the funds exclude or bury the sales cost factor—that is, they don't take into account how much, if anything, is tacked on as a purchase charge—the famous "front-end load." A misconception, incidentally, is that the so-called no-load fund (without a purchase charge) is necessarily a better buy than a load fund (which typically charges about 8%). Actually, it comes down to net performance. You can find load funds that best the no-loads.

To get a further idea of the selection problem, look at the basic types of funds that must be analyzed in view of personal objectives:

▪ Growth funds: These are mostly varied common stock funds for the investor aiming at long-term capital gains.

▪ Growth with income funds: Here again you have varied commons, but with somewhat greater stress on yearly payout.

▪ Income with growth funds: These include mostly mixed commons that give you still greater stress on income.

▪ Balanced funds: If you want to have your cake and eat it, too, these mixed stock-and-bond portfolios place equal emphasis on growth and income.

▪ Income funds "flexibly diversified": Here you find highly varied stock-and-bond portfolios.

There is also a small class of income funds owning bonds or preferred stocks, and sometimes both.

These five classes—along with a few specialized funds mainly in insurance, and several international funds—cover the lot. And though it makes sense to review them class by class, you'll be wise to keep in mind that a good deal of blending exists between the groups. Also, over a period of several years, a fund is apt to alter its policies gradually. The overall trend has been to broaden the range of investment, with fund managers leaving themselves a lot of leeway. Apart from these basic features, many funds offer special added attractions. Switching, for example, is a special feature to look at. A single management will operate two or more funds with varying investment objectives—say, one for growth, one for income. One example: An investor might own growth fund shares, retire at age 65, and—needing more income—shift to the company's income fund. Switching usually costs just a few dollars. This, of course, is better than selling one fund and paying a full 8% load (purchase charge) to buy another. But note that there is no tax advantage: Any profit is taxable at the time of conversion.

Withdrawal plans "guarantee" a fixed income per year and are often used by retired persons for extra income or by parents to cover a span of college years. But make sure that a high withdrawal does not invade principal (6% is sometimes suggested as the safe maximum).

Contractual accumulation plans let an investor pay for his shares in monthly installments. But he pays up to 50% of the total load charge of around 8% in the first year, and is thus heavily penalized if he sells out early. A "voluntary" accumulation plan levels out the load charge, and still gives you the advantage of long-term "dollar averaging."

Reading up: The bible of the mutual fund business is Arthur Wiesenberger's book *Investment Companies,* with quarterly supplements; available at public libraries and at brokerage offices. Leo Barnes' book *Your Investments* (American Research Council paperback) has a clear section on the funds.

Investments: in print

Books on investments, the market, and the Wall Street world are like stock tips at lunch. They come in bunches, and 90% of them are wisely ignored. Scratching for the valued 10% can be quite a chore. Here are a few books that may be worth your time and attention:

The Big Board—A History of the New York Stock Market, by Robert Sobel, glosses over nothing and aims at the reader who takes the stock market seriously. Jay Gould, Jim Fisk, Cornelius Vanderbilt, J. P. Morgan, among other giants of Wall Street's past, are given a close going-over. Result is readable history (Free Press, Macmillan).

The story of Gerald M. Loeb is told in *The Wizard of Wall Street,* by Ralph G. Martin. You can gain the flavor of a 40-year career on the Street—plus some insights into how he did it (Morrow).

The Intelligent Investor, by Benjamin Graham, is A-1, conservative in approach, aimed at the serious amateur (Harper). Burton Crane's *The Sophisticated Investor,* as revised by S. Eisenlohr, is frequently recommended to customers by brokers —it's realistic, reliable, with keen insights into the problems faced by a man building a portfolio.

The Stock Market, by Eiteman, Dice & Eiteman, is solid material aimed at the advanced reader (McGraw-Hill).

Leo Barnes' *Your Investments* is a sensible, readable review for the man who has looked at the market, and maybe made a bid or two—but who admits he has much to learn (American Research Council).

You and Your Stockbroker, by Robert J. Schwartz, makes sense for all but the most sophisticated investors. The client-broker relationship, and a broker's duties, rights, modes of operation are outlined (Macmillan).

Morton Shulman's *Anyone Can Make a Million* is fast-reading, full of ideas about making the stock market work in your favor. If you're an investor, it may shake you up a bit (McGraw-Hill).

A book with a delightfully candid title—*The $2 Window on Wall Street*—will whet your appetite for a quick killing in the market, or make an evening of fun reading: by Ira U. Cobleigh, an old-timer on the Street (Toucan-Doubleday).

Want to read some wild and woolly tales of Wall Street and

what makes it tick? *The Money Game,* by a Streeter calling himself "Adam Smith," is an evening's worth of half fun, half philosophy (Random House).

Albert Haas (a broker) and Don Jackson (a physician) have come up with some sharp views in *Bulls, Bears, and Dr. Freud* —or the psychological side of Wall Street. The market, they say, often is used to sublimate frustrations, and speculating has sexual overtones (World).

If you have always thought of puts and calls as two of the more arcane tools of the Wall Street trade, you're right, absolutely right. However, John D. Cunnion, editor of the J. K. Lasser Tax Report, has come out with a clear, readable 160-page explanation of these buy and sell options: *How to Get Maximum Leverage from Puts and Calls* (Business Reports, Inc., Larchmont, N.Y.).

Investing Abroad, a sort of traveling investor's guide to Europe, is fine if you want to cover much territory quickly; especially good chapters on London's City, the Bourse in Paris, La Borsa Milano, and the stock exchanges in Frankfurt, Duesseldorf, Hamburg—a book that unwinds some of the confusion about markets abroad (Harper & Row).

Patch of land: Don Campbell's *The Handbook of Real Estate Investment* is straightforward, readable, and covers the range of possibilities from raw land to a share in an office building (Bobbs-Merrill).

Insurance: Life, Health, Casualty

The insurance business is loaded with high-pressure salesmen (sometimes untrained), hundreds of competing companies that sell a confusing array of policies that seem to shoot off in all directions at once—and hokum in a public press that's too frequently afraid to rock the boat. But nevertheless you *need* insurance! You *must* buy it! Here are some tips.

Take a look at your life insurance

First look at your life insurance policies. A review may be in order. You might improve your present coverage by taking advantage of new features available (maybe at little or no extra cost). You can also make certain that your basic strategy is up to date, and that new family requirements haven't outdated any old provisions. You might even find out that you are overinsured—especially if you're a high-income businessman past 50.

As for family requirements changing: A new child or grandchild, or a death, obviously could require a beneficiary change. For example, a new secondary beneficiary may be needed.

In any case, if you've piled up several life policies over the years, a clear inventory of them all (including such items as projection of cash values to age 65) is the first step toward a coherent insurance plan. Your family lawyer or another key advisor should have a copy of this inventory if you make one, since insurance should be considered as part of your overall estate plan. Especially, it must be coordinated with your will (see Chapter 5, Estate Planning).

Buying life insurance isn't, of course, just a matter of how much. Sometimes you hear advice to sell your straight life policies with sizable cash values, invest the money profitably (maybe in a favorite stock)—then buy term-life coverage to give your family death-benefit protection.

This sounds fine and may, indeed, work well for you. But keep in mind that if you're middle-aged, you may find yourself virtually priced out of any form of life insurance. Term coverage at age 50 costs about double what it does at 40. At 55, it costs three times as much. Remember, too, that the cash value of a straight life policy may represent over 4% compounded—after taxes. Note the "after taxes." Any alternate investment of premium money would have to better this level of return.

Limited-term payment is another idea that looks attractive. Typically, you are told that a contract requiring you to pay for just 20 years, during your highest-earning period, would suit you fine. It may—and it may not. A point to remember is that straight life gives your family greater protection—per insurance dollar—than does a limited-payment contract.

As a rule of thumb, straight life—which means, of course, that you pay premiums until death—will give you over 50% more coverage during the first 20 years than will a 20-payment policy costing the same premium.

In any case, if you want it, you can get a straight life policy that has a built-in partial decrease in premium starting at age 65, when your income normally becomes limited. Many straight life contracts provide that at retirement age you can elect to use the cash value for an annuity. This gives you an income for the rest of your life—without the red tape and commissions that would ordinarily accompany a new contract. Often the retirement income can be paid to you and your wife for as long as either of you lives. Cash value of straight life at age 65 averages about $500 for each $1,000 of coverage. *Note:* Often you get a larger annuity return on this type of policy written today than if you wait to buy an annuity when you retire.

Remember, too, that there are many possibilities for special payment of insurance benefits. For instance, at no extra cost you can arrange for your family to get a fixed income until the children are through college, with the balance then payable in a lump sum or in reduced income.

But what if you're overinsured? Suppose your children are grown, and your investment portfolio has expanded. You may decide you want to part with some life coverage. An obvious way, of course, is simply to cash in a policy (with current cash value less net cost taxable), then reinvest the cash. Or you might get a paid-up policy with a smaller face value.

But there are other ways. One is to borrow as much as you can on a policy, then assign it to your children and let them pay both the premiums and interest on the loan. If you give them full ownership, the policy payoff will be outside your taxable estate.

It's wise to make sure that you have common disaster, double indemnity, emergency premium payment, home mortgage, and guaranteed insurability clauses. These are useful, often overlooked, and quite cheap.

Gearing your insurance to inflation

What about life insurance vs. retirement-income plans? "Gearing up the old retirement plan to meet inflation is the big news," says a top independent insurance consultant in New York. You don't necessarily need more life coverage—in fact, you could be overinsured. But updating coverage in line with some new policies on the market makes sense. At the same time, you might sidestep a pitfall or two.

The new type of retirement plan that pays out a variable amount of income each month—*depending on the performance of a common-stock portfolio*—gives you three choices:

- Combination life insurance and mutual fund packages.
- Variable annuities with payouts depending on investment yield (see below).
- Combination fixed-income and variable-income annuity plans.

A few small companies pioneered in selling mutual funds. Now you'll find such big names as Connecticut General, John Hancock, New England Mutual, Occidental, Prudential, and Travelers in the common-stock mutual fund business.

Here you get convenience and flexibility plus the feeling that you're dealing with a company you may have known for years. The idea, generally, is that you buy the fund shares and your life insurance from the same salesman and—as for the fund shares—you can quit buying them or liquidate whenever you choose.

If you continue to buy the fund shares up to age 65, you then begin to get a retirement income that depends on their market value at the time. *But note:* There's no special guarantee tied to the mutual fund part of the package—you can outlive the retirement income. The insurance coverage works just as with any ordinary life policy. These package plans have advantages, but the dollar performance of insurance-company common stock funds is largely untested. You would be wise to check on this, though—as far as possible.

A variable annuity, guaranteeing you a varying retirement income for as long as you or your wife live, binds you to a fixed contract. You pay so much a year until retirement, with the payments invested in a common stock portfolio. The basic idea, of course, is to ride up with inflation, year to year. But there's this drawback: It's a front-end load. If you cancel the deal in its early years, you pay a penalty.

Companies in this expanding field include Aetna's subsidiary Participating Annuity Life, Paul Revere, and Variable Annuity Insurance Co. If you want to mix a fixed retirement income (the old standby) with a pure variable contract, you might look at some new combinations being sold by Aetna Life and New England Mutual, among others. Here the portfolios are 50-50 common stocks and bonds–mortgages, so you have a floor if the market goes down—and still room to ride up.

Another new insurance "trend" has been sparked by Internal Revenue. Say you buy a life insurance policy and give complete ownership of it to your wife. Fine—the gift, if it has no strings attached, takes the policy payoff out of your taxable estate. But IRS has a string. If you continue to pay the premiums, part of the payoff—in some cases all of it—will be deemed subject to estate tax.

But there are at least two ways out:

1. Have your wife pay the premiums.

2. Have your premiums paid in advance so that you're four years ahead (see Chapter 5, "Estate Planning").

While checking over your life coverage, note these points:

■ College financing: It may be smart to use a retirement-income plan that will have ample cash value by the time your youngster reaches college age. You then borrow on the policy (at 5%). It's worth investigating variations on the college-insurance tie-in.

■ Juvenile policies: The idea here is that the low premium cost to a child continues after he becomes an adult. For example, you can get a policy on a boy age 14 for about $125 a year, giving him $12,500 permanent coverage at the same premium. Get a payor clause waiving premiums should you die.

■ Homeownership: Here you use decreasing term insurance covering the duration of your house mortgage. A man age 45 with a $30,000 mortgage on a $60,000 house, 20-year term, pays about $200 a year for this type of protection.

■ Guaranteed insurability: You attach this clause to your

straight life policy ($2 per $1,000 per year). It insures you future coverage in bigger amounts—even if your health fails.

Hedging bets for your retirement

Pay special attention to the individual variable-annuity contract. This idea will be big in the 1970–75 period, and may be worth a look. It's a long-range retirement planning idea, and already is available in enough variety to let you do some sensible shopping around.

After long delay, some big names in life insurance—Aetna Life & Casualty, Travelers, Lincoln, State Mutual, Paul Revere, and American General, among others—are now selling directly or through subsidiaries. Prudential, Connecticut Mutual, Massachusetts Mutual, and New England Mutual are part of a sizable list of top companies that are likely to move in soon.

But note: The individual variable contract—which is strictly a retirement-income investment, not ordinary life insurance— is variable in more ways than one. As noted above, the annuity payout is pegged to the performance of a common-stock portfolio. But the fine print varies from policy to policy, too.

When you buy such a contract, you're generally guaranteed an undetermined retirement income for as long as you, or you and your wife, live. You pay a fixed amount each year until age 65; your cash goes largely or wholly into common stocks. The advantages can add up:

▪ You have a chance to ride up with inflation, and you pay no current tax on the stocks' appreciation or dividend buildup before retirement.

▪ You'll be taxed on the yearly payout, but this comes when you're probably in a lower bracket; whatever you've paid in comes back to you tax-free.

▪ Your heirs get a break. Should you die before age 65, usually they get the current market value of your shares or the total premiums paid to date—whichever is greater.

If you don't want all your cash in equity investments, you can hedge and buy a portfolio mix: 50% in common stocks, say, and 50% in bonds and mortgages. Some companies let you vary the mix as you choose.

Here's an example of how a variable might come out. Based on past performance of the Aetna subsidiary's 100% variable portfolio (about 95% in commons), a man of 50 who put in $3,000 a year over the past 15 years would today have a fund of over $100,000. He would now begin to draw about $700 a month.

The result you get will depend on the items in the portfolio, its management—and on continued inflation. Says one pro: "You really bet that the stock market won't lag behind inflation."

You must also make sure that the fine print doesn't cross you up. For instance, there's the front-end load problem. You'll lose if you cancel the contract in the first few years, because sale commission and fees are taken out. The load varies. With Travelers, for instance, it comes to roughly 9% of the first year's premium. But some companies go to 25%.

Life coverage for the high-risk man

What you buy is one thing. Whether you can buy at all is another. Usually you *can* buy. If you were turned down for life insurance in the past as a health or occupational risk, you may well find that you can now get a policy. Many top companies have been easing their rules and going in heavily for what the trade calls substandard business. You pay an extra premium, and sometimes it's high. But often it will be just a couple of dollars more per $1,000 of protection.

Even a man who has had cancer can get a life insurance policy so long as he has had no recurrence of the disease in five years or more. The added premium he'll have to pay is about $15 per thousand a year. Thus, a man of 50 will pay about $50 per thousand instead of $35. If more than 10 years have passed since the cancer illness, the cost of coverage will be fairly close to normal with nearly all types of cancer.

You can get insurance today even if you have a bad case of high blood pressure, partly because of new drug therapy. A person 35 years old with a severe case will pay about double the standard premium of $18 per thousand; at age 50, the normal $35 premium jumps to $85. But the younger man gets close to the standard premium when his case is moderate and under control, and the 50-year-old pays only $40.

The 50-year-old has to pay $8 to $16 extra per thousand if he has diabetes; $2.50 to $5 if he has a duodenal ulcer.

A coronary poses the hardest case for insurance. The extra premium during the first year of recovery can be triple the standard rate. But this drops to less than double at five years, and gets substantially lower as more time passes.

Occupational risks still get slapped with extra life insurance premiums at times. But this usually won't affect the deskbound executive. Even a construction executive who visits mines or inspects high steel no longer has to pay added charges. However, if you travel fairly regularly to remote, unstable, or unsettled countries, you may be billed $2.50 to $7.50 extra per thousand.

If you fly a plane, the extra fee is based on age, experience, and hours in the air. The range is $2.50 for a Sunday pilot, and on up to $10 per thousand. If you scuba dive, you pay $5 extra if your maximum dive is 75 ft., and $7.50 for 100 ft. Most sports, though, mean nothing in the way of added insurance cost.

A way to save on life insurance

Prepayment of life premiums has appeal now that a growing number of companies are giving a yearly discount. One top company, for example, will give a 4½% discount for premium prepayments from one to 10 years, and 4% for the next 10 years. Thus, you would pay only 95.5% of the first year's premium; 80.2% at five years; 64.4% at 10.

The rate paid on dividends left to accumulate interest has gone up with many major companies.

On the juvenile life insurance front: A new policy quintuples coverage on the youngster's life by age 21, while premium doubles. The plan jumps the coverage of a basic $5,000 policy to $12,000 at age 16—with no change in premium—and jumps again to $25,000 at age 21, when premium is doubled. "Jumping juvenile" plans of this type are worth discussing with your insurance man.

Speaking of insurance for kids, the idea of building a child's own program for him when he is still quite young has some merit. Straight life costs about $8 a year per $1,000 at age 5, around $9 at age 10, and $10 at age 15—assuming at least $10,000 in coverage. This jumps to $16 at age 30 when your child, maybe as a young parent, might need to buy.

You can get some added values by attaching options to a child's life policy. As a simple example, say that you buy a $10,000 policy for a boy aged 10 for $90 a year. Adding an option charge of $9 a year will give the boy the right to buy more coverage, in $10,000 amounts, at option dates in the future, *regardless* of his state of health. Under a typical plan, his potential coverage is $70,000.

Beating a risk in margin deals

Buying stock on margin (where you put up part and borrow the rest from your broker) becomes even riskier than usual in a case where a family man dies leaving a large unpaid margin balance. His executor—and heirs—can be caught in a bind.

In recent years, some brokerage houses have introduced credit life insurance—it pays off a margin debt, usually within a fixed range, say, up to $50,000. Originally (a few years ago), Bache & Co., Shearson, Hammill & Co., and Shields & Co., came out with this idea. If you are interested, check with your customer's man.

The monthly insurance rate per $1,000 is pegged to age and the status of the account. It ranges under $1 for a man of 35 up to about $4 at age 70. In some cases, no physical exam is required. You can, of course, cover a margin account by simply upping your regular life insurance, or adding term coverage equal to your outstanding balance. But here the cost is considerably higher than by using "credit life insurance."

Raising cash on your insurance

Life-line borrowing—or cashing in on an old contract clause that the insurance company would as soon forget—has become a popular money-raisers' sport. With good reason, too. Your best bet for low-interest borrowing is life insurance. That is, if you haven't already used up this line of credit and don't mind upsetting your family insurance plan.

The rate is generally 5% simple interest. For example, say that you bought a $50,000 policy at age 35; today—at age 50—you have about $12,500 in cash value. You can usually borrow from the insurance company up to 95% of this amount, and later pay back the principal—or not, as you choose. If you don't repay, but continue to pay your regular premiums, your family's protection is only cut by the amount of the loan (25% in the example).

If your life policy is one that pays dividends, usually you are able to play safe and use the coming year's dividend to buy one year of term insurance to cover you up to the amount of the loan. With some insurers, this can be done without any further physical examination.

And note this point: The borrowing isn't in question if your contract says you can do it. It isn't optional with your insurance company. You have a contractual right—signed, sealed, delivered. Most policies written in the past 25 years have the 5% clause. But you can hardly expect the companies to be rushing to your door with loan papers. Higher legal rates on this type of borrowing are coming in, of course (6%, maybe higher in the future). But a change won't erase the 5% clause in your old policy. *Remember:* If you're middle-aged, with each $1,000 of life coverage owned 15 years, you have about $250 in current cash value—and you can borrow that much at a sweet 5%. That's the point to sing about in this day of the costly bank loan.

Doctor bills ride an escalator

Next, take a close look at your family's health insurance coverage. You can start with *costs*—which are up alarmingly and heading higher. Doctor bills and hospital charges are up more than 50% over 1965, in most urban areas. A high-income man—especially one who wants a private room at the best hospital in town when somebody in the family falls ill—may discover that his medical coverage is outmoded.

The Blue Cross–Blue Shield type of protection is basic, "first-dollar" insurance. You need it. But with its limited per-accident-or-illness payoff range, you most likely need considerably more.

"Major medical" which gives you and your family adequate protection in case of costly, long-term illness, is essential—unless you're prepared to self-insure to, say $5,000 or $10,000 or more.

First, check to see exactly what your company provides. Some company group plans, for example, pay a maximum $5,000 per accident or illness, or per year, often with a $10,000 or $15,000 lifetime maximum.

The same applies to hospital room-and-board charges under major medical. Some plans peg these allowances at, say, $35 a day; often they should be at $40 or $50 or higher, to stay in line with local hospital charges. Also, group plans should include items omitted in the past, like nursing-home care.

Some insurers now are offering private major medical coverage to executives who want more than their group plans provide. You might check with your insurance agent.

Another idea to consider is an individual income-continuation policy. This gives you added protection in the event of long-term disability. There's generally no conflict with any type of company group coverage. Benefits to replace lost income can go to $1,500 a month; and there's a clause that guarantees future insurance if your health declines.

Most major medical plans can be bought only to age 60, but a limited number are available at any age. If you're planning to retire in a year or two, you might arrange in advance to have private coverage take over if your company has a group plan that cuts out at age 65.

Aetna, Guardian, and New York Life are among the leading companies offering 65-plus plans that dovetail with Medicare benefits. Companies that sell individual major medical with payments in the executive's range include American National, Bankers Life of Iowa, Equitable, Hartford Accident, Mutual Life of New York, Phoenix Mutual, Provident Mutual—and the list is growing month to month.

Tip: In picking a plan, look for one that has no "internal limits" (daily allowances for hospital room, etc.)—a point to your advantage, especially as private hospitals raise their rates.

Top-dollar medical plans

Today medical insurance for higher-income people covers even such high-cost surgical procedures as kidney and heart transplants.

New major medical policies sold to individuals are pushing higher limits. With life companies such as Aetna, Equitable, Prudential, and Travelers, you can get benefits up to $25,000 or more per accident or illness for each member of your family. And the trend is up. Guardian Life, for example, has a $50,000 maximum-payoff contract.

If two or more in the family are injured in an accident, you get a full payoff for each person. With some policies only one deductible is applied.

Premiums, like coverage, are going up, too. With coverage of, say, $20,000 per accident or illness, a man of 45 with a family will pay about $135 to $200 a year, assuming a $1,000 deductible. There's a good choice of policies to age 60, a narrower choice to 64.

Executives' medical coverage: a new trend

Medical insurance for individuals is due for some changes in the next few years, and one important shift will be to an emphasis on benefits both in the hospital and out. Up to now, executive-type coverage has stressed in-hospital benefits.

Comprehensive high-ticket family policies are just beginning to cover such items as diagnosis in your own doctor's office, including the cost of lab tests and x-rays; regular house calls and office calls for everybody in the family; nursing care at home; and convalescence in a nursing home.

One line of policies is the "New Century Series" by Mutual of Omaha. It provides hospital room and board for 180 days per accident or illness for any family member up to $50 a day; surgery up to $1,000 with $2,000 for a transplant; maternity benefits including coverage of the infant from birth—plus the out-of-hospital items. Total dollar protection under this plan goes as high as $15,000 per accident or illness. Assuming a $300 deductible, the cost for a man age 45, with a wife age 40 and two teenagers, comes to about $500 a year. That's high, but remember it does cover doctor calls and other out-of-hospital expenses.

Other leading companies, such as Aetna Life & Casualty, Continental, Metropolitan, Travelers, Connecticut General, and Occidental Life, can be expected to enter the field soon with variations on the same concept. *And note:* This coverage can be designed to supplement an executive's company group protection.

A "super" major medical policy called Excess Med—paying you and your family up to $100,000 per accident or illness—has been introduced by Northwestern National. For a modest premium over the regular cost of your major medical coverage, you get a protection payoff that will take care of the longest-term, inflated-rate medical expenses. With a $10,000 to $15,000 deductible, the cost runs up to $100 a year.

Income protection

Income protection is an executive's and professional man's coverage that has become big in recent years. A new disability income contract points up a trend in this field that's worth checking out with your insurance man.

The policy, introduced by Aetna Life & Casualty, pays you up to $1,500 a month in replacement income if you are sick or injured and unable to work. If the disability begins before age 45 and continues the rest of your life, you receive the benefits for life. After 45, your benefits run until age 65. *Note:* The policy guarantees a total refund of premiums at age 65 if no benefits have been paid in the meantime.

For $1,500 a month in disability income, the premium is roughly $1,150 a year, with a 90-day wait before benefits begin, or $1,050 with a 180-day wait for benefits. The age-65 refund provision accounts partly for the high premium.

The trend has been up and up in the field of disability income protection. Another move in the business makes such policies more attractive to the executive under age 35. One example: If you're in this age bracket, you can now boost your income protection from, say, $500 to $1,000 a month by using a new option plan. The idea is that if your income-level supports it, you can exercise the option for up to 10 years after you buy the policy.

For disability coverages such as these, besides Aetna check Continental Assurance, Guardian Life, Monarch Life, Mutual of Omaha, Paul Revere Life, and Provident Life & Accident, among others.

A new income-protection insurance policy has an inflation hedge added to the usual package. Provident Mutual Life, of Philadelphia, introduced the idea. You buy income-replacement coverage to take effect in case of long-term disability, with benefits payable if needed to age 65. But under the new plan, you get a 2% boost in this monthly payout, starting at the end of each year.

A $1,200-a-month payout plus the 2% feature costs a man of 50 $1,070 a year with a 30-day wait for benefits, and $925 with a 90-day wait.

Note: The "guaranteed insurability" idea—which lets you increase your coverage at the standard premium rate, regardless of future health—is now being sold as part of disability income protection plans.

Up to now, this idea has been limited to life insurance. Now, with the new option, a man under age 40 can buy coverage to make up for income lost because of accident or illness—and at the same time, get a guarantee that as his salary goes up in the future, he will be able to buy proportionately more income protection. Several leading health insurance companies now offer this extra.

New twist in wife insurance

If illness—or an accident—should disable your wife, you would probably face the need to hire extra household help. And nurse-maids, housekeepers and other domestics come high these days.

With this in mind, some insurance companies now have "income" plans that pay off each month while a non-working wife is on the disabled list because of accident or illness. Benefits are generally conservative, but are on the upgrade. Aetna, Continental Casualty, and Mutual of Omaha are three leaders.

Health coverage for high-risk men

Health insurers—like the life companies—are getting more lenient when it comes to selling insurance to high risks. You can buy coverage—despite a poor medical history—from Aetna, Continental Casualty, Guardian Life, Insurance Co. of North America, Mutual of Omaha, and New York Life, among others. The history can include everything from ulcers to emotional disorders. Again, you'll usually pay a higher premium. But some companies, such as Mutual of Omaha, will take you on at standard rates, with a waiting period before benefits may begin.

Where there's a premium boost, the extra rate can vary a good deal. Typical example: A man of 45 who buys a $500-deductible hospital-doctor policy with maximum benefits of $15,000 per accident or illness gets a standard rate of about $110 a year. If he has had a coronary, this goes to $165 or more. Income protection insurance paying $1,000 a month in case of accident or illness costs the same man $750 standard—and about $900 with a coronary history. *Note:* A full return to normal health usually means going back to standard cost.

For the family member over 65: Medicare

The government's Medicare program has wider scope than you may realize, and frankly, might alter some of your personal insurance planning—and this holds true even if you have a high-bracket salary.

In effect, Medicare is a paid-up insurance policy for both you and your wife, beginning at age 65—covering hospitalization, post-hospital care, nursing at home, and outpatient diagnostic services performed in a hospital. It does not cover private physician or dental bills, most drugs, or such items as eyeglasses, hearing aids, and the like.

The aim is to protect all people 65 and over, regardless of income, and whether they are retired or working. Eligibility for Social Security benefits is not a factor for people 65 or over. Here's what you and your wife could get under Medicare—for each separate siege of illness:

Under part A:

Up to 60 days of hospital care—with a one-day deductible—figured on a national cost starting at $40 a day. Thus, for a hospital stay of 60 days with a bill of $2,400, you would pay only $40.

Up to 60 days of post-hospital care in a facility such as a convalescent home, figured on a national cost range—$10 a day. Thus, you would pay nothing if a 60-day bill came to $600.

Outpatient diagnostic services, less cost of a half-day in the hospital. This would cover x-rays, blood tests, and such.

Up to 240 home visits a year by nurses or physical therapists. On the basis of today's charges, your annual protection could run over $1,800—even if you had not been hospitalized.

If you had used up your paid-hospital and extended-care days, you would be eligible for another round of benefits after 90 days had passed, figured from your last hospital day or post-hospital-care day.

Under part B:

With protection optional—and a nominal monthly charge—doctors' bills are covered. Here it is important to check with

the local Social Security office; get the current part B enroll-
ment date.

. . . and Social Security

The 15% boost in Social Security payout—effective as of January
1970—affects everything from a retiree's monthly check to the
benefit paid a 40-year-old widow with small children. Here's
a quick review:

First, note the basic benefits. A man who has all along paid the
maximum tax and retires at age 65 in 1970 gets $190 a month—
up from $165. He can get 80% of the full payment if he retires
at 62 years of age, $86\frac{2}{3}$% at 63, and $93\frac{1}{3}$% at 64. His wife, starting
at age 65, gets 50% of her husband's benefit, or $95—with the
family total, $285. She can get 75% of her age-65 benefit start-
ing at 62. When her husband dies, she gets $82\frac{1}{2}$% of his post-65
benefit ($157) for life.

Under the new law, a man who pays the maximum tax and
retires at age 65 in 1975 will get $204 a month, and for a 1980
retiree this goes to $213—figured on the present $7,800 taxable
wage base. (The Administration has proposed a $9,000 taxable
base starting in 1972, with future top benefits upped accordingly.)

Disability benefits are higher. If you become disabled in
1970—at any age under 65—and have a wife and one or more
children under 18, you get $354 a month maximum. The same
maximum applies if you have children 18 to 22 and in college
or themselves disabled. If your children are grown and your
wife is under 62, you get $190 a month; when she reaches 62,
the family benefit is $261. Disability payments are made until
you recover and are able to return to work, or until you reach
65 when regular retirement benefits begin.

If you die at any age under 65—again assuming you have paid
maximum tax—and have a wife and two or more children under
18, or 18 to 22 and in college or disabled, the family gets $354
a month. With one child, or with two aged, dependent parents

only, it's $284. A lone widow gets $135 beginning at age 60. Your 1970 tax; 4.8% of $7,800, or $374.40—taken from the first $7,800.

Here's a footnote on some misunderstood points: When a man retires, he gets full benefits—$190-a-month maximum—no matter how much income he has from investments, pension, deferred pay, or from exercise of a stock option. If he works just some months in the year—say, two months as a consultant for his company—he can get benefits for the nonworking months no matter how much he earns. He might earn $10,000 a month, and still qualify.

Casualty insurance: the third and final segment

After life and health insurance, you need casualty insurance to complete your protection. Casualty insurance covers everything from a broken water pipe in the basement to the theft of your wife's mink at a convention—to your teenager's auto liability protection.

Start with a fast review of homeowner's policies. With real estate values (prices, anyway) so high that even seasoned real estate agents blush when they show a house, you'd be smart to check on your present homeowner's package plan. You could be underinsured.

Has inflation trimmed your home protection? Say that five years ago you bought a house for $60,000. Today—assuming it's like most property in its class—it might be worth, say, $80,000. This means roughly a 30% jump in value, or 6% a year. "For some areas this is quite conservative," says a Homerica, Inc., executive.

Suppose you now have a total loss by fire. If you haven't increased your insurance, you're out of pocket at least $20,000 on the structure alone, and more if you didn't insure to full value when you bought the house.

If you have a partial loss, with fire or storm damage of $10,000, say, you'll meet up with the "80% rule." Generally this means that to collect fully on your loss you must be carrying insurance up to 80% of the current market value of the house. If you are just a shade under 80%, the payoff may be somewhat under $10,000; it varies depending on the case.

But if your coverage is substantially under 80%, you get a "depreciation recovery" in case of a partial loss. If you have a $10,000 fire, you might recover only about $5,000 or so. Don't underestimate the danger of finding yourself underinsured.

In executive neighborhoods, 5 to 10% annual increases in value have been par all over the country for the past five years. In the past three years, values in some posh suburban areas have inflated even more.

In Connecticut towns such as New Canaan, Greenwich, and Westport and in New Jersey towns such as Short Hills, Saddle River, and Ridgewood the yearly price boost in some neighborhoods has run as high as 15% in some cases. Move west and the same holds—for instance, in places like Lake Forest and Lake Bluff near Chicago.

The cost of more insurance runs about $2.50 to $5 per $1,000 a year.

Homeowners get a break

Lately some new fine print has been tacked to the homeowner's standard policy. At this writing, the changes are in effect in 45 states, and the list is still growing.

One of the major new built-in benefits—for which you pay no extra premium—raises the payoff limit on personal property from 40% of the coverage on the house to 50%. This means that "unscheduled" personal property which is not listed for special floater protection, such as furniture, china, silver, arts works, clothing, and sports equipment, now gets better protection. For example, if your house is insured for $80,000, your unscheduled property is covered up to $40,000, instead of $32,000.

Another break helps the man who moves from one house to another. Formerly, personal property was covered only in transit, pending a new homeowner's policy. Now the coverage extends for the first 30 days up to the 50% limit. The in-transit part, however, is for just 10% of the usual protection.

The rule on theft from an unlocked car turns a bit in your favor. Formerly, a car had to be locked. Now you're protected if you leave the car keys in the hands of an authorized parking attendant. But you are still without protection if you leave the car unlocked and unattended.

Finally, "mysterious disappearance" is defined a bit more liberally. Say that your wife leaves a ring on a wash stand in a restaurant, returns a bit later and finds it gone. The policy now presumes a theft, so you're covered. But note: Protection in case of simple loss—where you have no idea what happened—now takes a special floater policy, under a somewhat tighter rule.

The new limitations add up, too. On standard policies, there's a maximum recovery of $500 for all jewels and furs lost in any one theft—formerly $1,000. You might consider broadening your list of such items already insured by a floater policy which covers virtually all risks (see below).

There's also a change that affects many of the unlicensed vehicles that people are buying these days, such as golf carts, snowmobiles, and some beach buggies. Such vehicles are no longer covered for theft and property damage—under a home-owner's package plan—unless used for service on the premises. Riding lawnmowers and riding snow plows, which have a distinct maintenance function, are covered.

Some policy basics: A Form 3 policy will give you broad coverage that's usually ample. Form 4 is for a tenant, and Form 5—the broadest protection—may overshoot your needs. The Form 5 covers all risks, but it may cost double or more the premium for a Form 3. The point is that with a Form 3 you can add floater coverage tailored to your needs, paying only for what you buy.

Special feature: Instead of the usual $50 deductible in case of a loss, you can get deductibles of $100, $250, and $500. This lets you save up to 20% of your basic premium cost.

Fighting inflation

Homeowner insurance that gives you an inflation hedge—announced a few years ago as an experiment—is now gaining favor. In most states you can buy a rider to attach to your homeowner policy that jumps the face value of the coverage 1% every three months.

Cost increases will vary; but here's a typical example: Say you have a house in the $60,000 to $70,000 bracket, with your homeowner insurance costing about $650 for a three-year term. You can contact your insurance agent and ask for an "inflationguard" endorsement that will jump the coverage 12% in three years for an extra 5 to 8%.

Such big names in the business as Aetna, Continental Casualty, Fireman's Fund, Hartford, State Farm, and Travelers are on the list.

Fighting crime—with personal property coverage

With house and apartment burglaries forever at a new high, clearly it behooves you to look into your protection. If you have more than the usual run of valuables around the house and fear that you can't keep burglars out, one defense is your personal property coverage.

Caution: Avoid the common mistake of relying too heavily on your homeowner or apartment-dweller "package" insurance: It puts a limit on how much you can recover for valuables (usually up to $500 each). It also limits your coverage on property that's stolen away from home. You may need a "personal articles floater" policy for valuables worth over $500, with each item separately appraised and listed.

About the only thing not covered by a floater is wear and tear. Nor are there geographical limits: If your wife's handbag is stolen at the opera in Paris or a thief takes your watch from a hotel in Caracas, you're protected. Also, there's no dollar limit on this coverage, if you're willing to pay the premiums. Rates vary. Insurance on furs costs about 50¢ a year to as high as $1.45 (in Los Angeles) for each $100 of value. Jewelry runs around $1.50 per $100 in most places—but in New York City this is now up to $2.80.

What you pay depends partly on the local crime rate. Whether you live in a house or an apartment, there'll be no rate difference within the same locality. Highest rate areas today are Los Angeles and New York, with Washington and Chicago close behind.

Besides furs and jewels, floater policies can cover costly cameras, musical instruments, silverware, stamps and coins, expensive sports and hobby equipment, and art works. Fine arts rates vary widely, but a fairly typical premium would be $2.50 per $1,000 of value, or $25 a year for a $10,000 Picasso.

Obviously, you should stick to reputable dealers when you have any kind of item appraised for insurance (art works require particular care). And it's wise to keep all bills of sale for new items in your safe deposit box.

Note: You get lower rates for investment jewelry or other small valuables kept in a bank vault—but this doesn't hold for furs kept in cold storage.

You could have trouble buying floater coverage. It might take some shopping around to get coverage on just two or three top-value items, especially in a high-risk area such as Manhattan. And an insurer will certainly be hesitant about taking on any customer who has a record of repeated claims under a standard homeowner's package policy. In any case, with crime rates way up, insurers can be expected to check more closely than ever on people who apply for sizable amounts of floater protection.

Installing antiburglary gadgetry—everything from double-duty locks to electronic alarms—will make coverage easier to buy, though it won't get you a cheaper rate. Having a wall safe also helps ($150 to $350 installed).

If you're traveling, your basic duty—so far as your floater insurance is concerned—is to use "ordinary care." But this boils down to using common sense—it doesn't mean keeping things locked away. Example: If you and your wife check into the

Savoy in London or the Drake in Chicago, you don't have to put your valuables in the hotel safe overnight. The floater still applies.

Fighting vandalism, riots

Vandalism and looting outbreaks in cities may concern you. Generally, a homeowner can breathe easy over the question of damage claims. Your homeowners' package policy—or separate fire and "extended coverage" policies—protect fully against damages caused by riot or vandalism.

If your auto is damaged by vandalism, you'll be fully covered under the "comprehensive section" of your auto policy (this coverage within such a policy typically costs $20 to $30 a year). If you are injured in a riot or civil disorder, your standard and major medical health policies, as well as disability income coverages, will provide full protection.

"Umbrella" coverage: for the high risk

A liability judgment that wipes out a family's assets is a terrifying thought. You're a sitting duck for a big damage suit if you have (1) substantial assets, (2) high visibility in the community, (3) high exposure to risk. That means a big house, prominence in public affairs, extensive travel, a plane or a boat—and perhaps teen-age drivers.

But you can buy protection. A number of insurance companies now offer broad personal liability policies, over and above basic liability insurance—"umbrella" protection. This blanket liability protection—from $1 million up to $10 million—covers everyone in your family, around the world. Policies protect against all the usual hazards, plus such risks as slander, libel, contractual liability, invasion of privacy. Costs of investigation, defense, and settlement are included.

The amount of basic liability coverage you must maintain before you get the blanket policy varies with the company. It might run $100,000/$300,000/$10,000 covering auto accident liabilities,

$50,000 comprehensive personal liability, $100,000 watercraft, and so on. The minimum yearly premium (for a family whose exposure is average is about $70 to $100 a year for $1 million coverage, with $250 deductible. It can be a smart idea—a lot like a big spread of "major medical."

Some companies to contact: Liberty Mutual, St. Paul Insurance, Aetna Life/Casualty, Continental Casualty Insurance Co. of North America.

Slicing your way into a courtroom

There's another reason to have umbrella protection: the sports accident. A short time ago at a Midwest country club a Saturday golfer sliced a hard shot and felled another player close by. The prospect: a serious, permanent injury, as well as an ugly, drawn-out lawsuit, with claims running into six figures. Said a top negligence attorney: "With a jury, liability could go sky-high."

Hashing it all out in a courtroom could also take a staggering amount of time and cause strain for both parties. Any executive ought to know the risks he runs in such a situation.

Say you're on the tee and send off a wild shot that hurts a waiting player. Here the chances are that the legal concept of "assumption of risk" frees you of any liability. The law says, in effect, that the other player assumed all reasonable risks of the game when he left the clubhouse.

But say that you fail to shout "fore" out on the fairway and hit another golfer. Here you'll probably face the basic test of negligence: Did you use ordinary prudence—what the law calls "reasonable care"? If you carelessly ignored the other man, you could be knee-deep in a damage suit. But you also might be able to respond with a claim of contributory negligence.

If you can show that the injured man also was negligent—if, say, he saw you about to swing—then his negligence erases yours. And note: You don't measure it finely; just a little negligence will kill his case.

But you can't count on a standoff, even if your man was negligent. Say that you're with two or three others deep-sea fishing. You haul in a catch and in the process another man is slashed by your hook. First, did the injured man "assume" such a risk when he boarded the boat? If not, then did you use reasonable care?

Suppose that you were, in fact, negligent—and that he was equally negligent. Despite his own carelessness, he may be able to recover damages. How? By showing that you saw he was vulnerable in time to have avoided the accident. Seeing his position, maybe you shouldn't have hauled in at all.

Broad personal liability insurance is, of course, part of the general answer to sports accidents—though the time, sweat, and strain of a court case will come only out of your hide. Your homeowner's package plan routinely provides $25,000 in coverage, and this can be raised to $50,000 for $1 or $2. A high-bracket man may want more. For him, "umbrella" coverage may be a must.

And what about life on the patio?

Cocktails in paper or plastic cups may be insipid bartending, but outside by the pool it makes good sense. A foot deeply cut by broken glass is just one patio possibility that can land a homeowner in a courtroom.

What with pools, kids' tree houses, swings, charcoal fires, dogs—plus youngsters and their elders—filling your backyard in summer, you can ring up quite a list of potential legal liabilities.

Again, insurance may be part of the answer. Basically, you must supervise your property in what the law calls a "reasonable" manner that avoids harm to outsiders. That sounds clear. But getting down to cases may be far from clear. A big question is: Just who got hurt?

You have some steaks grilling on a charcoal fire. A guest sidesteps a running child, topples onto the grill, and is seriously burned. Here you probably stand clear of any legal liability. The social guest assumes a reasonable amount of risk. You needn't make things especially safe for him—like, say, isolating the grill in a far corner.

You can become liable, though, if you fail to warn a guest of any concealed dangers you know about—from a broken stair to slivers of glass in the lawn. If you knew of it, you're hooked. Generally, if you didn't know—it's the guest's risk.

A poolside babysitter takes a little more guarding. She's a business visitor and—like the deliveryman or caterer—has a right to find your property reasonably safe. The theory is, the business visitor must be protected from dangers you should have been aware of—even if you weren't. Your liability is greater.

Live-in domestics are in a special class. They're business visitors—but since they know the premises, they're more open to your counter-claim of contributory negligence. So their protection is limited.

A trespasser (unless a child) takes your property as he finds it, even if he's an innocent wanderer. So, he can't collect damages if he falls into an empty pool. A homeowner's only duty, in effect, is not actively to harm him. Even a suspicious prowler rates his consideration: You can't shoot him without giving him a chance to explain or get out.

Kids and swimming pools, of course, get special attention from the law. Usually, you can't defend yourself in a lawsuit by proving that the youngster was an uninvited guest, a trespasser. The risk is apt to be yours anyway—and this may hold even if you have installed elaborate fences. The law is hard on pool owners, and in some states having a pool means that you're maintaining an "attractive nuisance" strictly at your own peril.

As for pets, some state laws give you a defense the first time your dog bites somebody: You didn't know the dog was "dangerous." In other states, from Maine to California, you get nary one bite—as owner you're liable.

And the lady next door who takes you to court to have you stop those late-night patio parties—she isn't too loved by the law, either. Here you have considerable leeway, short of obvious, out-and-out harassment.

Suppose your 10-year-old son gets too wild with his baseball and lets go a pitch that injures, say, a friend sunning in your yard. Here your liability—or lack of it—as a parent may surprise you. The rule is that you're not legally responsible just because you're the lad's father. (The boy, though, might be sued and have to pay damages—if he has property in his own name.)

You become personally liable, generally, only if you knew that he was pitching too close to your guests—or that he was often careless with a baseball. It's a case of your knowing of a likely danger. The same rule holds, for example, where your child carelessly hurts someone with his bicycle. You might pay heavy damages—if you knew he was often reckless with the bike, but still let him use it.

Special rules cover licensed teen-age drivers who operate their own cars. Generally, the parent can't be held legally accountable.

Insurance won't keep you out of laborious, drawn-out court cases. But you may need comprehensive personal liability coverage—for safety's sake, at least $100,000 to $150,000 worth. Maybe a great deal more is needed—umbrella protection, for instance.

The traps that await directors

What about the corporation director? Anybody who's an "outside" corporate director may want to re-examine his personal obligation in the light of what some lawyers are saying.

Personal liability is wider than you realize. Stockholder's lawsuits are launched more often these days. That's partly because there are more complex mergers being made, partly because of greater shareholder sophistication. An outside director, for example, may sometimes be held liable as the result of such things as inaccurate information in the company's report. If you're a director of a parent company, your personal liability may even extend to suits brought by shareholders of subsidiaries.

Insurance can be one answer. Coverage protecting the outside director can be bought from such companies as St. Paul Fire and Marine, and Lloyds of London. St. Paul's cost range is $225 to $520 per year per $1 million. There is, though, a limitation to this protection.

You're not covered as a director (or officer) of your own company. Corporate policies for this purpose are sold by St. Paul, American Home Assurance, Employers of Wausau, Liberty Mutual, and Lloyds, among others.

Note: "Umbrella" liability coverage (which costs $50 to $70 per $1 million a year, and takes over when your basic auto and homeowner insurance runs out) generally doesn't cover stockholder suits.

Worrying about car theft

Detroit is joining the insurance industry in worrying about auto theft, and some new models have gadgetry to thwart the rustlers. GM, for example, has a warning buzzer for careless folk who leave keys in the ignition; some 60% of the half-million or more cars stolen last year had the keys in them. Ford has steering-column locks for some models. There will be more key-lock combinations (GM will have 4,000 vs. its 200 of 10 years ago), and serial numbers will be easier to check—right on the dashboard.

You can even do it yourself. On the market: auto burglar alarms (horn or siren $30), electrical system cut-outs ($7). Such gadgets are mostly quite effective, but there's a catch. You may forget to flip the switch.

Moreover, car thieves are a resourceful lot. Your car may be next, gadgets or no. Businessmen are especially vulnerable, since it's the late-model cars that are stolen, mostly in urban areas. Nor are the affluent suburban towns immune—even your own driveway is a risky place to leave the key dangling from the dashboard. So lock your car—and check your insurance.

Even if you leave your doors wide open and the motor running, you're usually covered by your auto policy. Comprehensive coverage (fire, theft, etc.) is one reason the adult city driver pays so much for ample auto insurance.

Theft protection varies somewhat, but reimbursement usually is based on cash value of the car as of the date of theft. You have some room for negotiation with the adjuster. But generally, figure 20% to 25% depreciation from cost the first year, 15% more the second year, and a good 10% a year additional thereafter. In any case, don't take an adjuster's first offer without some argument—and maybe a bit of investigating.

Though your auto coverage may seem the best on the market, you can run into vexations if your car has been stolen—like the amount of time it takes to be reimbursed after the police are notified. This can be three days, 30 days—sometimes as long as three months.

Some companies pay $8 or $10 a day for alternate transportation after a theft (frequently there's a $300 maximum). Since this is in addition to what you get for loss of the car, the company is likely to pay off faster.

A good insurance man will steer you away from companies with drawbacks (like slow payoff records or tough claims-adjustment records) and coordinate your auto coverage with other insurance.

Another problem is that although you're covered if somebody steals the tires or car radio, your auto insurance won't help if valuable personal property is taken along with the car, or from within it. Your homeowner's (or apartment owner's) package policy should take care of most such items—within limits. You may need a "floater" for, say, a $4,000 mink (at $12 to as high as $40 a year, depending on your city).

What if a thief steals your car and then is involved in an accident? Are you free of any liability? Generally, yes. Even if you're found to be liable, your insurance covers. The one who stands to lose most is the third party who's injured by the stolen car. Conversely, if you carry "uninsured motorists' protection" (cost: to $5 a year), you are covered if you're the third-party victim.

High cost of a teen-age driver

Think twice before giving your teen-ager a car for graduation. Besides the obvious worries ("Lord, it's one o'clock and he isn't home yet!"), there's the unpleasant question of auto insurance.

Most insurers are loath to take on teen-age drivers, especially boys. Not only must you search for coverage, but when you get it, the cost is sky-high. If you have an unmarried boy under 20, his auto insurance will cost about triple the adult rate, if he is the principal driver of a second or third car in the family. *And note:* This is true even if the car is registered in your name.

One example: say that in a typical case it costs roughly $100 a year to $100,000/$300,000/$25,000 auto coverage with one car and no teen-agers. This goes to $200 if a 17-year-old boy drives his father's car "with permission." It jumps to $300 if the boy becomes the principal driver of a second car.

Obviously, you're better off—in every way—if you tie the boy down to the family car. This way you can insure him under your policy as an occasional driver. If you give the boy a car of his own, even your own insurance company may refuse him a policy.

There are other advantages to keeping a boy tied to a family car. The records show that a youngster is more careful if he uses a family car than if he drives one of his own. Besides, if he has a good record for two years or so, your insurer will probably be willing to cover him under your policy, even if he becomes a full-time driver. *Caution:* In any case, keep him away from the "heap" or "hot rod." This type of driving will likely put him into the state's assigned risk pool at much higher insurance rates—if not in the hospital.

Penalty premiums start to go down for a single man after age 20. At 20, the principal-driver rate is about two and a half times the standard adult rate. This drops each year to just 10% extra at age 29.

However, if you have a boy entering college, he may have a tough time getting coverage if he takes his car away to school.

Best idea, if you can work it, is to keep his car at home and maintain it as a second family car, insured under your own policy.

As for teen-age girls, the family-car rule is still a good idea, at least for a couple of years. A policy covering a girl age 17 as principal driver costs about 50% more than the standard rate for adults. True, this excess premium goes down to 10% for a girl at age 20. But surveys also show that girls are getting more careless at the wheel.

Take a look at some other cost-saving chances:

▪ The multi-car family plan usually saves you 10% in premiums on a second car insured under your policy—even with a teen-age driver. It saves you up to 20% on the husband-wife "family" car.

▪ Teen-agers who have had accredited driver education training often get a premium reduction of about 10%.

▪ Merit-rating plans that pay off for good driving records can save you 10% to 15% on steep teen-ager premiums, given an accident-free record. Conversely, premiums can jump this much after a single accident.

▪ If your son is in the military and able to drive only when home on leave, he'll usually get the standard rate.

Frequency rather than severity of accidents will guide an insurer. If your boy, for example, produces one total wreck, he may be deemed a better risk than if he causes a string of very minor accidents.

Many major carriers guarantee not to cancel a policy after it has run for 60 days, unless your license or car registration is suspended. But if your boy does have a couple of accidents, the company probably won't renew his policy after one year.

Credit-card insurance

Are you responsible for bills run up on a credit card that you never requested? Unsolicited cards have been flooding the mails lately, so this is a question that has many executives wondering.

The answer: If you sign the card—or use it—the law in most

places says you have accepted a contractual obligation. You're liable for all reasonable charges made if the card is lost or stolen. You're generally not responsible, though, if you haven't signed or used the card—even if you have received it and it carries your name. Generally, any card that you have either requested—or accepted by signature or use—carries a liability. You're responsible for charges on a lost or stolen card until the issuing company gets notice of loss.

Some companies now include liability insurance along with their cards. American Express, for example, has coverage that limits your liability to $100. In any case, you can have a rider tacked onto your homeowner's insurance policy; cost runs under $10 per $1,000 per year.

The Land You Live On:
Swinging Real Estate Deals

Grim scene on the buyer front

If you're a novice at the usual tug-of-war over even the simplest real estate deal, you may find some small solace in knowing that a residential property transaction breeds more ulcers than almost any kind of dollar transfer. The middle men alone frighten most people, and for good reason. To help ease this situation, here are some bits of knowledge on buying, leasing, selling, improving—pick your own spot.

Today (circa 1970), the market a buyer faces is grim—especially if he's an executive or professional who wants to move into an upper-class suburb. At this writing, it might even be said that 1970 was the year they hid the key to the house.

Prices today in most big cities are still wildly high. Mortgage rates in a 7 to 10% range are a disaster (and when state law puts a lid on, a buyer is frequently faced with "points"). Down payments, mostly 25 to 50%, are getting stiffer. And the prospect—for now, at least—is generally gloomy.

Forget any notion that buyer resistance has had much softening effect on home prices—in most places, it hasn't. Buyers have for many months been reacting in anger and frustration, but not really enough to put a sizable dent in prices. In the New York City tri-state area, for instance, a survey by Area Consultants shows that prices in suburban bedroom towns went up 13% in the year ending in mid-1970. Westchester County was up 16%. Meantime, cities such as Washington, Chicago, and San Francisco have been showing a 10% annual jump in some top locations, with smaller cities not too far behind.

Timing your purchase

If you must buy, you should try to do your house-hunting early—meaning some weeks or months ahead of the big buying season that gets under way in April–May of each year. Michael Schell of New York's Metropolitan Relocation Associates notes that "real estate brokers will give a 'pre-season' buyer much closer attention." The broker has the time and needs the commissions. More important is the price jump: Between, say March 15 and June 15, an upper-bracket house may well jump 5% in cost to a buyer. Since you're buying a standing house, you aren't faced with the disadvantage of a parallel boost in construction labor costs.

Also, there's a better chance for negotiation in the off-season months when fewer buyers are trooping through houses. A seller who needs to make a move may loosen up on such items as fixtures, carpets, drapes, garden and game room equipment. He may even leave a piano behind—and if you get a real break, he will slice off a bit of the house price because you have a jump on the selling season. *And note:* Sometimes you will do a little better with lenders for your mortgage loan—with fewer home buyers crowding the waiting rooms of banks, building and loan companies, and such.

In any case, if you will be buying in a strange city, always allow a good two or three weeks to pick your suburban community, then two to four weeks more to find a house if you want something really worth your dollars—and figure a month more before the closing.

Cutting costs

In some states usury laws hold mortgage rates down to 7 or 7½%. In New York, for example, the maximum for conventional mortgages is 7½% (8½% for FHA). But the trouble is that "points" are often charged. The points, each worth 1% of the mortgage, are deducted by the lender from the proceeds of the negotiated loan that are paid to the seller. So the seller pays the points, but usually he passes them right along to the buyer.

Today, deals are being made with as many as 5 to 10 points.

In states where there's no maximum on mortgages, the interest rates go sky-high. In Connecticut, for instance, the range is 9% to as high as 9½%.

What can a buyer do? A big down payment may not swing a lower rate, as many people believe. The lender may still need its maximum yield, no matter the amount. Making the rounds of lenders may not be productive—shopping may shave a quarter-point from a mortgage rate, but there's no guarantee. Even an executive's company contacts may not help much: He may land the mortgage, but at the top rate.

One chance for at least modest savings is to assume an owner's mortgage that has a lower rate of interest. The drawback is that the buyer may need extra cash. If the mortgage loan is down to, say, 50% of the value of the property, you—as buyer—must come up with the other 50%, cash on the line. *But note:* If you get advantage of the difference between, say, an 8½% loan and 6%, you save a shade over $2 per month per $1,000. So, on a $30,000 loan, you save $720 a year.

Another way to save on a house deal is to make certain that there's top value in the house itself. It's smart to hire an expert for cellar-to-attic inspection. A builder or engineer will charge $50 to $200. Nation-wide Real Estate Inspectors Service, Inc., with offices in major cities, is one of several growing companies in the business.

Housing abroad: Besides screening suburban bedroom communities in the U.S., such operations as Homerica, Inc., and Previews' Executive Homesearch (a division of Previews, Inc.) are expanding home-location services in Europe.

Sizing up a bedroom community

Aside from home prices and swinging mortgage money, the most painful part of a deal for many buyers is the business of relocation—a problem that plenty of executives have to face every few years. Sizing up a new bedroom community in a new metropolitan area takes more than simply checking in with the local mortgage banker and looking over the local school system.

Executives who have lived through lots of moves—and the professionals who advise them—give these prime suggestions:

▪ First, visit three or four towns in the new area where you expect to live. Then narrow your choice down to one town before you start looking at houses. Reversing this can lead to troubles, they warn.

▪ Take patience along with your bankroll. Says one top Chicago realtor: "Figure on making a few compromises—but let them be in the house you buy, not so much in the town you pick."

You may well find that smart selection of the town you live in will get you more for your money in terms of services, surroundings, convenience. That can be vital now that real estate prices in executive suburbs are way up. Buying a home in a "name" town, say some experts, might easily cost you one-third more than buying in a neighboring area where surroundings are similar and services are likely to be just as good, even better.

Note: Some very well-heeled communities, you'll find, can have weak local school systems because their affluent residents use private schools.

Part of town-shopping depends on the future. If you'll be moving on in four or five years (par for many executives in their 30s and 40s), then you'll want to buy where the resale potential is good. This means, of course, a town or neighborhood that will maintain its character. Says Mildred Janice, a Washington relocation adviser: "A village with good resale features can quickly become a dead duck if the woods bordering it suddenly turn into a 500-house development." Another pro points to the danger of buying in neighborhoods bordering golf courses — the club may sell out to a developer. It happens frequently.

Agents: Generally, the local bank is your best bet for leads to real estate agents. But usually, in town-shopping, you'll want to compare towns yourself, and use a different real estate man in each. Says a Connecticut adviser: "A real estate man is bound to 'sell' his own town. You'll find yourself getting talked out of other possibilities."

There's a rule-of-thumb on taxes. In top-rank suburban towns you'll generally find annual tax bills ranging $20 to $40 per $1,000 of market value. Be sure to ask the real estate agent the dollar amount of taxes last paid on the house you're considering, and if there has been a tax boost since.

If the tax bills in a town seem low, check carefully whether such projects as new schools are being planned. If tax bills seem high, make sure that the houses you have looked at aren't unreasonably taxed within the area. In any case, warns relocation consultant Robert Stahl of New York, don't rely on general "tax rates" published by the town. "They can be terribly misleading."

Whatever guide you might get on taxes, it's a good idea to visit the town hall for information on such things as zoning and planned projects. Usually you'll get candid, straightforward answers from people such as planning board clerks or assistant school supervisors. Moreover, an inside view of the town hall can tell a lot about the community. Says one pro: "Spend an hour in the municipal building, thirty minutes in the library, have lunch in the town restaurant—and you can get a surprisingly clear picture of what the place is really like."

Fire protection?—this you can gauge by comparing insurance rates.

Latest twist in real estate is the small metropolitan-area firm that has no real estate tie-in and sells information on bedroom communities. For example, Area Consultants (New York)—with fees in the $200 range—advise on everything from zoning to commuting headaches. Similar firms are spreading.

That new home: a project you can't delay

Anyone who has ideas about building a new house—instead of buying a standing one—had better start the ball rolling a year in advance. Don't wait until spring if you want to build in summer. *Note:*

▪ If you want an architect, you'll have to find him and sign him a year in advance. Top architects are scarce, over-booked, and work on a long lead-time.

▪ If you want a construction mortgage, you should get your commitment from the lender as soon as you find your architect—don't let time slide.

▪ If you take a look at today's housing scene, you can shape this rule of thumb: Delay costs cash. For instance, if you let months go by before starting your new-house project, chances are that you'll face construction costs—and maybe material costs—that will be higher.

▪ If you do some early digging and find that custom construction in your town is a poor prospect (it is in some areas), you can get busy on a smart alternative: the top-quality prefab house that today has new advantages, and goes easily past the $50,000 range.

When you undertake the project, remember the vital role of the architect. His primary job is to help you find the land and then put your design on paper. But he's also a very valuable bridge between you and the contractor. This can pay off. He can help you pick a reliable builder, then follow through and prevent the project from falling into needless and expensive construction delays (a tormenting problem lately for many people). He can also see that the contractor doesn't use cut-rate methods or grade-B materials.

Finally, if the architect has a reputation for quality design and execution, he'll help your construction financing go through a local lender's office with greater ease. This won't get you a lower mortgage rate, but it will mean quicker handling and more workable terms (perhaps a bigger building loan, if you want it, say 70% instead of 50%).

An architect's fee generally runs from 10% to 15% of house cost (excluding land), with the trend these days to the 15% side. Example: For high-quality custom design, construction cost is roughly $25 to $30 per sq. ft. of floor space. So, for an 8- to 10-room house of 3,500 sq. ft.—at the $25 figure—you would pay $87,500, and the architect would get from $8,750 to $13,125. The fee is paid in installments. A typical scale: 25% when you accept a rough sketch, 50% when the work begins, and 25% when you move in.

How do you pick an architect who will give you the maximum? This gets purely personal; it depends on what you want in a house. But, say the top pros in the field, there are really just two types to consider.

■ One does only contemporary, strictly modern houses—the kind that you see mostly on the West Coast, in the Southwest, in Florida and Hawaii.

■ The second is the traditionalist who does authentic copies of early established styles, like Georgian or colonial. This man is getting to be a rare bird, and if you find one you should cherish him.

What you want to avoid is the compromiser whose work is a

weak blend of old and new. His product will be little more than a standard development house, plus frills. Here's where you waste money.

For a really good result, you need to develop rapport with the architect. He must know your mode of living, and this whole process of understanding takes time, patience, maybe a dozen or more visits—and a bit of arguing. If you and your wife aren't willing to hammer out this kind of relationship over a span of months, then buy a standing house, say the pros. In any case, before you pick your man, see some of his work. And while you're about it, ask two or three of his clients how well he managed to stay within the agreed budget for their houses. Some architects go overboard.

Old houses: charm isn't cheap

The opposite approach is up the garden path—to the old house with the gazebo, the quaint fireplace, and the sagging slate roof. But that charming old house—the one with lots of space and character that your wife wants to "make over"—can turn into a disaster when you get down to restoring and modernizing.

It's a case, of course, of first eying the timbers before you become at all serious. Remember, there's only one sure way to avoid trouble with an old house: If it's on a prime site, and the price is low enough, tear down the house and build a new one.

In any case, a simple—but thorough—layman's inspection can be helpful (before you hire an appraiser at $20 an hour).

First—especially if the house is quite old—line up the top ridge of the roof to be sure it's reasonably straight. A sag could mean a partial framing collapse, and maybe a sizable—and costly—rebuilding job. Lopsided house corners and outside walls that bulge mean foundation weakness and probably a weak frame. Costs can be even higher.

Next, go to the basement. If the walls are of laid-up stone (pre-1900), at least be aware that they may one day pose an expensive problem—even if they haven't started to bulge inward.

If solid masonry, check for cracking, which means dampness, weakness, maybe termites. To test for termites, probe the basement timbers with a knife, especially the "sills" running flat along the top of the cellar walls.

The point is, if you want the house in good, safe, durable condition—for general family use—you can live with just so much deterioration. Remember, too, the problem of resale in 10 or 15 years. Here are some further checkpoints for your inspection tour:

- Ventilation: Peeling on the outside of a frame house means poor ventilation in the walls with too much moisture retained—a new paint job will peel, too. New venting is no major problem, however.

- Firestopping: Without some type of in-wall cross-framing to break the updraft, the fire hazard is apt to be serious.

- Chimneys: Thin-walled, single-brick-thickness types are dangerous; so is lack of fireclay lining, top to bottom.

- Wiring: An eight-to-12-room house needs 16 to 20 circuits—and a circuit-breaker panel—for modern operation; if you see a fuse box in the basement with only four or six circuits (typical), the wiring is inadequate, outmoded.

- Plumbing: After checking basement piping for heavy corrosion, go to the topmost floor with a bathroom and open all faucets; a strong flow of clear water means at least usable piping—and adequate pressure.

Say that you finally call in an appraiser, get his tentative O.K. (he usually will have reservations)—and decide to buy. You'll likely end up doing more restoring and modernizing than you counted on. Costs vary, depending on locale, but generally you can figure on these ranges:

- A quality bathroom costs $3,000 to $5,000 if entirely new space and piping are needed, and $2,000 to $3,500 if you can use an existing layout.

- A kitchen, depending on fanciness and existing layout: $3,000 to $6,000.

- A basement game room with bar runs $3,000 to $4,000 deluxe (wall paneling, suspended ceiling, recessed lighting). Important: For a good livable job, you need reflective insulation behind the paneling.

- A new wing in quality construction costs $22 to $25 per square foot; and $30 or more with bath, electrical units, and such.
- A complete rewiring job for eight to 12 rooms runs $1,000 to $1,500.
- Blown insulation can cut your heating and cooling bill by 30% or so; it also tends to prevent spread of fire. Cost is about $1,500 for eight to 12 rooms; installation time is one week.

As for heating, consider radiant wall heaters if you open up unused space or add a wing—instead of installing a new heating plant. For an 8-to-12-room house, a new furnace (often needed in a pre–World War II house) will cost about $1,200 to $1,500, including automatic controls and labor. A central heating-cooling system runs about $3,000 if ducts are already in; $5,000 if new ducts are needed (assuming that walling construction makes it possible to run ducts at all).

If you have no buying experience with window (or wall) room air conditioners, count on at least $1,000 to $1,500 for enough tonnage to cool the bedrooms and other hot rooms. *Note:* All of these costs are rough, and can vary by as much as 25%, depending where you live.

One more tip: If you intend to create new space instead of just improving old space, hire an architect. Among other things, an architect can avoid a "remodeled house" appearance that quickly gives away a redone house. If you add only modern equipment, or a bathroom or kitchen—hire a contractor. Check his references, and work on a contract basis.

Second homes: good buys, but not cheap

If you have ideas of buying a second home—for summer vacations and year-round weekending—you'll find prices up, from the Hamptons on Long Island on out to California's Big Sur country.

Still, you can find good buys, if not cheap ones—and there are some tips on how to get the best location, comfort, and value. There may even be a rewarding investment angle—where, say, you want a summer place to sell later on when the youngsters are on their own. Speaking of later sale: If possible, get a "winterized" house—with heating usable in cold weather. The summer retreat without winter possibilities is nowhere near so salable. Decidedly, the trend is to all-year-round.

On timing: In most upper-level resort areas—such as Cape Cod, Woodstock (Vt.), the Glen-Torch lake section of Michigan, and on west to Pebble Beach in California—the best house-hunting is in July and August. The sensible idea is to look around the area you want during a summer vacation (maybe renting a place in the meantime), then sign a contract after Labor Day. Avoid a quick, early-summer buy (particularly in June), if possible.

Choice waterfront properties—ocean and lake—have been going up in price from 5% to as much as 20% a year since 1960. What with the supply fixed and demand pressing heavily, the next few years—during the early 1970s—may see more of the same.

Good-quality oceanfront land in southern Maine, for example, is up from $125 a front foot five years ago to at least $150 or more. This is for the land alone; you build your own villa. Prime-location vacation houses in Big Sur have as much as doubled in price in five years; at Stowe, Vermont, where you sun in summer and ski in winter, choice land is up around 50% in the past five years; and in good locations, it can cost over $10,000 an acre (plus what you pay for a lodge).

If you want to be within daily commuting distance of a city (say, on the shore of Long Island Sound in exurban Connecticut), you pay a sky-high price. If you go further away—to the weekend commuting circle (say to some place in Dutchess County, two hours up the Hudson from New York), you'll pay roughly 40% less for comparable property.

Finally, if you go past the weekend circle to a more remote spot, you'll get another cut in price, sometimes sensational. If you want a current example of such buys, contact, say, Previews, Inc. (New York)—they often list properties in remote locales where bargains exist.

Just where, then, is your best buy? The haven far from civilization may be tempting—but may have enough drawbacks built in to outweigh any price break. Such things as insurance and repairs can be a headache—not to mention the question of future salability. And, say old hands, the travel time can become downright painful. On balance, your best buy is, first of all, probably within present-day weekend travel distance (not too far beyond), and second, a standing house instead of a bare piece of land that calls for new construction.

Overall, you will certainly get more value for your money, in space and quality, if you buy a solid shelter instead of hiring a builder. In resort areas, material costs can be quite high, and local labor may do you few favors unless closely supervised—and who will do that? A possible solution: the vacation prefab (see below).

In most vacation areas, cash down payments run 40 to 50%—up to 100% if you have your eye on a retreat that is miles from a crossroad.

As for mortgages, they're tough—especially if the place lacks winterized construction. Sometimes (and this helps, particularly in remote areas) the seller is willing to take back a mortgage himself. Mortgage rates in resort localities are running $7\frac{1}{2}$ to 10% in most sections. (In the Caribbean, they're up to 12%.)

Sometimes a city bank—where a buyer lives—will make a vacation-house loan by lending on the basis of the buyer's local residence in the city. This means extending the first mortgage, if there is one.

Insurance can be a headache, too. In distant areas of Maine, for example (and this is typical), full homeowner's coverage on a $40,000 house will cost about $800 for three years, as against roughly $400 in the city. Sometimes you can't get full homeowner's protection, and you may have to do a lot of shopping for straight fire and storm insurance. On the oceanfront, flood-and-wave coverage is virtually unavailable. A shore house, incidentally, should be protected by sand dunes a good 16 to 20 ft. high—a heavy storm can level a 6- or 8-ft. dune.

Brokers: There tend to be some fly-by-night, part-time real estate operators around many vacation areas. The best idea is to ask the president of the local bank for a recommendation. This can make a world of difference.

Second homes that come from a factory

Another idea on the summer-home front is the smartly designed prefab. It's a growing trend and one well worth looking into. You move the prefab to your site on a flat truck, put it up fast, and save time, money (some, anyway), and maybe a lot of headaches trying to locate a resort-area builder for a quality original job. *And note:* By and large, the prefab will cost you less than a standing house—a deal where an owner has sales profit in mind.

More and more prefabricators—from Acorn (Concord, Mass.) to Serendipity (San Francisco)—are turning out the $15,000 to $25,000 beach cottage, mountain hut, or hunting lodge. Tech-built Homes (Boston area)—makers of exceptionally fine prefabs —even has a chill-proof package that can double as a summer house and ski lodge. *Timing:* Take a few months to examine a few prefab catalogues, and possibly pick a future site during your next regular vacation.

Prefabs come in all sizes and shapes. They can be as simple as a pier-foundation fishing shack. And they have also moved into the luxury class: Hamill Homes (Grand Ledge, Mich.), for example, has summer houses in the $50,000 range. And nowadays you can find summer prefabs that are the work of leading architects—for example, Carl Koch of Boston and Charles Goodman of Washington, D.C., both designers of contemporary styles, and such traditionalists as Herman York of New York City.

For, say, $25,000 (plus land cost), you can get an expertly designed prefab summer place. A comparable custom job—by a quality architect (if you could find one willing to do it)—

would cost you a good $10,000 more in fees and extras. And it could easily cost you up to $20,000 more, especially if you landed a contract with one of the top architects in your city. Besides, with a prefab you should be able to count on an overall saving in construction cost of 10%—maybe as high as 15%, as against the cost of an original construction.

The average prefab company will have a dozen or so basic plans, plus variations, in several styles. You can pretty much pick your own layout—and get a design that will enable you to start small, and add to the summer house in future years. You get a semi-custom design.

There are more advantages: If you stick with the leading manufacturers, you'll also find the quality of materials generally good. Besides wood, there's a new trend to the use of aluminum parts for durability and easier maintenance.

The residential prefab can be finished six weeks after the foundation is set—same for a small summer cottage. This is a good 50% faster than even speedy conventional construction.

Finally, you will learn that financing a quality prefab is easier today than a few years ago, when lenders looked down their noses. The deal may take some doing, but it can usually be handled.

But buying a prefab isn't all clear and easy. First, you'll want to check on the possibility that a zoning ordinance or building code limits or even eliminates your freedom to put up a prefab. Sometimes deeds have this restriction. Also, despite new materials, you are most likely limited to frame construction. You can't get solid brick or fieldstone!

Plumbing, heating, and electrical equipment sometimes must be installed at the site in the usual way (and often by local workers) so that a lot of the potential saving of a prefab may be lost. Check carefully. You are also obligated to use the crew of the prefab company's builder-dealer in the area. Generally they are quite good, but if they do a slipshod job, you're in trouble. *One safeguard:* Hire an engineer to make a few brief inspections.

Other companies that sell quality, higher-priced prefabs include: Deck House (Acton, Mass.); Kingsberry Homes (Atlanta,

Ga.); Leisure Homes (Youngstown, Ohio); and Blackstock (Seattle, Wash.).

Riding the boom in vacation condominiums

There are more choices on the real estate scene than there are stock options in an executive suite. The second-home front is alive with all sorts of ideas. Example: There's a vacation condominium craze going on. Today you can find apartments and "town houses" and fancy vacation villas on the condominium plan in scores of choice carriage-trade locales—from California's Lake Tahoe to the Fajardo–Las Croabas section of Puerto Rico. They're a booming part of the real estate business— and they're selling fast.

Winter could be a good time to get into the swim: You visit the area you like, check the plans on the drawing boards, and sign a deal that will have you comfortably installed by the following winter season. Why winter? Buying a winter vacation condominium offers a chance to plan smartly for retirement some day. But you can play it the other way too: Buy an apartment and sell it in a few years at handsome capital gains. Pick right and you can get:

▪ An automatic wintertime vacation site amid compatible neighbors, with no tedious trip planning or reservations needed.

▪ Built-in recreation facilities, domestic services, and property maintenance.

▪ A chance to profit from management-supervised rental of your property when you're not there.

▪ A workable, warm-climate retirement plan—you buy at, say, age 50 or so, and with little effort have the condominium paid for before age 65.

You'll find a vast variety of locations and prices. In Acapulco, for example, beachfront condominiums by Playasol range from $20,000 (one bedroom) to $140,000 (four-bedroom penthouse). In the San Juan area of Puerto Rico, high-rises range from $20,000 to $75,000 (you can buy an option for $1,000 or $1,500).

World Resorts, Ltd. (New York), is building a 2,000-unit complex in St. Croix at $60,000 to $90,000 and has plans going as far afield as the Greek Islands.

Away from the ocean you can find such condominium centers as the Tennis Club and Rim Crest developments at Palm Springs ($35,000 to $70,000), the Woodmont ski lodges at Snowmass-at-Aspen ($60,000 range), or Lake Village on Lake Tahoe—only a half mile from the casinos ($35,000 up).

Having the management rent your property part-time each year can bring down the cost of purchase. But check the details—one point is that rental commissions will vary from 10% (most usual) to as high as 50% of your income.

Take pencil and paper to any proposed rental deal. Here's a fairly typical example, based on sales at the Alphorn ski condominium at Vail, Colo. Say that you buy an Alpine ski lodge costing $38,000. This takes a downpayment of 30%, with financing of 70% at $9\frac{3}{4}$% over 20 years, for $272 a month. With the $50 management fee added, the monthly payment comes to $322—or $3,864 a year. You can rent to vacationers in winter for 60 days at $75 a day, and in summer for about 20 days at $50 a day. Total rental income: $5,500. Rental commission, maid service charges, and linen charges are taken out—bringing your income from rentals down to $3,600. Your net cost comes out to $264 a year. Ideal? Yes, and it can be done—given smart selection of your property. Also, you should get a tax break. In most cases, you can deduct for insurance, repairs and maintenance, and depreciation as an owner of rental property.

Your chance for a hefty resale profit is good, judging by some current sales. In Acapulco, apartments that cost $32,000 in 1968 have been selling for $50,000. Similar results hold for south Florida, where some high-bracket condominiums have jumped in value 12 to 15% a year.

But note: The pattern is uneven. Puerto Rico, for example, where condominiums are numerous, shows annual boosts in value of just 5% in most cases.

Checking the fine print: The biggest problem for a buyer is quality of management, and the record of the condominium outfit should be checked out, as in any business deal. Rental results, especially, hinge on management. You should know precisely what is and isn't covered by the monthly maintenance charge. See how it covers such items as group insurance on common areas, painting and repairing of the building exterior, landscape maintenance. Ask about special assessments for such items as pool construction and upkeep and new tennis courts— you can be stuck for features voted in by others.

Get a good lawyer for the closing, and watch for special closing fees.

Homesteaders rush to Spanish Main

How about a beach house someplace between the Bahamas and Barbados? A new wave of real estate activity rolling across the islands is carrying with it escape-minded vacationers and prospective retirees. You'll find them three miles from Nassau on Cable Beach, or 1,000 miles off the beaten track in Tobago or Bonaire.

Many Caribbean pilgrims like to talk about finding "new, unspoiled" islands. It sounds intriguing. But remoteness may not suit you if you have retirement in mind. Most Americans, it seems, wind up in centers of activity such as Montego Bay, St. Croix, and even the outskirts of San Juan. Anyplace in this area, you will find prices high and heading higher. *But note:* In the Caribbean and Bahamas the summer "sell" is softer, and by seeking your property during the summer "off" season, you get a jump on the tide of affluent buyers from the U.S. and Europe. They make the trip south in wintertime when it's fashionable. And summer in the islands is pleasant—usually in the high 80s, with a trade wind.

The buy-and-rent-retire idea is one approach. You buy an acre, build a house, and have an agent rent it when you're away. This takes some sting out of the cost, which can run to, say, $90,000 for a quality house near Nassau. You use the house two months a year and rent it for 10—at $5,000 or $6,000. This pays light bills, air fares, and a little on your investment. The advantage over the condominium approach is that you can pick your own location and your own particular style of construction.

One way to get started is to pick likely islands and write to each local chamber of commerce for the names of land developers and agents who deal in your price range. But first, note some basics:

▪ *Inflation can hit like an autumn hurricane.* The asking price for an acre in, say, Montego Bay may be 20% more than last year —or 40%. So far, no letup in this boom is in sight, especially since more jetports and small-craft landing strips are being built in the islands.

▪ *Bargaining is a must.* You have to haggle to unearth the truth behind the "asking price." An advertised $10,000 acre might be had for $6,000 by the time you reach for your checkbook. But the reverse holds, too. You can get caught in a bidding trap, and pay $15,000.

▪ *Good quality land is important.* You may want to sell later, and lower-grade property in the islands tends to stay lower-grade. Also, some "bargain" locations may end up too near a future industrial development.

▪ *Politics can be a factor, too.* In the spring of 1970, for instance, Trinidad had a flare-up of street violence. Also, the very alluring tax shelters that some islands have offered foreigners could be modified by future governments.

With these ground rules in mind, scan the sea of islands.

At Lyford Cay outside Nassau—one of the posh spots of the Bahamas—people pay up to $50,000 for homesites, plus $100,000 and up to build. But you can travel at a slower pace. On Windemere Island, off Eleuthera, for instance, $65,000 gets you oceanfront plus beach house. On Norman Key in the Bahamas, you can even do well for $40,000.

At Dorado Beach, 10 minutes by air taxi from San Juan, golf-course lots are going at $25,000 to $45,000 and construction at $50,000 and up. More modestly, in the surrounding Dorado area you can find quality locations and spend about 40% less. In any offbeat locale, though, shop with great care.

In St. Croix's two towns, Christiansted and Frederiksted, figure $30,000 and up. Jamaica, Antigua, and Barbados are, of
course, popular. At the Tryall Club near Montego Bay, Jamaica,
for example, you'll easily spend $100,000. But at Port Antonio,
down the coast, you can get by for $40,000.

Caution: In any month, go in person. Never buy site-unseen
in the Bahamas or Caribbean—even if your cousin is a backer of
the development.

Got a yen for the good earth?

There's yet another second-home path to follow. Go the way of
the cow-barn-silo-woodchuck—buy a farm. Make it weekend
distance away, of course—and when you're 65 (or will it be 60?),
retire there.

Handle it right, and you may even swing a good long-term
investment, some tax benefits (*if* you run a regular farming
business)—and you may even pick up some current income.
But if you're serious about the farm idea, not just casual weekending, be prepared to plow a lot of money into the project.
Farmland prices are up an average of 50% since 1960, and they
were up 10% in 1969 alone—at least in many locations. The
steepest price rise, of course, has been close in near the big
cities.

The trick: Go just far enough—and in the right direction—
from your city to get acreage at a good price, and pick up maximum future appreciation possibilities. But don't get stranded in
farmland Siberia, meaning so far away from where you live that
a weekend trip to the farm becomes unbearable. Isolation will
get you no place.

Some examples of what you can do: Farmland within 50 mi.
of Chicago goes for $2,200 to $2,500 an acre. Go a bit farther and
it drops to $1,000 or $1,200. Another 25 mi. to 50 mi. and it's
$850 an acre. About 100 mi. out of San Francisco, choice land
goes for about $500 to $700 an acre. It's $1,500 to $2,000 near the
city. The same holds true, generally, for Atlanta, St. Louis, and

other cities. Soil quality and water—lake, well, irrigation—also affect price, of course.

For an idea of land values, see the free publication *Strout Nationwide Property Values* (311 Springfield Avenue, Summit, N.J.). For leads to farms and brokers, try the National Institute of Farm & Land Brokers (155 E. Superior Street, Chicago) and the United Farm Agency (612 W. 47 Street, Kansas City, Mo.).

Note: Often the local bank's trust department has a farm ripe for sale, and you save commission and get financing.

You can get a 50% mortgage for five to 15 years from insurance companies and the Federal Land Bank. But you get better rates and terms by financing through the seller with a "sale on contract." A small downpayment and mortgage installments let the seller spread the tax on his profit. As a buyer you pay less outright—yet get all benefits of appreciation and full depreciation. Keeping your investment spread thin with, say, a $10,000 downpayment on a $100,000 farm gives you big leverage possibilities. This is the angle to work.

Before buying, get an appraisal. The American Society of Farm Managers & Rural Appraisers, DeKalb, Ill. can give you leads. For $250 to $1,000—depending on the property—an appraiser will estimate the farm's income potential, its market value, and will study its present—and future—tax structure.

Caution: Along with faster appreciation, farmland close to a city frequently switches from rural to urban assessment—and taxes shoot up.

A city slicker sometimes forgets basic economics in his return to the soil. Farming is a complex business today, and needs to be managed like one. This means starting out with an "economic unit"—enough land to support costs such as taxes and interest, and still return a profit. Area, climate, terrain, soil, market, and crop determine how much land you need. Near St. Louis, for example, you would need 400 acres to raise soybeans profitably. Fewer acres, say 300, would tightly squeeze your profit potential—even if you managed the farm like a pro.

Non-tillable land is best put to grazing or trees. Both call for little risk, but bring little profit (and with trees you have to wait a long time for it). With crops and livestock, prices fluctuate. Still, cash crops, such as alfalfa, soybeans, hay, corn can return nice profits. Feeder cattle farms are lately popular with weekend farmers near metropolitan areas, who buy calves (about 500 lb.) for fattening (to, say, 1,100 lb.). But experienced full-time help is needed. Orchards and dairy farms are more sophisticated operations.

Professional management is almost essential if you want income out of your farm. Few weekenders have either the time or knowledge to handle the complexities of today's farming. This means finding a competent farmer to handle your place on a contract basis, or turning the whole operation over to a professional farm manager such as Doane Agricultural Service, St. Louis. Or you can turn to the farm management staff of a bank like Chicago's Northern Trust Co. They'll hire the farmer, do the paperwork (keeping tabs on federal and state farm programs), and manage the operation so it returns a profit—typically 4% to 6%. For this, you pay an annual fee per acre or a percentage of the gross, say 7% to 10%.

If you can demonstrate to the Internal Revenue Service that your farm is a business, not just a hobby, you get tax advantages. But you must show that profit is your motive—and get specific advice on the ins and outs of the 1969 tax reform law.

Real estate can be a tricky investment

In the 1960s, real estate investment made millionaires—and it created some financial quagmires, too. In the 1970–75 era, the same basics apply, but more finesse is needed to turn a smart dollar. In any case, There's more to real estate investment than an inflation hedge. Some of the activity today ties into retirement planning (like buying a six-unit apartment for income and living in one unit). But most investors are just out for cash profit.

Raw land holds the most opportunity—and the most risk. Pick the right spot (say a couple steps ahead of city expansion) and you can make a killing. You may pay $1,000 an acre a few miles out of town, and sell it in 10 years for $10,000—or more. Or you can sell it for the same $1,000—and be out of pocket for taxes at about 3% a year, plus closing costs and installments on a mortgage (if you can get one on a raw land deal).

Pinpointing property that's just a few years from development takes careful research on population, planning, traffic, zoning— plus a sound hunch. Too close to town and you're priced out of the market. Too far, and you will have a long wait for appreciation. And remember, in buying raw land you must figure what your money could earn elsewhere. One source of help: Income from leasing to someone such as a driving-range or filling-station operator, or farmer.

Apartments, stores, and other rental units are short on appreciation, but give you income, tax depreciation—and a little less gamble. You gain the most advantage from tax depreciation by buying land-plus-building with the building amounting to a major part of the value—say 75%. The depreciation factor is even more attractive if you pay the minimum down—maybe 25%. The 25% is possible this way: You get a 20-year 60% mortgage (currently at, perhaps, 8½%), and ask the seller to take an additional "purchase money" mortgage covering 15%. The fact that you are left with an effective down payment of 25% means you're getting top depreciation. This gives you big leverage possibilities. A 10% annual return (the range for well-managed property) translates into 15% if you have this kind of high depreciation and low down payment.

Aim to have about 75% of gross cover costs. For example, with a 12-apartment building, the rent from nine of them should take care of management, maintenance, taxes, and mortgage, giving you a net income from three units.

Note: Cooperative and condominium apartments have a live-in feature that's getting popular. You buy two units, or a whole floor of a building, live in one and rent the rest. With a condominium you get a deed that provides reasonable freedom to rent or sell as you choose. With a co-op you get a proprietary lease (a cross between a long-term lease and a deed), and this may mean you need approval of an owners' committee before sub-letting.

In an ideal setup, each of two apartments might cost you $50,000, with monthly carrying charge (for maintenance, taxes, interest, mortgage) coming to $400, or $800 total. Your tax and interest deduction might amount to 30% to 40% of the $800, or $240 to $320 a month. Living in one unit and renting one for, say, $600 gives you a cushion.

But note: Condominium and co-op deals frequently surprise an owner with hidden costs (for insurance, heavy outlays for renovating lobbies).

Real estate investment trusts (REITs) and syndications are—for the average investor—complex and risky. What you do, in effect, is buy a unit of ownership in, say, an office building. You pay from $5,000 to $20,000 or more for a unit, and hope for a payout. A 10% return is quite possible. So is losing your shirt. Success turns on the quality of management, its expertise and integrity. It's a case of thorough investigation on your part—in advance.

Some starters for reading up: *How to Make a Fortune Today —Starting from Scratch,* by William Nickerson (Simon & Schuster); and *Making Money in Real Estate,* by Lawrence Beneson (Grosset & Dunlap).

Quick look at a lease

Leasing an apartment—or a house, if you can find one—may be one way to sit out the high-priced housing market for a year or two. With house prices rising at an annual rate of 10% in many top-grade suburbs and conventional mortgages at 7½% to 10% interest, you might be smart to become a tenant for a spell. It depends on your personal circumstances and where you live, but you could be better off leasing—even if you had to break the lease later on. The penalty is usually one to three months' rent, maybe a bargain in view of current mortgage rates.

Note: If you follow this route, you are banking on softer prices for houses—in a certain section of a city—and softer or "easier" mortgage loans, in the future. It's a calculation.

But no matter why you lease instead of buying, you will want to check the fine print in the lease with your lawyer, and get every scrap of advantage you can. Note that even your rent can be upped before the lease term ends—if the fine print says it can.

If you have been a homeowner for years, you may be surprised by all the details a lease can cover. For instance, an apartment lease should spell out the question of redecoration—even down to the number of coats of paint. If you'll be putting in a partition or installing, say, a special lighting fixture, it should give you permission and tell who will own any new fixtures when the term is up.

Look for special house rules buried in the lease; things like use of the garage, late-hour entertaining, and so on. The trouble is that such rules—if reasonable—can become grounds for eviction if breached. If it's a new building or an old one being renovated, get a safeguard that won't let you be without utilities (heat, light, water) for longer than is absolutely necessary for emergency repairs. It can be an important protection. Generally, you can sublet unless a clause prohibits it. Try to get a firm statement giving you the right. You would continue to be liable for the rent—but you would have an out if you found the right house to buy.

In a suburban town, go directly to the building manager; a real estate agent isn't apt to list many apartments. And sometimes if a broker does handle a rental, you (as tenant) may have to pay his commission or finder's fee. *Tip:* If you're leasing a house, try hard to swing an option to buy—sometimes this will work, and provide a break if and when mortgage terms soften.

Leasing land: buying concept

The "residential leasehold"—where land for a new house is leased for terms of 20 years or more—is an idea that's been used around the country from Connecticut to California. If (as expected) land prices move up, you'll see more of it. Advantages apply especially to *high-bracket real estate deals*. Both buyers and sellers often get a good break.

As a buyer, you pay less down, and generally less per month. For example, in a choice California residential area, a lease for a prime waterfront lot costs about $6,000 yearly. The $100,000 the site might otherwise have cost can be profitably invested. In Connecticut, a leading builder sold house and lot for $65,000 —or house alone for $45,000, with a long-term lease on the land. With the lease, a buyer saves $5,000 in down payment, and his monthly payments can be reduced by as much as a third.

Or say you are a land holder. Suppose you own an acre or two in your neighborhood, purchased years ago. If you sell it outright, you likely would pay a sizable capital gains tax—not so with a lease. What's more, in this kind of lease deal, real estate taxes are paid by the lessee. And you, as owner of the land, retain control over its future development—and pick up an annual income as high as 10% of the current fair market value of the land.

Terms of residential leaseholds vary widely around the country. Leases generally run from 20 years to 75 years, although some run to 99. Often there is an option to renew the lease at 5-, 10-, or 20-year intervals. You would want to check with your lawyer first because state laws, of course, play a part. In Maryland, for example, a new law says that lessees will have a right to purchase after 20 years. But in this day of mobility, who stays in a house for over 20 years?

Decorators: new look in
design, style

Move for a moment to a vantage point at one end of your living room. Does it look a mite down at the heels? In fact, does the whole blasted house need the going-over inside that your wife says it does? Redecoration is, of course, in a woman's bailiwick—

but as a husband, you will find it pays to get involved. You'll be paying the bills, and today the bills can be higher than the sky-light.

In the hands of a top interior designer, a complete living room job could set you back $5,000; the entire house, $30,000. It can go higher, of course. Then why use a professional at all? Why not simply redo the rooms yourselves?

The reason is that it's good business. A first-rate interior designer (the top people disdain the term "decorator") provides purchasing savvy in a complex, specialized market. Thus, he (or she) can spare you costly mistakes. And the designer's artistic talents give you the benefit of his knowledge of scale and proportion, color harmonies, furniture, the newest materials and their durability. Today's preference for blending traditional (including antiques) and contemporary pieces takes a particularly astute eye and skilled hand to carry off well. Above all, you get individuality. First-rate designers deal only in exclusive merchandise, buying at sources generally not open to the public.

The ideal way to find an interior designer is through a friend who has worked with one and is satisfied with the results. Be sure to see examples of his work—either in a client's home or in color photographs. Other sources are the professional societies: National Society of Interior Designers (136 East 57th Street, New York, N.Y.) and the American Institute of Interior Designers (730 Fifth Avenue, New York, N.Y.).

Better department stores have interior designers, too. But using their services usually entails an obligation to buy most, if not all, your furnishings from the store. Fine—if you like the selection and it's big enough to fit your needs. *Note:* There's no exclusiveness with big-store merchandise—except in a few stores such as W. & J. Sloane and Lord & Taylor.

First, the designer comes to your home to study the family's manner of living, likes and dislikes in furnishings, color preferences, and existing furnishings you want worked into a new scheme. Standard consultation fee is $25 or more an hour, but top designers command a flat $100 to $200. But the fee is often dropped if you retain the designer. Remember that the designer's job is to reflect your taste, not to impose his own. If there's no initial rapport, he's not your man. And be prepared to spend considerable time seeing the job through (from two to four months).

If you're pleased with the designer's ideas and they fit your budget, the next step is a contract. This should state the services and furnishings you will get for an agreed-upon price, method of payment, date of completion. Be sure to insist on a target date.

Financial arrangements vary. Some designers bill only for furnishings, charging you the list price and taking a profit on the markup from the manufacturer's wholesale price. (Markups run 40% to 50% on furniture, 30% on fabrics, 25% on carpeting, 10% to 20% on antiques, 50% on decorative accessories.) The better designers tack 15% to 20% on top of that. A handful even charge by the hour. In rare instances, designers charge only for the furnishings at wholesale cost (ask to see the manufacturer's invoice), then tack on a fee (10% to 20%) or a flat design fee ($1,000 to $2,000)—or both.

Before you get too far into the planning, ask for a color rendering of what the designer has in mind (this will cost you $100 to $150). And within three weeks after signing the contract, you should get a detailed presentation of the whole design scheme— floor plan, pictures or sketches of furniture and accessories, fabric swatches, pieces that are to be refinished or reupholstered, and the budget.

At this point your wife may want to do some looking on her own, although designers generally discourage this. But most designers will either make an appointment for the client or accompany her to the showroom. Or she can use the designer's card to get into certain closed showrooms. Designers outside the "market areas" (New York, Boston, Chicago, Atlanta, Dallas, San Francisco) often stock samples. The client foots all the bills if the designer is asked to accompany her on a shopping tour to another city.

Customarily, final payment is made upon completion of the work (one-third when the contract is signed, one-third when furnishings are ordered). Long deliveries (at least a month) can drag the job out, especially when you order custom-made items.

Note: Custom furniture, say, for a particular corner, is more expensive and may be difficult to place if you move.

How to clear the air inside your home

Curbing "pollution" is another type of renovation that's becoming more popular. You can't do much about air pollution in the streets except protest. But at home—in an apartment, townhouse, or close-in suburb—you may want to make the air totally fit for breathing. Obviously, many diseases ranging from asthma to heart disease can be caused by polluted air. And it does have a bad effect on furnishings.

In a house, central air purifiers are attached to the air-duct system in the basement. An electrostatic precipitator takes 75% to 90% of the dirt, pollen, and smoke out of the air. It will filter the air in your home four to six times an hour (Carrier Corp., General Electric, Chrysler Airtemp; $400 for 10 rooms). Portable room air purifiers can be plugged into a socket, are under one sq. ft. in size, and make very little noise (Puritron Corp., $30 to $45). Double-duty units humidify the air and collect dirt. One type is installed in the duct system (Carrier, $100). The other is a room humidifier to which effective air-filtering gear can be attached (Presto Industries, $60 to $100).

Standard air conditioners do a fair job in hot weather. They can filter out about 80% of the dirt—but *only* from the air coming in, not the air already in.

As for noise pollution, the most highly recommended home remedy—soundproofing—can be costly but often well worthwhile. If you want to soundproof a room, the best way is to install inner walls about 6 in. from the existing walls, with acoustical materials in between (about $2 per sq. ft.). Then weatherstrip the doors, or even better, install sound-resistant doors made by such outfits as Munchhausen Soundproofing Co., New York ($200 to $600). Windows need the same treatment, of course; the best material is Thermopane—which is two ¼-in. panes with

2-in. to 4-in. between ($125 and up per window). Accoustical ceiling tiles will run you 50¢ per sq. ft.

It costs $1,500 to $2,000 to soundproof a bedroom or study effectively. But if the job is done properly it will eliminate 75% to 80% of all noise. Machines that "mask" noise by means of a steady, pleasant sound may be effective. But accoustical and medical experts note that the long-range effects of these gadgets aren't known.

Putting a roof over relaxation

A specialized kind of house renovation—one that falls in a man's department—is the "rec room" job. Start the job in September if you want to be in time for the winter season.

Converting basement space, putting a new room over the garage, or even adding a new wing to your house will give you the space you need. But you'll have to allow at least two weeks for the remodeler to get started on the job. Then he'll take four to six weeks for the average renovation, and six to eight weeks for a major job.

Here are some starting points:

▪ Cost of a recreation room in a $50,000 to $100,000 house can run anywhere from $2,500 to $10,000 or more. Rule of thumb: To remodel existing space, figure $10 to $15 per square foot; $20 for a floor over the garage, and around $25 for a new house wing (put on the backyard side).

▪ The value of your property will be increased nearly dollar for dollar if you add a new wing; or, if you renovate space, you'll get back a good 50% of cost if you sell.

▪ Cost of equipment can go sky-high. A top-grade pool table, for example, sells for up to $2,500. Figure roughly 40% to 50% more than basic renovation cost if you get everything from the latest indoor sports gear to stereo and color TV.

Finding the man to do the work may take a bit of doing. Some tips: Get recommendations from a local bank or a top architect; get three bids (to weed out the man who's too high or cut-rate), and be sure to obtain a contract that itemizes all phases of the work and gives a completion date. If you're spending $5,000 or more, let your lawyer look over the paperwork. The "blanket" contract should be avoided.

If you're adding a wing to the house, or even a second story to the garage, to get rec room space, an architect should do the basic design. Generally he'll charge 10 to 15% of the building cost, and he will supervise the contractor.

Before you redo a basement, garage loft, or any other space, be sure you have a full 8-ft. ceiling; one of 7 ft. isn't good enough. Latest trend is the luminous, suspended ceiling with lighting built in, so figure this in your calculation.

Paneling can be high-quality—and high-priced. Teak, rosewood, or walnut veneer sells for up to $100 per 4- by 8-ft. panel. Plainer vinyl-plywood is just $8 to $10. In carpeting for basements, ask about hydrofoam (a moisture-absorbent covering) or vinyl tile placed over concrete.

In laying out your plans, remember that indoor sports gear can take up plenty of space. A professional-size pool table is 4½ by 9 ft., and with a heavy slate bed weighs 1,000 lb. You'll need a total of about 14 by 18 ft. for a comfortable game.

If you're a bit cramped for space, a family-size pool table is 4 by 8 ft. ($500 to $1,000 for good quality), takes less space, partly because shorter cues can be used. Table tennis outfits run $100 to $200 for top quality, with sturdy kids' models in the $75 range. Besides wood, see a metal-framed composition table with easy-to-fold top (Abercrombie & Fitch, $200 up).

A regulation-size table tennis is 5 by 9 ft. But you should have 8 ft. at each end and 3 ft. on each side for a good fast game. For a space saver, add a table tennis top to your pool table. Have a carpenter rig it, or check your sporting goods store.

The latest in poker tables is octagonal, seats eight, has a padded surface and hidden trays that hold drinks and chips (Brunswick, $200 up). A movable bar with built-in refrigerator and the usual gadgetry runs $200 to $400. A custom-built 8-ft. bar with sink and refrigeration costs $1,500.

The home gym has become a big rec room item, especially for the middle-ager. Here space need be no real problem. All you need is a cubicle (maybe 8 by 8 ft.) to mount a horizontal bar, and a vertical one for isometrics. After that come higher-ticket items. Among the possibilities: an indoor jogging machine with adjustable treadmill, meter, and timer ($135 to $250); rowing machine, manual ($90) or hydraulic ($250); bicycle machine with timer, speed switch ($300). Check Sears, Montgomery Ward, Abercrombie & Fitch.

For less strenuous relaxation, you can fill a corner with a basement piano and drum combination. A 63-key cocktail piano costs $400 to $1,000, and a complete drum outfit, $500. *Tip:* A dealer trade-in basement piano (a full 88), guaranteed tunable, costs $200 to $400—or check the garage-sale ads (but have a piano tuner check it first).

Green thumb

Paul Voykin's *A Perfect Lawn the Easy Way* (Rand McNally) looks over the back yard with considerable skill; his clear instructions take you through the whole year.

Gardeners World (Random House), by Josephine von Miklos and Evelyn Fiore, is beautifully illustrated—and practical, too—if you're interested in laying out flower beds, combining various shrubs and flowers, and such.

Where to look for home protection

Home protection has been a big item in the past few years. It's a serious side of home ownership that has makers of locks, electronic switches, and similar gadgetry working overtime. Here are some pointers for those seeking sensible and effective ways to protect their families and property from burglars and vandals.

At the outset, most experts say this: Keeping a gun is rarely a safe solution to the home protection problem—despite the fact that in California, for instance, 90,000 pistols are legally bought in a six-month span of time. Says a senior Washington police official: "If you're a novice, there can be no argument for keeping a gun." The pro-gun arguments of the National Rifle Association fall on deaf ears at the FBI.

So look at some of the alternatives. Electronic systems can signal an intruder's entry by means of sound-and-motion detectors that trigger alarms, switch on yard floodlights (especially effective, say pros), and even make mechanical phone calls to the police.

A transistorized "Radar Eye" covers up to 20,000 sq. ft.; any movement will activate it and set off an alarm (Pinkerton's, Inc., $600 up). A sound-detection system with microphones in the house sets off warnings of an entry (Alarmtronics Engineering, Inc., Newton, Mass., $1,800).

Combination units that detect movement by infrared ray and by sensing the pressure of feet on the floor will automatically dial the police and simultaneously warn the family (Ballistics Control Corp., Long Island City, N.Y., $600 to $3,000). You can even get a system that will alert the police or a private agency if your phone line is cut. Special monitoring services can help. Holmes Electric Protective Co. (New York–based), for example, will monitor your alarm system.

Some other electronic ideas to inquire about:

▪ A master light switch in your bedroom. If you hear a noise during the night, you can immediately light up the house and grounds.

▪ A portable, easily plugged-in time switch to use when you go away from home for a weekend or vacation. The gadget will turn TV, radio, and lights on and off at odd times, day and night.

▪ A phone answering service that can hoodwink a burglar trying to "case" your house by phone in your absence. The service — if you line it up properly — can answer as though someone is at your home, or give the caller a false return-time. (Casing by phone, incidentally, is on the rise.)

As for locks, a "jimmy-resistant" deadbolt that can't be pried open with a thin blade or strip of celluloid should be on all outside doors. Also ask about chain locks with attachments that let you secure the chain from the outside. Windows can be protected by magnetic contacts that will sense slight movement and trigger an alarm.

If you want to protect cash, jewels, securities, and so on, the best idea is a fire-insulated wall safe (Mosler's highest-quality safe costs about $1,000). *But note:* "No location in your house will hide the safe," says an expert, "and a skilled crook, given time, can open almost anything."

What about a watchdog? You can, of course, get a big, deep-barking boxer or German shepherd. But keep in mind that unless he's trained, he may be a sound sleeper. Sometimes a yappy terrier or poodle is better. *Tip:* Whatever breed, feed him his daily meal in the morning so he won't sleep on a full stomach throughout the night.

If you live in a sparsely settled and lightly patrolled neighborhood, you and a group of neighbors might consider hiring a private policeman to patrol the area. They generally do eight-hour shifts, earning about $3 an hour.

Depending on a gun for home protection raises many hazards:

■ Overreaction is a danger. "You might shoot your own son returning from college unexpectedly at 3 A.M. — it's happened," says one expert.

■ Inexperience in handling weapons can make you the target of your own gun if you try to use it on an intruder.

■ Gun theft is a fast-increasing crime — yours may be stolen.

Anyone who, after all this, buys a pistol should know these points: The safer, more practical type is the .38-caliber revolver. An automatic pistol is more dangerous partly because you can't tell whether it's loaded or if there's a bullet in the chamber. Also, firing-range experience is a must.

And there's always the overriding problem of keeping the gun safely away from children and others. The trouble is that you may well find that if you're to store your gun safely, you can't reach it in an emergency — a sort of double-barreled disadvantage.

Selling a house in a rough, tough market

You're hitting a rough market these days if you are putting a house up for sale. Finding a buyer who can pay the price — and swing the needed mortgage deal—may not be easy. Keep in mind that to help your house sell, you might:

▪ Hire an independent appraiser (whose fee will be somewhere in the $100 range). Check his appraisal against what two or three real estate men say the house is worth. This will help you price it right—and not scare away buyers by reaching for an unrealistically high price that an agent might suggest. Rule of thumb: If it's a $50,000 to $75,000 house, allow maybe 10% for "horse-trading." Ask, say, $60,000—if you're willing to go as low as $54,000. But don't start by asking $70,000. *Note:* A suburban bank often will be able to give you the name of a good appraiser.

▪ Take a "purchase-money" or second mortgage yourself. Say that you are selling for $60,000, and the buyer puts down a third of that, or $20,000. He has trouble getting a $40,000 mortgage. You take, say, $10,000 of the $40,000—in the form of a second mortgage. The lender takes a first mortgage of $30,000. Lenders will often go for this. There is some risk, of course—which you must weigh.

Also, keep in mind this selling pointer: If you do sales-appeal repairs and fixing up—quite often neglected by sellers—you will usually stand a much better chance of seeing the house move faster. Put in some new lawn seed, paint the gutters and worn trim, fix the stuck window that won't open or the cracked pane in the garage door. Call it psychological repair work—it counts. And once you've picked a good broker, follow his suggestions as to showing the house to buyers. *One tip:* Don't walk around with him; you'll spoil his sales pitch. Incidentally, local suburban banks also know the best brokers in town.

You don't want a high-pressure salesman (or saleswoman)—not for the type of property you'll be selling. The financially responsible buyer, possibly an executive coming in from out of town, will steer clear of the fast-talker. You do want a reliable, conservative agent. Besides, you want an agent who won't forget for a moment that he represents you—not the buyer—and one who won't try to pressure you into a quick sale at a lower price than the house deserves for the sake of a fast commission. The kind of agreement you sign with the broker can make a difference.

You might want an "exclusive contract" that gives a single broker the right to handle the deal, though generally this has limited appeal for a seller. It's useful when you have a property that needs some special sales effort—an estate, for example.

In some affluent communities, there are agents today who make a specialty of handling properties in the $100,000 range, and, of course, there are a few national brokers (such as Previews, Inc.) to consider. But most likely, you'll want a "multiple listing" agreement. On balance, it's best for most sellers. Under this system, all "listed" brokers can handle the house, though you deal with just one. He shares the commission, no matter who sells the house.

In any case, be sure your broker's agreement spells out (1) his commission—often 6% in a large metropolitan area, and (2) the time element, lest you get hung up with a broker who can't move the property. If you have an exclusive agreement, two to four weeks is advised; if it's a multiple listing, then maybe 60 to 90 days. It varies.

As seller, you will, of course, have your lawyer approve any contract of sale between you and a buyer—no matter how clearcut the deal looks. When dealing in real estate, a handshake is a mere sentimental gesture that won't cut any ice in a courtroom. You need it in writing.

To the mobile executive, it's a mover's world

Easings in the new tax law should save you at least a small bundle if you'll be selling your old house and moving to a new city. Until 1970, you could deduct only "direct" moving expenses: cost of the van, packing, and transporting you and your family, with meals and lodging included. Now you can deduct three additional kinds of business-related moving expenses: Costs related to the sale of your old house and the purchase of the new;

travel expenses for pre-move house-hunting trips; and temporary living costs covering up to 30 days before the day you move into your new house. For more detailed information on moving expenses that may legitimately be deducted, see Chapter 4, "Income Taxes: How to Treat the Bite That Hurts."

Income Taxes: How to Treat
the Bite That Hurts

It's surprising how much about income taxes can be packed into a few pages. Obviously nobody can review the whole tax law—point by point—in one medium-sized book, let alone in one chapter. But it's possible to signal a few warnings, and to single out some special pitfalls.

One point at the outset: There is no single, magic formula for smart tax work. There is no "inside" way to cut way down on what a man must inevitably pay to the Internal Revenue. There is no secret gimmick that a few informed tax lawyers and CPAs know about. What there is, though, is the possibility of reducing your taxes to a minimum level in a given situation.

And one warning: The tax man—CPA, lawyer, or self-styled

"expert"—who promises you a windfall in taxes saved, and who suggests that he has all kinds of methods for tax reduction that you never heard of—may be a man to avoid. True, there are gray areas in the tax law, and it's possible to color them pure white and make them work to your advantage, if you use some sharp techniques. But the sharp techniques can bite back, and every year a few thousand otherwise honest people find themselves in a federal courtroom. And thousands and thousands more— though they stay out of court—end up paying stiff dollar penalties for paying too little, too late to the U.S. Treasury.

The idea is expressed by the tax lawyers this way: It's perfectly proper to *avoid* taxes—that is, to pay just as little as you can within the bounds of the law; it's *not* proper, or even legal, to *evade* taxes—which is what the sharpies and know-it-alls attempt to do. With this much tucked away, it's possible to review some sensible, dollar-saving pointers.

Tax advice, or how to fight the 1040

First, what about seeking tax help? Say that you're an up-and-coming executive or professional man, in the $25,000 to $40,000 income range, and this time around you dread the April 15 filing date. You're wondering why in blazes you have never hired a tax man. You're far from alone.

But help is at hand. Says a top Washington tax adviser: "If your 1040 has outgrown you, contact a CPA or tax lawyer promptly—and don't let a late date scare you off. A real pro in the field is prepared to help a man who comes in as late as February or March for the April filing."

But sort your papers in a logical, businesslike fashion before you take them in (even executives muff this). Then your adviser will be able to work faster and more effectively—and his bill will be smaller.

And note: April 15 need be no do-or-die date. If the man you hire is terribly rushed, he probably will get you a 30- to 60-day filing extension, though the price you pay for being late is 6% interest on the tax due.

Your big problem is to find the right tax expert. To find a good man, you can, of course, ask your company's attorney or chief accountant to recommend someone. A business friend might be able to name a tax specialist in a leading firm of lawyers or CPAs. But your best bet probably is to find a small, top-quality outfit. The big firm—not overly anxious for the small account—will usually give you the name you want.

Don't count on your family lawyer for tax advice. This is important to remember. The average attorney in general practice is no income tax specialist—and he isn't shunting you aside if he says he's unable to handle your 1040 problems. Computerized tax services, incidentally, are aimed mostly at the specialist, not at the individual taxpayer.

If you're on the way up in terms of income and have never employed a tax adviser, it may be best to get a younger man. He'll be more interested in the smallish account. Most important, he'll be able to keep working with you in the future. But before you pick anybody, consider the scope of the service you need.

There's more to it, of course, than simply filing a 1040 each April. If you want just this, it's a case of taking your papers to an accountant's office, and, barring complications, exchanging a few phone calls. This is the routine part of what you can get.

But many executives with increasing incomes and growing investments have knottier tax affairs to unravel each year. They need tax service that goes beyond the routine. This means an overall strategy, not just April 15 thinking. For example, a skilled tax man can make certain that you're getting the fullest possible advantage of all capital gains that the law allows. He can give you the tax side of investments other than securities, including everything from real estate to diamonds. He can unscramble charitable donations for you—in terms of the new 1969 tax reforms.

The point is this: You don't simple hire somebody to figure out your best possible April 15 result—after the fact. You get a tax program that—with advance planning—ensures a favorable April 15 result.

You can get into some pretty hot arguments over who can best do your tax work, a CPA or a tax attorney. The more candid experts put it this way:

The CPA has the top accounting credentials. There are reliable, licensed accountants who aren't CPAs, but however competent, they lack first-rank rating. A CPA will usually have a closer knowledge than a lawyer of the details of the tax law and will give you highly skilled technical planning and paperwork. He will also know all the ins and outs at Internal Revenue. He's your skilled, pragmatic tax pro.

The tax lawyer provides similar services, but is less of a tax technician. At the same time, he offers a different advantage. He can help you with long-range tax-related affairs: estate planning, the setting up of trusts, and so on. This is a plus.

No matter who you hire to do your tax work, remember that you can rely on him and his expertise—but only up to a point. In a recent case (little noticed but important), the U.S. Tax Court laid down the law in no uncertain terms to the prosperous taxpayer who leans too heavily on his professional adviser.

Say that you negligently fail to report some element of income: a stock dividend that's taxable because of an option to take cash, a taxable reimbursement from the company that you thought was nontaxable, or the like. You are hauled in by Internal Revenue and hit with a stiff penalty. You claim innocence because your 1040 was prepared by a CPA or tax lawyer. This is no excuse, warns the Tax Court. Mailing in an accurate 1040 is *your* duty, nobody else's. Your tax man certifies the accuracy of his work—not your recordkeeping.

This type of case—where the taxpayer fails to give full and accurate information to his own adviser—has been plaguing high-bracket people in the past three or four years. A good tax adviser will try to warn you in advance of such chances. How far he gets really depends on a clear understanding of your affairs—and your recordkeeping habits—usually gained only over a span of years.

Note: If you've switched tax men frequently, as many people do, you might be wise to settle down with one. And why not try to find the ideal combination?—a young, bright pro who is both an attorney *and* a CPA.

The fee you'll pay: Some people pale at the idea of spending money on tax advice and service, But it's fair to say this: If you are in the $25,000 to $40,000 income range—and are heading up —you are foolish to ignore the idea of lining up a good man.

The fees range widely around the country. Generally, a qualified pro will charge $150 to as high as $500 or more (tax deductible) for a straightforward job on your form 1040. The hourly rate for general tax work is about $20 to as high as $100 — it varies that much, depending on the seniority of the man, the firm, the city. A bright young practitioner will most often fall some place at the lower end of the fee range. And he may well give you the 1040 work you need *and* some tax advice—depending on your situation—at what amounts to a bargain rate. He'll be thinking of your business in the years ahead—and *you* should be thinking of this, too.

Another point on seeking tax advice: Instead of getting simpler and less complex, the U.S. tax code has steadily gone from bad to worse. It's now tougher to understand, even for the pros. The new 1969 tax reform law chopped up parts of the code (see below) and the results might well enter your own tax picture. Even the routine tax paperwork has become more and more obscure. The revised 1040 filed in April, 1970, for instance, was supposed to be simpler for everybody. It turned out to be a small disaster. So on this basis, you *need* tax advice today, more than ever.

There's still another reason for picking up a tax man, one that's of growing importance, but almost entirely overlooked. Today 26 states (including California, Illinois, Michigan, New York, and Pennsylvania) plus the District of Columbia, get IRS tax-return information on tapes that are fed into computers at the state tax offices. This means fine-tooth-combing of your federal returns by the state—and the chance of being picked up for audit on a state tax return if there is even a small discrepancy between it and your federal 1040. Eighteen other states get IRS information on a less sophisticated basis.

What's more, it all works in reverse. IRS is getting more and more state filing information. *Moral:* Make sure your tax man handles all your returns, and carefully combs out any and all discrepancies. This is, if you have a tax man.

For executives, professionals:
a personal audit

The idea of hiring a tax man for *more* than just tax services makes sense. If you're on the upswing in corporate management or rising to the top of your profession—moving ahead in terms of property and income—it might be wise to take a look at the *personal audit.*

A professionally prepared audit—by a CPA—can work for you in many ways in addition to its value as an aid in tax planning. This holds true for a higher-income man, especially where it's become clear that his personal business affairs have been handled in a jumbled, piecemeal way. With the audit, you get a great amount of basic information that is valuable in any first-rate income tax program, year-to-year and long-term. But you get much more. An audit can help you make surer decisions on monthly budget, savings, investment objectives, insurance—plus such items as college financing and how much you can pay for a new house. It can even help you decide if you need estate planning—and how much.

The first step is to find an experienced CPA. You get from him a personal balance sheet showing assets and liabilities in detail—everything you own from art objects to insurance policies, as well as even small amounts owed for, say, interior decorating or having new wiring installed in your house—or taxes. This plus consultation and general recommendations make up the service.

Generally, you'll need two sessions with the accountant to get the audit started, and two visits a year thereafter: one for the annual chore of filing tax returns, the other to update the audit. Getting all the paperwork together to begin with may be tedious —but it can pay off.

The CPA won't come up with any ironbound rules for planning your dollar flow, but he will give you some reasonable guidelines. Take a typical case. Jones is 45, married, has two teen-agers in high school. His salary is $50,000, and by 1975 he will probably be getting $75,000. He has an income of $1,000 from cash savings and a small stock portfolio. Assets include $35,000 of equity in his house; life insurance cash value, $10,000 ($50,000 in coverage); cash savings, $10,000; common stocks, $10,000; personal property, $10,000 (including two cars, paid for); vested pension funds, $15,000. Liabilities: $2,000 in debts and $2,000 taxes payable. So, his net worth is $86,000.

Advisers say that a $50,000 man, in average family and financial circumstances, should save at least 10% of his after-tax net. So Jones—who pays about $16,000 in taxes—should be putting away at least $3,500 a year. *Note:* A $30,000 man might be advised to save a minimum of 5%. "It should be 10%," says a CPA, "but few people hold to that, what with today's prices."

On the budget side, one rule of thumb is that an executive in the $40,000 to $60,000 income range should give his wife 40% to 50% of his net after both taxes and savings to run the house (excluding mortgage payments and utilities).

Our man Jones has $2,625 a month for his budget—after taxes and savings. If he compromises and gives his wife 45%, she gets about $1,200 a month, leaving Jones with $1,425. The $1,425 must cover the mortgage, property taxes, all types of insurance, household repairs, new furniture and equipment for the house, auto expenses, husband's expenses, and outside entertainment.

The audit will help to sharpen investment objectives, too. It will give you a clear idea of how much you can safely put in the market each year, and how prudent you should be with it. Since Jones' $3,500 savings is a bare minimum, it should probably go into safe growth investments—*not* speculation. "Some clients find it almost a relief to know that they really shouldn't speculate," says a Chicago CPA.

College financing comes into the picture, and many people find that they are aiming under the mark. Jones, with two children in high school, needs $40,000 to as much as $60,000 for college, allowing for inflation and the possibility of graduate school. Also, his audit shows him that he should stay clear of any house that costs more than $80,000. And though he needs some basic estate planning, he hasn't reached the point where formal trusts are required. The list goes on.

You put your general affairs and tax problems into one package for close review. You then seek legal, investment, and other advice as before, but on a sounder basis. A CPA will charge $300 to $1,000 initially, and each year thereafter, for the auditing plus his work on your 1040 in April. Fees vary greatly.

Don't panic if IRS calls you in

Next, there's the question of facing up to the opposition—the Internal Revenue Service. And, for most people (sharpies aside), it really isn't *all* bad. If you filed your last tax return with a nagging doubt, don't become too up tight if the IRS calls you in. This can happen, especially to an executive or professional who's income is healthy, even if his 1040 is as innocent as a Walt Disney cartoon. (If it's more like a Scandinavian "X" film—he's in trouble.)

Obviously, unusual deductions and offbeat transactions, such as income-averaging, may flag a return. But so can high income alone. The rules on who gets audited (or partially audited) are not clear-cut. Figure that there's at least a 50-50 chance of your return being flagged for possible audit if your income is over $25,000. An IRS examiner makes a quick personal check—an "eyeball check"—of a flagged 1040. Only if he sees something amiss is the return tossed on the audit pile.

If you get a notice by mail naming a time and place for an examination, you're probably in for something less than a full audit. The odds are with you; one or two items in your 1040 will get a going over—and the notice will most likely tell you what they are.

"The big blunder is to take in your whole file of paperwork," says a New York tax lawyer. "You might open up a totally unnecessary line of inquiry."

Assuming you have an adviser—do you go alone, with your tax man, or have him represent you? You might be smart to have him along. "Let him be a personal buffer, if nothing else—don't risk letting off steam," says a Washington adviser.

As a novice at tax review, you obviously assume quite a risk going it alone, if a sizable amount of money is involved. In some cases it may be wise to stay away and let your own man take over—you won't get in the way of the tax talk. But let your adviser decide this.

On an involved case, where many records are needed, IRS auditors may visit you if you request it. But the pros say you should avoid such visits. If the agent comes to your home or office, your records (past and present) are all too accessible. "Also, affluent surroundings can work against you," says an experienced adviser. "Call it psychological—but it's a point."

The telltale call: If an IRS agent phones and then appears in person at your home or office, you may well be in line for a full audit, no holds barred. Get on the phone fast and check in with your tax man—or try to get one if you have none.

Suppose that, after all, you end up alone at a local IRS office—what's the risk? First, keep in mind that in his own realm the IRS examiner is a professional. He has inspected countless tax returns like yours. He won't push you rudely—but he won't miss any chances to pick up extra tax dollars, either. He has wide discretion and in many cases exercises his own judgment over your affairs.

Good rapport can count, and much can depend on his attitude. A favorite beef among IRS agents is that the businessman sometimes "talks down" to them. "It hardly pays—an agent can say 'no' too often," says a pro. So don't go in with a VIP attitude—it may cost you money.

If you think you owe less than the agent claims—and if the disputed amount of tax is $2,500 or less—you now can ask for a simplified "district conference." Here you talk privately with an arbiter and file no petition. Chances of compromise are good, but if it doesn't satisfy you, you can go still higher inside IRS.

When a dispute involves more than $2,500, you must file a

statement for a district conference—and you'll wisely have this prepared by a professional. Next step up is a hearing before IRS's "appellate division," and at this level you would be foolish to appear without a tax man at your elbow. At an appellate division session, you confer with an IRS expert who has great authority: he acts as both judge and jury. It isn't as dire as it appears, though. Usually the theme is bargaining aimed at settlement. In an average year, over 60% of these appeals are settled for less than the IRS had originally demanded.

Going any higher takes you into the federal courts; and there is a new speeded-up Tax Court procedure for disputes involving $1,000 or less. But this is a way to consume time, expense (tax man), and nervous energy. Besides, going to court poses a dilemma: You have no guarantee that the final tax owed will be a cent less than IRS's original bill for tax due. It may be more.

Silver lining: Keep in mind, as you view the whole business of sparring with IRS, that even a full audit of your 1040 need not cause you to become coronary-prone. Usually, about 6 or 7% of all audits actually end up in producing refunds for the taxpayer. And around 40% produce no change in the amount of tax owed the government.

If you look back at your last 1040 filing, and get a slight sinking sensation for fear that you may have botched the paperwork and even yet be hit for another big cut of tax dollars (and penalties), don't just sit idle. If real money is involved, sit down with a tax adviser and talk it over. You can always anticipate an audit by gathering every scrap of additional evidence you might need to support your position—in case. And if you think you're really in a bind, you can erase your 1040 as filed by filing an amended return (1040X).

Tax woes: avoiding an audit

Now, getting down to audits—and how to avoid one. There is no *foolproof* way to avoid the procedure, but there is a way to give yourself, say, a 90% chance of being passed over.

It's true that if your income is over $25,000, you've got a good 50% chance of having your 1040 flagged automatically for checking by an Internal Revenue man. The trick is to make sure—or as sure as possible—that he'll scan your tax return, and then tuck it back into the file without embarrassing questions—or an audit. At the outset, the tax professionals stress two points.

The first seems improbable, and just a bit naive. It isn't. It is the question of neatness in making out the 1040. "It means a lot," says a Cincinnati tax man. "It gives the agent more confidence in your return, and he is more apt to pass it by."

The second point concerns the occasional big item that should be, but often isn't, checked over with an expert. Such things as how to report a sizable sale of a security where there's a later repurchase, a real estate deal where capital gains tax is due, the use of income-averaging, or such. The idea, of course, is to consult somebody if you have any doubt about how to properly report the item—or to what extent it needs to be reported. "But," says the Cincinnati expert, "you needn't necessarily rush out and line up a man to do your entire 1040—especially if you realize your problem on April 14, the day before you must file." He adds: "You might pick up enough advice in a 10-minute phone call to stay out of trouble."

Deductions can get you involved in an audit, even if the amounts aren't excessive. IRS agents look for certain tipoff items. On contributions, for example, bunching items under "miscellaneous" is a sure way to attract attention. Instead, attach a list. If you donated property (a painting, shares of stock), explain how you arrived at the value. If it's over $200, state clearly that there are no conditions attached to the gift, and clip to the 1040 a signed copy of any appraisals. Ignoring this may get you an audit.

A high interest deduction can trip you up if it's not logically explained by a sizable house mortgage or other loan. If you have such a deduction, add a brief explanation to your return.

On state and local sales taxes, note: (1) If you bought a big-ticket item (car, boat, or such) give purchase details; and (2) though you are allowed to deduct more than amounts shown on the sales tax tables in the 1040 instructions, you're asking for a call from IRS if you fail to explain clearly the excess.

Casualty loss claims can make your return liable to audit, especially if you fail to itemize and explain how you arrived at the loss. Theft and vandalism losses have been way up. If you deduct, give the date and details of the police report. If you made no police report, you're asking for trouble at IRS. Also, claiming household accident losses, such as dropping a ring in the garbage disposal unit, may mean an audit.

Remember too: Don't deduct for termite damage. It can't be supported, and may bring you an audit—or a partial audit.

For the businessman, heavy travel and entertainment deductions remain a pitfall, and the mixed business-pleasure junket gets special attention. *One tip:* Use IRS's special form for "T&E" items—it may save you from an audit. And put unreimbursed business entertainment items down as itemized deductions—don't mix them up with travel expenses, which go down as deductions from salary. Muffing this point will flag your return.

Business education deductions generally are safe—if they're clearly job-related. Again, you can avoid trouble by a clear explanation.

If you changed jobs, you can deduct a consultant's fee provided he helped you relocate. If he didn't get you a new job, the question is closer. New cases show a liberal trend.

Deductions for the cost of investment advice will bring you no trouble—provided your return shows capital transactions or proportionate investment income.

Attaching original records to your 1040 is a blunder. The same applies to machine copies of most records involved in your tax return.

Also, keep your explanations of items on your 1040 brief and concise. "If you attach long, detailed explanations," says an old pro, "the agent may be tempted to toss your return on the audit pile."

Remember to keep your tax paperwork for at least three years following your April filing. IRS can audit your 1040 at any time in this period. The delayed audit—especially more than a year after filing—frequently comes as a shock to higher-income taxpayers who may have breathed easy a little too soon. Stock purchase and real estate records should be kept, of course, until you sell the property, no matter how many years. Note, too, that if you expect to someday use the liberalized income-averaging rules, you must keep all income records for at least five years.

Getting a filing date extension

Suppose that the April 15 filing deadline looms just ahead, and you discover that the task of dropping your 1040 in the mail by deadline is impossible. You're not alone, of course—but what you do about it makes a difference. What you may need is a filing-date extension. Here's how to get one:

Promptly—before April 15—send a registered return-receipt letter to your District Director of Internal Revenue. If you have a good reason for delay, you can get an extension ranging up to 90 days. In some cases, this can go even as high as six months. (If abroad, a man automatically gets two months.)

Valid excuses include personal hardship such as serious illness; loss of tax records or inability (on provable grounds) to assemble your records on time; and inability to obtain essential 1040 assistance, for example, where your tax adviser lets you down without warning. *Make your case.* Put down all your reasons—and if you send a personal letter, add two points of information: whether you (1) filed 1040s on time in the past three years, and (2) paid your estimated tax installments when due—and if not, why not.

Even with an extension, the late filer doesn't get off scot-free. You'll have to pay interest at 6% on the amount of tax due, covering the period of the extension granted to you. But the penalty for late filing *without* an extension is worse. On top of the 6% interest, IRS will demand 5% of the tax owed for each late month, up to 25% of the total amount due. The 1969 reform law tacked on a small additional penalty, but its applicability at this date is in doubt.

Your request for an extension may, of course, be turned down. If it is, you still can put off filing for 10 days following the date of refusal—without paying the added penalty (above the 6% interest).

Caution: Inability to pay in itself is never an excuse for late filing. If, for example, you had expected to pay the tax by selling certain securities, but have been unable to liquidate—promptly file your 1040 anyway, paying as much of the tax as you can. You will then be billed for the rest within two weeks to 30 days —or for the whole amount, if you paid nothing as of April 15.

Tax refunds

Many people file a 1040 that establishes their right to a refund— and about a month later begin looking in the mailbox for a check from Internal Revenue. *Tip:* Wait a while before you write to IRS about it. The point is that it takes a good six to eight weeks for a refund to appear in the mail, and lately IRS has been warning that you should wait 10 weeks before making an inquiry. This means no sooner than about June 25, if you filed on April 15.

The trouble is, if you write too soon, you'll clutter the paper-work process and may cause even more delay. It's like dropping a pencil down into the gears of a Xerox machine.

Or, suppose that you have already received the refund check. You may not be scot-free. The fact that you have the Treasury's check in hand doesn't in the least rule out a later audit of your return. Each year IRS does a certain number of post-refund audits—and the moral here is: Keep your records within arm's reach. An estimate is that as many as 250,000 taxpayers on the refund list will have their 1040s audited in 1971. The stress, as usual, will be on people in higher income brackets who have complex tax returns.

Estimating this year's tax: a puzzler

Of all the paperwork detail a man must attend to if his 1040 affairs are to be in order, the declaration of estimated tax prob-ably causes the most confusion. It's as bad as the tax portfolio of an oil well lease-back—to some people. Also, the estimated-tax foul-ups of businessmen and professionals shake up more dollar penalties than can be traced to any single section of the tax law, save late filing. Here are some pointers.

With your 1971 estimate, you can pay the tax in full by April 15, of course; or you can choose the usual four installments—due April 15, June 15, September 15, and January 15 (1972). A point often overlooked: On *any* of these dates, you can change your estimate simply by filing a new declaration. Anyway, don't forget the penalties for filing incorrectly. If any quarterly payment of estimated tax (plus withholding) comes out to less than 80% of the tax due that quarter—computed from your final tax return—you can be assessed 6% on the difference.

If you follow one simple rule—that for some reason, many people tend to botch—you will avoid the 6% penalty: Just compute your new estimate on the basis of the tax paid for the previous year. If this usual method isn't practical to use, it's still possible to protect against the penalty. You can base the estimate on last year's income, using the current tax rates and your current personal exemptions. Or you can base any quarterly installment on at least 80% of the tax that would be due if income continued at the year's current rate. For example, suppose that your income is $8,000 for the first quarter of 1971 (January–March). That would mean $32,000 of projected income for the year. Say that exemptions and deductions cut this to $28,000. On this amount, the joint-return rate is $7,100 (not allowing for a surcharge). If you paid ¼ of 80% of $7,100, or $1,420, by April 15—via withholding plus cash—you would be safe.

Another technique is to base the installment on 90% of the tax due on income earned to date. Say that taxable income is $8,000 up to March 31. You treat this as if it were an entire year's income and figure the joint-return rate—in this case, $1,380. Paying 90% of this by April 15 would safeguard you from penalty.

With both the 80% and 90% methods—which may be practical if you have relatively high non-withheld income—you repeat the formulas for computing each quarterly installment. There's one other out if you find, *toward year-end,* that you have been underestimating. Arrange with your company to withhold a large amount before December 31 to offset the low payments. (If it suits your purpose, you are always free to have your company hold out a bigger bite than is owed for the month.)

A special warning might be directed to the junior executive or the young professional just starting out. Even with a modest income, he may have to estimate. The rule: You should file a declaration (form 1040-ES) for 1971 if your estimated tax is $40 or more for the year, *and* (1) your estimated gross income for 1971 includes more than $200 not subject to withholding, *or* (2) one of the following applies:

■ You are single and your estimated gross income exceeds $5,000.

■ You are married and file a joint return and your (combined) income exceeds $10,000.

Note: In no case must you file if your tax due upon non-withheld income (dividends, interest, etc.) is less than $40.

Incidentally, a husband and wife may file a joint declaration of estimated tax, and still file separate tax returns for the year. If separate 1040s are filed, then estimated tax payments can be split between them as they see fit.

Saving for your own pocket

Tax withholding by an employer is straightforward enough. But the part of it that has to do with *extra withholding allowances* is another place where taxpayers get confused. The basic idea: You get to cut your company withholding—if you wish—to compensate for exceptionally high deductions. Instead of having more withheld and picking up a refund after the year is past, you have less withheld.

This, in effect, puts more cash in your pocket today—money that otherwise would rest in U.S. Treasury coffers at a zero interest rate. It also has the advantage of tipping you off to the need for a general review of your itemized tax deductions.

What you do—but only after filing your 1970 form 1040 (and

this might be some incentive for early filing)—is to revise the withholding exemption certificate (W-4) that's on record with your company.

IRS will grant you one extra exemption, or "allowance," for each $700 of itemized deductions above a level fixed for your salary bracket. Each allowance cuts salary subject to withholding by $700 a year. So if you're in the highest withholding bracket, 30%—for salaries roughly over $25,000—each allowance means $210 more in your pocket (30% of $700).

To get one allowance with a $25,000 salary, deductions must be at least $4,425, assuming the taxpayer is married. For two allowances, they must be up $700, to $5,125—and so on, for three or more. In the $30,000 to $35,000 salary range, you start with deductions of at least $5,700, for one extra allowance, and go from there. The $35,000 to $40,000 range starts at $6,550; $40,000 to $45,000, at $7,400. A man earning $50,000 starts figuring allowances at $8,260.

A typical case: Smith's salary is in the $32,000 range. He files jointly, and allowing for exemptions, his monthly withholding is, say, $630. On this basis, with one extra withholding allowance, the $630 drops down to $615; two allowances drop it to about $600; with three, it drops to $580, and with four, to about $560.

Looking at your own situation, there are these rules of thumb: The itemized deductions of people in higher income brackets—meaning $25,000 and up—average about 20%. On this basis, the odds are at least 50-50 that you're entitled to extra allowances.

If you fall far short on this—say, 20% or more below the required deduction total for even one allowance—then (1) your situation puts you in a small-deduction minority—for example, you may have exceptionally low tax and interest deductions; or (2) you need a review to make sure you're not missing some deductions that could save money.

Deductions are money in your pocket. For instance, if your taxable income is, say, $20,000, and you file a joint return, each dollar of deduction saves you 28¢ in taxes. If your taxable income is $28,000, you save 36¢; at $36,000, you save 42¢. Yet ac-

countants and tax lawyers note that many people in higher income brackets fail to fully cash in on the deduction bonanza.
They miss entirely such items as office-at-home deductions
and some less apparent investment-related deductions; they
fail to take the full amounts allowed for such items as medical
deductions (that go over 3%), and casualty loss deductions.

Note especially: Tax deductions usually don't fall with pre-
cision into black-and-white compartments. The rules often are
gray. The thing to remember is that there is considerable flexibility.

Some items, of course, cause trouble: claiming large "miscellaneous" charitable contributions, for instance—with poor
paperwork to back it up. Or, taking offbeat business "entertainment" expenses that look a little fishy on paper. Also, it's true
that you can't count on getting by with a doubtful deduction because a friend tells you at lunch that he picked it up; too much
depends on the individual IRS agent who happens to scan your
form 1040, and too much depends on the whole complexion of
your tax return.

But there is flexibility, and oftentimes it can work in your
favor. A top tax consultant in Washington has this word: "It
comes down to common sense in many cases. If you have a doubt
about what you think is a reasonable deduction—take it. Con-
strue the law in your favor. Just make sure you have the records
to support your position."

The risk? In most cases it will be 6% of any additonal tax due,
for the late months only—which may be a risk worth taking,
on the chance of your picking up a money-saver.

The tax breaks you can find at home

Next look at some *business-related deductions*—a sizable item
for executives, managers, salesmen, business owners, and professional men. It's rare these days to find an executive or businessman who seldom if ever entertains associates at home, who
has no business book shelf in his library, or hasn't set apart even
a corner of his den for office work.

It's just about as rare to find the man who picks up all the possible tax deductions allowed for such expenses. And these deductions are now more important than ever, since both the Internal Revenue Service and the courts have lately eased up a bit in these areas.

- For 1970 and later, be sure to keep a clear diary of business entertaining at home, with receipts, plus other records covering office obligations that follow you to the front door. Much depends on your records.

- For your 1970 return—and here's where many people will slip up—you can *reconstruct your deductions.* You can't create a tax diary, but you can recover records, fill out incomplete ones, make a few phone calls, and come up with most of the paperwork needed by next April 15.

To deduct for entertaining at home, you must—if IRS challenges you—show that your guests were business associates who were there for business purposes. And "associates" means customers, clients, suppliers, employees, advisers such as company lawyers and CPAs, plus fellow executives. It also includes prospective associates: a possible customer or a young man you've invited to the house to size up for a junior management job. It includes associates' wives, too (and yours), if it's a party.

Note especially: Goodwill entertaining at your home counts. You needn't show that after dinner the men departed to your den to "talk business."

Let's say that last summer you had a patio party for 50 business contacts and their wives. By phoning the caterer, local liquor store, and agency that supplied the bartender, you come up with bills totaling $500 for 100 people ($2 a person for hot canapes, $2 for liquor, $1 for extras). Attach the bills to your cancelled checks (if you've lost the checks, explain it), have your secretary list the 50 men and their business relationships—and you should have a clean-cut $500 deduction.

Don't forget your wife: Her help with recalling guest lists, dates, etc., might turn up (on paper) a surprisingly sizable business-entertainment calendar for the past year. But make your records especially clear if you mixed business contacts with personal friends at a party. This can trip you.

The club: If you have business associates and their wives to, say, dinner at home, then drive them to your country club for dancing, the club expenses are as readily deductible as the cost of the dinner. But you may run into trouble over deducting your club dues for business purposes. First, more than 50% of your total club use must be for business. The rule gets sticky, and all in all, it's an item to check with a tax man.

For "T&E": try records

Much depends on recordkeeping wherever "T&E" is involved (travel and entertainment deductions). This holds, of course, whether the entertainment is at home, in a restaurant—or aboard your boat.

However businesslike, deductions for entertainment aboard a boat may easily run you on a reef at IRS. The rules are strict. To deduct any part of the cost of maintaining the boat, you must be able to show that its use is over 50% business-related. If it's anything less, then such items as depreciation, upkeep, and insurance can't be deducted. Even business use in excess of 50% gives you just a proportionate deduction. For instance, if the boat is 60% for business and you spend $2,500 a year on its maintenance, you can deduct just $1,500.

Tip: Writing off only food and beverages used in business entertaining—afloat *or* ashore—will probably bring less of a squawk from an IRS examiner.

A slightly disastrous Tax Court case (that is, for one taxpayer) points up the need to keep complete, accurate records. The taxpayer was a shareholder in a company and used a boat owned by the company for entertaining some customers. Part of the expense was admittedly personal, part strictly business. The taxpayer made one mistake: He kept no records of the outings. Not only was no tax deduction available, but the cost of operating the boat became a taxable dividend to the shareholder.

Generally, the rules on deductions for business-related *gifts*— at Christmas or at any time of the year—are fairly liberal. You can deduct as many gifts as you wish up to $25 each—and this covers gifts to business or professional associates, clients, customers, and such. And you get an added break: If you give a present costing no more than $25 to a family member of a customer, etc., you can deduct its cost. This allows you to give, say, a toy racing car or a doll to the child of someone with whom you do business, and still take the deduction. The rationale is, of course, that you wouldn't be giving the present if it were not for the business relationship. But, as always, keep clear records, showing the name of the individual to whom the gift is made, the date, the amount, and *especially* the business relationship and purpose.

Claiming deductions for combination *business-vacation trips* can cause tax troubles. If it's in the U.S., you can deduct transportation costs plus meals and lodging en route—if the *primary purpose* of the trip was business. If vacationing was primary, you still can deduct any direct business cost—for instance, for a short side trip to call on customers.

On a business-vacation trip *outside* the U.S., you can deduct full travel expenses if business was primary and the trip took less than a week, or—if longer than a week—you spent less than 25% of your time vacationing. Beyond this you deduct only a percentage of costs. Example: If 10 days out of 20 were for business, you deduct 50% of your total round-trip costs.

But what about a business-pleasure trip with travel divided between U.S. and foreign mileage? The rule: If an executive flies, for example, from San Francisco to New York, stops over, then flies on to London, the San Francisco–New York cost is fully deductible—assuming the trip is primarily for business. Only the New York–London cost is subject to allocation. But if he flies nonstop San Francisco–London, the whole transportation cost comes under the allocation rule.

Incidentally, you'll have a hard time deducting travel expenses for your wife, especially if you're claiming for a business-pleasure trip. This is true even if she acts as your hostess at business functions or performs some secretarial duties.

Who's to say what a trip's "primary purpose" was? To prove your case, if called in by IRS, muster such evidence as correspondence with businessmen you visited, a copy of your appointments schedule—plus all the bills.

Records: The general rule of recordkeeping for "T&E" is to clearly show dates, amounts, people involved and of course, the business purpose of the transaction. Besides these diary details, bills, cancelled checks, receipts, etc., should be saved. And it's a good idea—in case you're hauled in by IRS—to save *all* T&E supporting records, no matter the amount of money involved. This general rule holds for all types of travel-expense deductions, as well as any kind of business entertainment or gifts. *Suggestion:* J. K. Lasser (1 West Ave., Larchmont, N.Y.), for example, puts out an excellent tax diary. It can pay for itself many times over. Or a 25¢ note pad can turn the trick—if you're willing to make the entries.

An office at home

The office-at-home is another place where business-related taxes enter the house. Late-night and weekend work at home is a regular chore among top managers; IRS and the Tax Court have recognized this and softened some hard rules. Today it boils down to this: If you (1) regularly do office work at home (and there's no fixed rule on how many hours a week), and (2) have a room set aside solely for this purpose, you can take what is sometimes a sizable deduction.

A crucial point is to show—should an IRS man appear—that you actually have an office, not just a library or den. This means some visible signs: desk, files, typewriter, dictating equipment, a business phone. If you use an antique desk and a typewriter with a teakwood cover, you won't lose the deduction—but it must prove to be a working office.

In deducting for an office-at-home, you can use a floor-space formula. Say it's a sizable room that takes up 10% of your total house space. In this case, you can deduct 10% of your total depreciation, insurance costs, heat and light expense. (Real estate taxes and mortgage interest are, of course, deductible in full.) You can also deduct the full cost of painting and repairing the home-office, plus the cost of all business furniture and equipment (via depreciation). Also, deduct your business library: books, magazines, tapes, films.

If you live in the distant suburbs and keep an apartment in town—used partly for business meetings and late work—you may have still another deduction. But, again, check it with your tax man.

Note: Recent Tax Court decisions point to liberalization of the deduction for costs of maintaining an office-at-home. It now appears that such expenses qualify for a tax deduction *whether or not* the office is required or recommended by your employer —so long as company policy assumes that the employee will incur unreimbursed expenses in the course of his work.

Business education

Business-related education is a deductible expense often botched on 1040s. More and more in the past few years Internal Revenue has backed down a bit from a hard position and decided that rules for deducting the cost should be, if anything, eased a little.

A quick rundown: A business executive who takes a college course, day or night, or attends a college-sponsored seminar, can deduct his costs if (1) his company required the effort, or (2) he decides that the course is necessary to enable him to keep up with developments in his field or improve his *present* job skills.

There's this limitation: If you take a course to prepare for an entirely *new* line of work or profession (say you're an advertising man and decide to become a lawyer), IRS says *no* deduction. But the fact that the course has an academic degree tacked on doesn't preclude a deduction—even if the degree is the mark of a new profession. If it doesn't lead to a new type of work, you're safe with IRS.

Most appealing to the businessman is what can be deducted in the way of education expenses: Besides tuition, books, and fees, you can deduct cost of travel to and from the college, plus living expenses out of town. A seminar, incidentally, needn't be on a campus. What's more—assuming you take a reasonable number of course hours—you aren't limited to a local college. You could get the deduction, for instance, if you traveled from

St. Louis to Cambridge for an advanced management course at Harvard. You might even study abroad and get it.

There's no limit on the dollar amount, nor on the number of years. IRS will likely take a liberal view of business education expenses in the 1970s.

Moving: for the company's sake?

If you have a business relocation coming up—city-to-city—the 1969 tax reform law should save you at least a small bundle. Until 1970, you could deduct only "direct" moving expenses: cost of the van, packing charges, and the cost of transporting you and your family to the new location, with meals and lodging en route included. Now, under the revised law, you can deduct three additional kinds of business-related moving expenses: (1) Costs related to the sale of your old house and the purchase of the new; (2) travel expenses for pre-move house-hunting trips; and (3) temporary living costs covering up to 30 days before the day you move into your new house.

Costs for these three items may be deducted up to $2,500, with $1,000 of this allowed for the temporary living costs and house-hunting trips. One less beneficial change is a tighter distance requirement. The rule now is that deductions can be made only if you move more than 50 mi.; the old limit was 20 mi.

Note: The ICC, too, has some new rules. Now, if your moving bill turns out to be more than 110% of the original cost estimate, you have up to *15 business days to pay*—instead of facing an immediate threat from the van line not to unload. Also, the mover must deliver with "reasonable dispatch." These rules have dull teeth, so your best bet is to have your company arrange the move. Anyway, if you do have trouble with a mover, contact the nearest ICC office. It's one way to put some pressure on the van line.

Now turn to some deductions that are *purely personal:* medical, charitable, casualty loss, and such. Some areas—like medical

—get fairly gentle handling by International Revenue, if not velvet-glove treatment.

Medical bills get sympathy from the IRS

When it comes to doctor and hospital bills, even the government's tax collector appears to realize that a family's cost can go sky-high these days. So the IRS position is somewhat easier than in the past. Note two points:

▪ *You have more items to deduct now,* including even such things as clarinet lessons to help cure a child's dental ills. It may pay you to go over the list, which has all sorts of entries that many people miss.

▪ *You're on firmer ground when talking medical deductions* to a tax agent than when trying to sell him on, say, the merits of travel-and-entertainment expenses or large office-at-home outlays.

In other words, the law is a bit more on your side these days when you start totting up medical expenses to see if they exceed 3% of adjusted gross income—the point where the deduction begins. This is especially significant when you consider that medical costs have gone up, on average, nearly 50% in the past five years, with high-income men paying top prices all the way. Added to this is the fact that a great many costly items aren't paid for by insurance, even for the businessman with good "major medical" protection.

Some of these non-insured deductible items may surprise you: First are the routine—but often endless—office calls for kids' shots and quick checkups by the pediatrician (which can add up at $10 each). Next come many drugs and medicines, maybe vitamins, and annual physical exams for everyone in the family.

Some items can send the cash really flying. There's "total" dental care: everything from cleaning teeth, to partial plates, to orthodontics for the children (where you can easily spend $1,500 or more per child). And there's the occasional long-term hospital stay, with its added costs (for such things as a needed private room) that even high-quality insurance doesn't cover. The list goes on: "practical" nursing care at home for an aged member of the family; psychological treatment for a child; and equipment such as hearing aids ($500 to $600), portable air-conditioners to help an ailment, stair-seat elevators for heart patients ($1,000 and up). *Note:* Even part of what you pay for *central* air-conditioning is now deductible, in some cases.

The tax agents, you'll find, will even allow a dram of Kentucky bourbon at specified times each day to be deductible—if you have an MD's word that it's to treat an illness. A physician's prescription can mean much. With one, you can also deduct such noncompensable items as health-club costs (special exercise routines, steam baths, rubdowns, etc.) and the expense of traveling to a warm climate to relieve a *specific* ailment.

The point, of course, is to review your last year's outlays carefully; you may find yourself considerably over the required 3% of adjusted gross. A man with $35,000 adjusted gross income can begin to deduct his medical bills starting at about $1,000, which is not hard to exceed these days.

Caution: You can carry it just so far, of course. It's true that even a drink of whisky may be deductible, with a doctor's prescription. But one recent case, for instance, spells out a harder position and shows that you can't rely *entirely* on the fact that an MD prescribed it. On firm orders from the doctor, a man sold his multiple-story house so that his disabled son could move about in a one-floor home. The sale involved a loss for the father, but no part of the loss was deductible. This was pushing the medical deduction idea too far.

To charity: cash on the line may be best

The tax deduction is, of course, the selfish side of a donation to charity: to a church, hospital, school, college, home for the aged, or the like. When you give a dollar to charity, the after-tax cost reduces the nobility of the gesture—but it's there, so why ignore it?

For example, if you give $100, and have a taxable income of, say, $28,000, and file a joint return with your wife—your net cost comes to just $64. With $32,000, it's $61—and it works down to $50 for a man who has a taxable income of $50,000. And it is cash on the barrelhead that gets the most favored treatment, by and large, from Internal Revenue. What's more, the 1969 tax reform law put some gaping holes into some of the fancier "planned" donation ideas.

To show how cash donations get the better break: In a recent case, a taxpayer claimed a sizable church deduction for the year —but he had no records whatsoever to prove his case. He was able to show, though, that he was a steady churchgoer and had made comparable cash gifts to other charities. Result: The Tax Court allowed the full deduction claimed. The case is on the liberal side (he had *no* records); but it makes the point—you do, in fact, fare better when you've donated cash.

What of the planned-gift ideas? Despite the 1969 reform law, there are still some *limited possibilities*—and these are being eyed closer than ever today by colleges and other non-profit institutions. (*Note:* Colleges are in a particular bind with their fund-raising efforts, partly because of the recent law changes, and partly because of unrest and disorder on many campuses, from Cambridge, Mass., to Los Angeles, Calif.).

Anyway, you can go a step past the plain cash donation. Say that you own a block of stock and are willing to part with a slice of it. You show a paper profit on the stock. You decide to donate to your alma mater, say, $10,000 worth—shares that cost you only $5,000. The result is that you get a charitable deduction of $10,-000; and you pay no tax on the $5,000 appreciation. One caution: Under the revised law, for this to work, you must have held the shares for at least six months (so that they come under the long-term gain rules). Note: If you own shares that have *declined* in value, you would sell them first, then make your donation; this way you could use your tax loss on the sale to your advantage.

Past this point, you're on a shaky step. The next rung up the ladder is "giving capital gains." Here you sell the shares to the college (again, long-term) at your *original cost.* Say you own shares that cost $30 and today list at $60. The idea is to sell them to the charity for $30, getting back your cost—then deduct $30 on your tax return. Here, though, the revised law imposes an *extra tax* on you, the donor, and involves complex paperwork. Review this one with an adviser; you may find that such a plan is impractical in terms of net cost.

More complex are so-called "lifetime income plans." You donate a block of securities, but reserve the income from them for as long as you live. Again, the revised law hems you in— this time with some strict technical requirements. It takes detailed, expert advice. At this writing, even the specialists aren't sure of the precise results.

Another type of donation that has raised much dust is the gift of an art object to charity. Here you run in to more new-law restrictions—for instance, the appreciation in value of the donated art work will be cut by 50% for deduction purposes when the donation is made to certain types of nonprofit organizations. You can, though, still make the art donation to a museum and take the full tax deduction.

The Tax Court has also been hitting art donations hard. In a recent case, the taxpayer claimed that some donated paintings were worth—for deduction purposes—about $100,000. The court promptly cut this down to $30,000 even though the donor had employed a well known, experienced art appraiser. In effect, the court decided that the appraiser wasn't reliable. Moral, say the specialists: Hire *two* appraisers if a sizable sum of money is involved—and muster all other possible evidence of value.

How do you deduct a charitable contribution made by buying tickets to a benefit—a theater party, dance, sports events, or such? There's a lot of confusion on this score, according to Internal Revenue. IRS points out that often a taxpayer will be misled by the charity's simple claim that the cost is deductible.

Generally, you may deduct the difference between any regular price (standard box office) and the higher amount you pay the charity. If you tear up the tickets without using them, the deduction is the same. However, there's a way to deduct both the standard ticket price *and* added contribution: If you aren't interested in attending, simply return the unused tickets to the charity along with your check.

Comments on casualty losses

To get a casualty loss deduction (over and above the $100 deductible), keep in mind these basic rules:

- The loss must have been caused by a *sudden* destructive force or event—a storm, fire, explosion, etc. Or, by a theft.
- The loss is measured by the "decline in the value of the property."
- The loss must be supportable—that is, you must have clear *records* to back the claim.

Now back away from the three rules. You will find plenty of exceptions that make casualty losses more subtle than you might imagine. Take the first rule on *sudden* force. A recent Tax Court case—a liberal decision—says that a deductible loss can come from a *series* of such forces, like a whole winter season of high winds and storms. The point is, you may not be able to prove exactly *when,* for example, your summer cottage was damaged over the winter season—but still be able to get the deduction.

The *"decline in value"* rule—that is, the difference between market value, before and after the event—puzzles many taxpayers. But note: As a practical matter—at least in many cases—repair costs can serve as a measure of the decline in value. This means that you can use evidence already on hand after a casualty —without having to spend money and time on painstaking appraisals.

As to the need for *clear records:* A recent case adds a twist. A storm did heavy damage to an oceanfront house, and the owner on his tax return deducted nearly $100,000. Internal Revenue, claiming that he hadn't proved his loss, cut the figure down to less than $25,000. The lower federal court backed the IRS, but the taxpayer appealed. The appellate court gave him a break.

It said, in effect, go back, gather more proof of loss, and return to the Court. The taxpayer did—and *won*.

The point, of course, is that the rule on records is a must. You should get careful, detailed records on paper as soon as a casualty occurs, and *not* wait until tax time in April. In short, casualty loss deductions turn on recordkeeping.

What about a decline in the sales price of a piece of property? Look at a twist in casualty losses that has tripped up some people recently: Say you have a country house worth $50,000. It's hit by a mud slide or a flash flood, and the damage is pegged at $30,000. Your insurance payoff falls short: You get, say, $20,000 —so you're out of pocket $10,000 (assuming you want to rebuild the house). But you decide to sell instead, and find that the damaged property will go for no more than $15,000 because buyers look on the area as a risk. This leaves you out of pocket $15,000 ($50,000 less the total of $20,000 plus $15,000). What can you deduct?

In a recent case the Tax Court backs IRS and says that, in this example you may deduct only $10,000—not $15,000. Only a decline in value measured by direct physical damage is deductible: it isn't enough to show simply a decline in the current sales price of the property. In another recent case, when storm destroyed houses *near* a taxpayer's home, he claimed a casualty loss of $20,000—the amount by which his home's market value dropped. But the Tax Court disallowed it because his property suffered no physical damage.

In any case, the crucial point is to prove your loss. Gather photos (before and after), copies of police and fire department reports, and newspaper clippings. Add to this the statement of an expert who has inspected the property if big money is involved—an architect, builder, appraiser. *Silver lining:* His fee is deductible.

Political contributions

Each year, election campaigns are under way from New England to California. The burden of a political gift rests on *you*—no part can be shifted to Internal Revenue. In short, there is no deduction allowed. Moreover, "indirect" contributions to a campaign—such as advertisements in a political program and admissions to fund-raising dinners—produce nothing in the way of a deduction.

Not only do you get no deduction for a personal contribution, but you can even end up paying gift tax (2¼% to 57¾%). The tax will apply to anything over $3,000, unless you count the gift as part of your $30,000 lifetime gift tax exemption. In your giving, always remember that you can't deduct a gift to an organization unless the group has tax-exempt status. "Groups" that devote themselves to politicking don't have this status. They can claim to be public-service organizations, but this cuts no ice with IRS if their activities amount to supporting political causes and candidates.

Note: If you contribute to a political campaign, your company can reimburse you—but you must declare the reimbursement as taxable income.

You can give shares of stock that have appreciated—and let the political outfit sell the shares. It's a way to give more for a political purpose; but review this with your personal tax man first. You'll get no deduction, though, in any case.

Portfolio deductions will save you cash

Investment-related deductions are worth close inspection (see Chapter 1, "Investments"). Some of the tax angles are drawn on thin lines. Sometimes these small windfalls—writeoffs for money spent in connection with investments—get lost. This happens even where a businessman or professional pays for professional tax help.

One trouble is that a taxpayer will ship a bulging box of records to his 1040 man at deadline season (which means any time after Mar. 1) and omit some items that he himself doesn't know are deductible. The tax expert may not have time to investigate.

Here is a quick rundown:

First, the broad rule: You can deduct any expense that is reasonable and necessary to produce your investment income, or to collect, safeguard, or maintain it. This includes the over-all cost of managing and owning income-producing property—and the cost of producing any related tax returns.

Spelling this out gives you a sizable list of possible deductions. Generally, you can deduct fees paid for the active management of your portfolio, as well as for pure investment advice without management. Add to this the cost of any routine clerical help you may use in connection with either investment property or income—bookkeeping service, secretarial work, and the like. Also—despite a common misconception—you can deduct consultation fees involving long-range investments. The total transaction doesn't have to be complete in the current year.

Custodian services, too, are deductible. A safe-deposit box comes under this heading; so do the fees paid to a broker, bank, lawyer, or other agent who collects your bond interest or stock dividends. You can even deduct the cost of books you buy on the subject of investments, assuming they bear some direct relation to your own activities; also the cost of tax guides and weekly stock-market newsletters. *Note:* Fees paid to engineers and architects are deductible if their work relates to maintenance or repair of investment real estate.

The cost of a trip out of town to inspect your investment property may be deductible. This means transportation, meals and lodging, and items such as cabs, tips, and laundry. If you own rental real estate, for example, you may be able to deduct travel costs for a trip to consult with an adviser in the locality— or simply to inspect the property on your own.

But just routinely attending a stockholders' meeting won't give you the deduction, nor will a trip taken merely to visit casually the plant of a company in which you own some shares. You can't draw a fine line—it's a matter of good judgment. In any case, you'll want especially clear records to establish business purpose. You must show that attending the meeting—or making the trip—was necessary to preserve your investment, in some specific, practical way.

Though you can deduct custodian fees you may pay a brokerage firm, the broker's regular commissions are *not* deductible. But they can, of course, be added to the cost basis used when figuring the tax when you sell—and thus the commissions can eventually reduce your capital gains. You can deduct any interest paid a broker on money owed as a result of margin transactions. Also, costs that arise out of short sales are always fully deductible.

An exception to all this involves expenses in relation to tax-exempt securities—these are not deductible. This means, for example, the fee paid for a safe-deposit box used to safeguard municipal bonds, and the interest charges on a debt incurred to buy municipals. If you have mixed costs that stem from taxable and non-taxable investments, you should prorate to get the deduction. For example, say total investment income is $10,000 and expenses $1,000. If 50% of income arose from tax-exempts, you could deduct just $500.

Assuming you hold property for income purposes, you can deduct the related costs even if the property proves a complete dud and fails to produce anything but red ink. This is true even if the expenses are purely to lessen expected losses in the future. But clear records are a *must*.

Tax hints for executives on the move

Now take a fast look at your real estate taxes. If you are selling your house and moving, there are all sorts of special services these days to assist in making a move easier. Like the service outfits (often representing real estate agents) that help you relocate in a new city (see Chapter 3, "The Land You Live On").

But there's no service to help you with the *tax complications* of switching residences—except for your accountant and possibly the Internal Revenue Service itself. So it behooves the transferred executive (today's chronic house-jumper), the middle-aged couple seeking smaller quarters (with the kids out on their own), or the retiree going from house to apartment to bone up on real estate tax rules. This can be profitable.

Actually, the tax collector treats home buyers and sellers with occasional leniency. For example:

- Sellers in a bind have been getting a break from the Tax

Court. One taxpayer who had his home on the market for a couple of years was allowed to deduct for depreciation and repairs during that period.

■ Sellers age 65 and over get a sizable benefit. They can sell a house, move to a rental unit or in with the family (making no new real estate buy), and avoid any capital gains tax on the first $20,000 of the sale price less selling costs. This can easily cut any tax by 50% or more.

■ Sellers and buyers of co-op and condominium apartments get the same tax breaks that go to people changing houses. Thus, among other things, they can avoid capital gains when they sell and then buy.

When you sell at a profit you can, of course, sidestep a capital gains tax if, within a year, you buy (and live in) another house costing as much as or more than the price you got for the old house. This is basic. *But note:* If you see something on the market you like, you needn't wait to buy until after you sell. You can sign for the new house (or co-op or condominium) any time within a year *before* you sell—and still avoid any gains tax.

What's more, if you sell and then build a new house instead of buying a standing one, you have a year and a half following the sale to move in. Not so with the *summer house.* Tax avoidance under these rules holds good only if you sell your "principal residence" and buy another. So you're taxed on any profit from a vacation-house sale. This holds, too, when you sell your principal residence and buy a costly summer place.

Special rules apply where property is condemned for public use, say to make room for a new freeway. Generally, you're free of tax on any profit if you reinvest in "similar property" by the end of the year following the year of forced sale. Again, you can buy in advance of sale and avoid tax.

But here—for the tax advantage—it needn't be your principal residence. And if you find it hard to buy similar property within the time limit, the IRS often will give you a reasonable extension. In a recent case, a man replaced his condemned property in time but later sold back the new land as unsuitable. He still got the tax break.

What if you sell your house at a big profit and don't reinvest? You can squeeze the taxable gain by (1) boosting your cost basis, and (2) lowering your net sales price. But this takes some doing.

First, add to the price you paid for the house all capital improvements (new rooms, modern heating, cooling, new shrubs), plus your buyer's closing costs and any architect's fees (skip repairs). Next, cut your sale price by subtracting all sale costs (lawyer's fees, commissions, ad costs). The 5% or 6% broker's fee helps a lot. This is time-consuming (with much dusty record work), but profitable.

Transferee's lament: A transferred executive shouldn't lose a dime on moving expenses. *But note:* Not only is any loss on a quick sale of his house nondeductible, but if the company makes it up, the payment is taxable income. Maybe the transferee should ask the company for just that much more.

A tax guide for the summer season

Here is a slightly expanded view of second-home tax angles. Summertime activities can sometimes lead to sizable deductions, but only if you know the ground rules.

Fights over summer home real estate deals often land in the courts. The rules governing deductions don't always lead quite where you might expect. When you rent your summer place, you can deduct maintenance, depreciation, and insurance cost. The question is: How much of these costs do you deduct? Internal Revenue Service rulings and court cases appear to point up two main rules:

■ If you occupy the house part of the summer and rent it out for part, your expenses covering *only* the period of rental may be deducted. What's more, the deductions shouldn't exceed the rental income.

■ But if the house is up for rent at the start of the season and you don't use it at all during the summer, you should be able to deduct full expenses covering the whole rental season—even if you have a tenant for only a month or so.

Resale rules are tricky (see above). It's generally thought

that you can postpone indefinitely the capital gains tax from the sale of a house if you buy another costing as much within a year. But this rule applies only to your *main* residence. Sell a summer house at a profit and you owe tax that year even if you do buy another second home.

Casualty losses at a summer house can be tricky, too. They can be deducted in excess of $100 if not insured. You can deduct loss from fire, storm (including sand storm), flood, freezing, landslide, tidal wave, and theft and vandalism. Losses caused by insects, erosion, rusting and dry rot aren't allowed. Proof is vital. If you discovered damage at your summer place, take photos promptly, gather newspaper clips, and get an appraiser's statement. And report to the police any theft or vandalism—it will help support your case.

Tax-reform law demands some new thinking

Dust kicked up by the 1969 tax reform law has largely settled. If you have complex tax affairs—and haven't already gone over them—here is a list of some 1969 items that might be reviewed with a tax man.

A top tax rate of 60% in 1971 and 50% in 1972 and later will apply to *salary and bonus income.* In shaping his compensation demands, a high-paid executive may do better by stressing cash and putting less emphasis on fringe benefits—depending on his situation. He might even defer a large bonus due in 1970 and pick it up later on—with compensating adjustments—when the maximum rate on salary and bonus income is down to 50%.

Also, consider the new minimum tax. "Preference" income above a specified level is taxed at 10%. Add $30,000 to your regular tax paid for the year; preference items above that total are hit with the 10%. These items include half of net long-term capital gains and the bargain element built into stock options. Among other things, this means that more care should be taken in exercising an option. The spread between option price and market value may be taxed at the 10% rate—and at the time of exercise.

Note: For a top executive, tax-exempt bonds are now relatively more attractive. They're a "shelter" investment beyond the reach of the 10% tax bite. The 1970 bull market in common stocks makes this point all the more interesting.

Income-averaging is easier. To take advantage of this, your 1970 income must be at least 120% of your average for the past four years—down from 133⅓%. And note: Long-term capital gains and gifts may be averaged.

A single executive in 1971 faces a tax no more than 20% higher than that paid by a married man on a joint return. If he has the chance, he might defer bonus income to 1971.

Executive compensation needs a close review (See Chapter 6, "Careers and Compensation"). For example: The lump-sum payout under a pension or profit-sharing plan—to the extent that it represents company contributions—is taxed as ordinary income instead of capital gain. Note especially: There's an averaging rule that can reduce the tax—but the advantage of the lump-sum payout is cut down for many individuals. An executive will want to seek the payout that works most to his advantage. An annuity may make good sense, even though it's taxed at the higher ordinary rate.

Investments also get a shaking out. Maximum tax on capital gains stays at 25%—for gains up to $50,000. Above that, it's 29½% this year, 32½% in 1971, and 35% in 1972. One result is that the timing of capital gains sales will become even more of a fine art for many executives in the next two years.

There's a melange of investment provisions. Common stock dividends that are paid in stock instead of cash are now more often taxable, and all stock dividends on preferred are taxable. These new rules are retroactive to January 10, 1969.

Real estate investors will miss out on some tax breaks because of tighter rules on taking depreciation. The pros point out that the new law makes residential real estate—especially slum property—a much better bet for investment than commercial property. A five-year write off covers rehabilitation of low-income housing.

Weekend farmers won't do so well. The law curbs the use of heavy farm losses to offset nonfarm income. The big clampdown comes where the yearly loss is over $25,000 and nonfarm income is $50,000 or more.

Youths get a break. If you have a college-age son or daughter who works part-time or in the summer, he or she can earn up to $1,725 in 1970, tax-free—up from $900 in 1969.

For a first-rate review of the new law, see *Explanation of Tax Reform Act of 1969* (Commerce Clearing House, 4025 West Peterson Avenue, Chicago, Ill. 60646.

Tax help

There are many books published on taxes and how to handle them. Some are good, some not. An outstanding book is suggested: *J. K. Lasser's Your Income Tax,* 1971 edition (Simon & Schuster)—available at all book stores. This is the best known and best read book of its kind, and fully deserves its long-standing reputation. Written and edited by Bernard Greisman, member of the New York bar, *Your Income Tax* is clear, to the point—and isn't laced with gimmicks or tax dodges that too often are used to sell guidebooks of this kind. At the same time, the book has many "inside" tips and profitable tax ideas.

If you want a good tax newsletter, the *Kiplinger Tax Letter* (twice monthly, $24 a year) is quite good. So is the letter *Research Institute Recommendations,* by Research Institute of America ($24 a year)—though it tries to cover less ground per issue.

Most taxpayers can benefit from the U.S. Treasury's publication, *Your Federal Income Tax (1971) for Individuals;* it has 160 pages of explanation written by people in the Treasury and IRS. You don't get inside tips—but you don't get misled, either.

Estate Planning:
For the Long Haul

Plans that fall apart

"You're wise to review your estate plan," say the trust officer, the tax specialist, the CPA, the lawyer—and even your wife. The trouble is that many a prosperous man has precious little to review.

Robert Ferguson, executive vice-president of Pittsburgh National Bank and a top planning authority, points out that too often the executive or professional man lacks even a basic plan, let alone one that's of maximum quality. And a leading author on estates, Robert Brosterman, adds: "In a typical large corporation only 10% of the management group will have all-out plans that really conserve family wealth."

An executive may have a written will. But in many cases it goes off on a tangent and fails to wrap up what may amount to a sizable part of his property. The major trouble is that only a man's house (if it's in his name), bank accounts, and investments normally pass to his heirs via his will. His personal life insurance, plus company benefits—group insurance, pension, deferred compensation, and such—go to the family directly. "The company benefits," notes Brosterman, "can easily be worth $250,000 or more to the heirs of a top executive."

The will not only misses property, but can be self-defeating in the bargain. An executive frequently will set up a trust for his wife by will, so that she and the children have the advantage of professional property management and guidance—a smart idea. But unless the trust is tied in, it misses all property passing outside the will. The result: The widow gets much of her inheritance directly—and the trust idea falls apart.

What's needed is a coordinated plan. One solution: a fringe benefit trust. You set up a revocable, living trust—it takes effect today, but can be revoked at any time. You give the trustee detailed instructions for managing and distributing your property when you die—as you would in a will—and put in your company benefit payoffs and possibly your personal life insurance. At the same time, your will is adjusted to instruct that any assets not already in the trust will "pour over" into it at your death, when the trust becomes irrevocable.

This arrangement—which top planners believe is safer and more efficient than similar provisions in the will itself—won't reduce estate taxes at your death. But it will ensure property management for your family under a unified plan, and enable you to make provisions that will eliminate estate tax when your wife dies.

A more involved plan uses a double-trust setup, with some items falling into a revocable living trust and others into an irrevocable trust that takes property out of your taxable estate. This is technical, though, and takes close advice on how to split up the items—and it varies, depending on your case.

Reading up: If you want to review planning ideas before seeing an adviser, read Robert Brosterman's *The Complete Estate Planning Guide* (McGraw-Hill).

Time to check the clauses in your will

At the same time, check on the fine print in your will—assuming you have one. Here are some points for review:

The so-called "simultaneous death clause" in a will can be important for children in the family. This applies to an accident in which both husband and wife lose their lives. In such cases, the heirs under most state laws lose the benefit of the marital deduction—which allows 50% of a man's estate to pass to his wife tax-free.

There's a way to hang on to this deduction, however, even in the case of simultaneous death. Make sure your will contains a clause specifying that in a common disaster, it shall be presumed that your wife survived you.

How much money might this save? With a taxable estate of $200,000, for example, willed 50% to the wife and 50% to children, the children's federal tax bill would be $31,500 without the marital deduction—and only $9,600 with it. The saving: $21,900.

Note: When husband and wife own nearly equal amounts of property subject to estate tax, don't use the simultaneous death clause. Instead, each parent's will should leave the property directly to the children.

There are many other ways to ease the estate tax burden on your heirs. For one thing, you can make your children irrevocable beneficiaries of your life insurance—and assign full ownership of the policies to them. This will remove the death benefits from your taxable estate. By careful planning, you can usually avoid gift tax on transfer of the policies.

A long-range program of gift-making is an old favorite for lightening the tax load. Say a businessman and his wife join in a 10-year plan to give $6,000 a year to each of their three children for nine years—totaling $162,000. In the 10th year, they give another $38,000 to make a total gift of $200,000—entirely tax-free, thanks to their individual exclusions of $3,000 per child yearly plus their individual $30,000 exemptions over a lifetime.

Since the parents together have a $60,000 lifetime gift tax exemption, this plan has an added advantage: It leaves them $40,000 of the exemption for future gifts. The tax on a $200,000 estate left directly would come to $48,000.

There can be sizable savings in a one-shot gift. Say that you cut $50,000 from a $250,000 estate. This means money taken out of the top bracket of the estate tax—and the family saves $15,000 (tax drops from $45,000 to $30,000). If you take $100,000 from such an estate—say the husband gives full ownership of his life insurance policies to his wife—the family will save roughly $30,000.

Here there's little chance that a gift tax would apply; for tax purposes, only the current cash value of the insurance is given away (see below).

But estate planning is not without some cloudy areas. For example, when you give your wife an insurance policy on your life, the proceeds won't be in your taxable estate. But be sure her will is adjusted to allow for it. Her will should not give you an interest in the policy, even as trustee. A new case says that if you get such an interest and she dies first, the proceeds could later go into your estate.

As for group coverage, last year the IRS ruled that you can assign your company life insurance and get the proceeds out of your estate. But there's a hitch. State law must permit the move, and most state codes make no mention of this. You can go ahead, but get advice on local technicalities.

Another device is to sign over full ownership on your home to your wife—and take its value outside your taxable estate. Recent court cases have held, in effect, that this is feasible. But check with your adviser. There's a careful hand required here.

Of course, it's also important to make sure your heirs can readily pay any estate taxes you can't avoid. This means cash. And you don't want the heirs to be forced into unprofitable sales of assets such as real estate or securities—stock in a closely held family corporation, in particular.

One method is to use insurance with a trust agreement attached. Make the trust the beneficiary of a life policy; on your death, it takes title to the estate assets, provides tax money from the insurance benefits, and holds the assets until they can be sold at the best price.

In a family business, look into buy-and-sell agreements with business associates—to supply ready money without permanently diminishing the family's interest in the company. Such agreements should specify a fixed stock value—and should be checked carefully with a tax adviser.

Should you name your wife as executor?

In reviewing your will, take special care in naming the executor —and think twice before appointing your wife. Such an appointment does have the advantage of saving a professional executor's commission (usually 2 to 3% of the net estate). Frankly, though, it can prove to be folly—unless your wife is as capable as you are of managing your property and investments. The job of executor is no sinecure that should be assigned for sentimental reasons.

This rule applies even if your will provides for a trust, with a professional named to oversee your assets for the benefit of the heirs. A trustee, however skilled, must wait in the wings until the estate has been settled. And with a reasonably complex estate, settlement can take a good year or two, often longer. During this period, the executor is totally in charge. Even though there will likely be an attorney for the estate, he will lack real authority. And a lot can happen to an investment portfolio in a two-year span.

Happily, there are some alternatives to consider. You can name the family lawyer as co-executor, alongside your wife as executrix. This puts the attorney in a stronger position to protect your family's best interests until the trustee takes over. And by entitling him to the executor's fee, it gives him reasonable compensation for his efforts.

Or you can appoint a bank or trust company, or other investment professional, to serve as executor as well as eventual trustee. A corporate executorship, of course, can't be interrupted by death of the trustee. You can name your attorney co-executor along with the bank, if you want—though this would mean a fee of 2 to 3% for each.

A third way to get around the problem—but one to weigh carefully—is to provide in your will that your executor should (with court approval) turn over part of the estate's assets, say 50%, to the trustee sooner than normal. This is something to work out in detail with your lawyer.

Misconceptions about an executor's duties lead to many mix-ups—and poor appointments. The executor has two main functions: to collect, account for, and then distribute the assets of the estate; and, at the same time, to see that all debts are paid—including taxes. This often means selling assets to meet the tax bill. Usually this involves selecting the proper stocks out of a portfolio—clearly no job for a novice.

No matter whom you pick as an executor, however, he should be informed in advance—and he should agree to the appointment. In addition, he should be fully acquainted with the ins and outs of managing your investments. If he doesn't merit this full confidence, don't name him.

A guardian for your child—and a trustee, too

It isn't always enough just to name a guardian for your children in your will. Especially if you'll be leaving a substantial estate, you probably ought to consider creating a trust, with a skilled trustee, to manage the property—instead of naming a guardian for this task. You still would have a personal guardian, of course, to look after the youngsters themselves. This arrangement has at least two important advantages:

- A trustee can be given as much discretion in handling investments as you see fit. A guardian of a minor's property, by contrast, is hamstrung by state laws. Among other things, he has limited financial authority—and usually can put money only into highly conservative channels.

■ A trustee can continue to manage the property for as long as you specify. But a guardian automatically loses his authority the day the child turns 21.

Just about the only possible drawback is the cost of professional trusteeship. With a bank or trust company handling the portfolio, however, this comes to less than 1% a year.

Of course, it's as important as ever to name a personal guardian. If you fail to do so, a court might have to appoint one. Don't assume that your executor will become guardian—unless you say so in your will—or that some unwritten understanding with a favorite relative will necessarily hold up. Other members of the family—or even the child himself, if he's 14 or over—might overturn the agreement.

The guardian doesn't have to be a relative, as many people suppose. He might be a trusted friend of the family. No one can challenge your choice except by upsetting your entire will— which is most unlikely.

If you need to change your will to take care of a guardianship, it can be handled by a codicil. It might be wise for you and your wife to make the change in both your wills at the same time. And remember to name an alternate guardian.

A personal guardian who has been appointed by the court has a great deal of freedom in caring for a child. When you name your own guardian, though, you can make your views clear— in your will if you wish. You can be as specific as suggesting a church, prep school, or college. These directions, however, place the guardian only under a moral obligation—not a legal one. A court isn't apt to interfere with differing decisions by a guardian—except on the question of a child's religious training.

Legal marriage of a ward under 21, incidentally, ends all aspects of personal guardianship, at least in the eyes of the law.

Before appointing a guardian, you should, of course, obtain his agreement. And if you're naming both a personal guardian and a property trustee, make sure that they, in turn, agree to cooperate.

Joint ownership: often an attractive snare

Owning property jointly with your wife—that is, listing your-selves as co-owners—may be a convenient and harmless way to handle a family checking account. But if you carry the idea much further, you are inviting serious trouble.

The real difficulty begins when joint ownership is used as a short-cut substitute for long-range estate planning. That's because joint ownership gives you little or no flexibility. You forfeit your chance to direct the final disposition of your property. And in the long run it can be costly.

Here's an example of how costly: Where there's an estate of, say, $300,000 moving from husband to widow to grandchildren, the difference between effective estate planning and joint owner-ship might easily be over $30,000 in taxes paid by the grand-children.

All too often, however, a husband thinks joint ownership is a safe and simple way to pass property along to his heirs, since if either he or his wife dies the other immediately becomes sole owner of the property. So he decides to postpone making a will.

But look at the risk: When the husband dies, the burden of managing his property suddenly is placed in his wife's hands. She may not be able to handle this job wisely, especially where a range of investments is involved. Often the wife will get a lot of well-intentioned but frequently ill-informed advice from friends and relatives.

Thus, your hard-earned money—and the family's security— may be jeopardized by unskilled handling. The way to avoid this, of course, is to have a professionally drawn will containing advice and instructions, and possibly trust provisions.

Another danger of joint ownership, though a less apparent one, is that your property may even wind up wholly or partly in the wrong hands. Take this example: A middle-aged man puts his property into joint ownership with his wife. They have no children, but the husband has an aged parent still living, and the wife has two brothers. The husband dies unexpectedly. A short time later the wife dies without having made a will. Since the joint property was entirely the wife's at her death, it all goes to her brothers (under state law). Likely, both husband and wife would have wanted to care for the husband's parent as well. Here the result of rigid joint ownership is an illogical, unfair, and probably undesired distribution.

Warning: Once you have got yourself locked in with joint ownership on a wide scale, there is no easy way out. Having your wife hastily transfer joint property back to you would be a mistake—you might even wind up with a big gift tax bill. Your lawyer or other estate-planning adviser can steer you on this, advising which properties can be retransferred without tax liability.

Gift planning: using insurance

If you're shopping for a tax-saving, lifetime gift plan for your family, you may find that giving away your insurance is a smart idea.

First, take a look at the conventional approach, using some round numbers. You give, say, $50,000 in stocks to your two youngsters. The dividends paid on the stocks come to $2,000 a year. Each child can get over $1,500 tax-free (in the $2,000 low-bracket)—and you pay less tax yourself. If, for example, your taxable income is around $35,000, you save roughly $1,000 a year.

Besides, you cut your estate by $50,000, plus income that would have piled up. If these two total, say, $60,000—and you leave a taxable estate of $100,000 or more—your family saves at least $15,000 in estate tax. Not only do you save estate tax—you can avoid gift tax, too.

But suppose that you have good reason for not wanting to part with your shares of stock. This is the rub for many a man—and it's the point where some of them decide to drop the whole gift-plan idea. Unless you give other income-producing property, you can't pick up your yearly income tax savings—but there is a way you can preserve the estate tax advantage, which may be more vital anyway.

Use your life insurance as the gift property. Say that you own a $100,000 life policy and assign full ownership in it to your youngsters, or your wife. Again, this can automatically cut your eventual estate—by $100,000. To use round figures, if your remaining taxable estate turns out to be $100,000, the insurance transfer saves your family $30,000 in estates taxes. And usually there is no gift tax problem.

Remember that when you assign the policy you aren't giving away anything like $100,000. For example, if you're age 50 and have been paying premiums for 10 years, the cash value is roughly $16,000 to $18,000, depending on whether the policy pays dividends.

The point is that, for tax purposes, the gift is well below your own personal lifetime exemption from gift tax, which is $30,000 ($60,000 for you and your wife). Also, this is apart from the $3,000-a-year gift tax exclusions that permit you and your wife together to give two children $12,000 yearly.

So usually you can give the life policy tax-free. For comparison, if you give $100,000 in securities to your two youngsters (joining with your wife), the gift tax would be about $2,000. Thus a gift of life insurance allows you to maintain your securities intact, and at the same time, avoid any current tax as you cut a large slice from your taxable estate.

And there's a third point to weigh: If today you give securities that have appreciated in value since you purchased them, generally your family members assume your own original tax basis —so when they sell, they pay capital gains tax on the full measure of profit. However—pending tax law changes—if you hold the securities and your children inherit them at your death, their tax basis is the current value of the securities at the time your estate is settled.

Providing for the future of children by giving them securities —especially common stocks—is a fast-growing practice, and probably you've been well aware of two prime advantages: (1) built-in inflation protection for the child's benefit, and (2) income tax savings affecting the whole family. But what you may not be up on is the best way to carry out the plan.

A "custodian account"—recently made available under the

laws of all 50 states—may be your answer. A few years ago, the formal trust was about the only practical way to set up such a stock plan for a child. But this means the selection and appointment of a trustee, the expense and bother of drafting formal trust agreements, and the cost of accounting, etc. Today the streamlined "custodian account" can be a smart alternative to a trust, in some cases.

The plusses: First, the idea is simple, workable. Opening a stock account for your child takes only a few minutes in your broker's office. You just register the stocks in your own name— or in another family member's name (see below)—"as custodian for the benefit of . . . ," your child. Generally, as custodian, you can sell the stocks, reinvest the proceeds, and reinvest the income, year to year. There are a few limitations under the law— for example, the custodian can't legally use the child's money to buy stocks on margin. But these restrictions are not usually too burdensome.

Now, consider tax breaks. First, all states get the same treatment from the Internal Revenue Service in Washington, regardless of differences in state laws. And here is the prime tax advantage: As long as you use your own money, and not custodian-account money, to support the child (this being your legal obligation), the annual income from the custodian account is taxed to the child. That is, he files his own return each April, and pays tax in his own bracket.

This may mean a very low tax—or none at all. Allowing for exemptions and exclusions, no federal income tax is due on the first $1,725 of income in 1970 (assuming, obviously, that the child has no other income).

Another plus is the fact that even though you may serve as custodian of a large income-producing account, in your child's name, you still retain your tax exemption for the child—as long as he's under 19, or remains a full-time student.

There is one possible drawback—it may or may not cloud the whole idea. With a custodian account, when the child reaches age 21, the property is turned over to him. With a trust, this, of course, isn't the case.

A limitation

Thus the big selling point for giving securities to your child via a simple, streamlined "custodian account" is that you not only sidestep a formal trust arrangement, but also have a chance to save taxes. But be aware of a limitation that applies on the tax-saving side.

When you give to a minor using a custodian account, you can still split family income down to the child's lower tax bracket. But depending on how you set up this kind of account, you may be in danger of losing an important estate tax advantage.

The Tax Court now supports Internal Revenue and says that you may not appoint yourself custodian of the account in the child's name—and still have the gift stay outside your own taxable estate. If you—as donor—are custodian of the funds, and die before the child is 21, the whole value of the account becomes part of your estate.

Discuss with your adviser the possibility of naming another person (and this can be a member of the family) as custodian. *And note:* The step can be taken even for an established account.

Avoiding the probate court

There has been considerable talk among estate planners and their clients, in the past few years, about avoiding probate. The theory is that you should handle your property so that when you die, it needn't pass via your will and be taken by your lawyer to the county courthouse—for laborious and costly administrative procedure—before it finally gets distributed to your beneficiaries.

According to this theory, if you avoid probate, your heirs are saved time, trouble, and excessive expense at the hands of the lawyer-courthouse combination.

In all of this, there is something to consider. Probate reform is, indeed, needed to varying extents in many areas of the country. Costs often are high. And most important for you, there are situations in which passing property to avoid probate makes sense:

- You can set up a "living" or inter vivos trust to operate while you are still alive to accomplish what a testamentary trust can accomplish—and avoid probate.
- You can buy a life insurance policy, and name your wife or child or any individual (but not your estate) as beneficiary—and avoid probate.
- You can own property jointly with your wife and avoid probate—if you're willing to assume some risks.

Property handled this way "passes outside the will" (in lawyer lingo)—and so sidesteps the courthouse on its way to your family. The same holds true for fringe benefits from your company.

But the idea that probate is always onerous can be vastly overdone. True, lawyers earn fees from the probate process—but they also would earn fees helping people avoid it (for example, setting up lifetime trusts). Also, it's highly questionable whether you can safely handle your own paperwork in connection with the disposition of your property. For higher-income people especially, do-it-yourself estate planning can be risky. There's more to it than just filling out some standard forms.

The trust is the be-all, end-all, do-all—for anybody who takes a stab at long-range estate planning on behalf of well-heeled clients. The trust can do everything but sit up and talk. And it can do *that* if you consider that a trust lets a man talk loud and clear long after he is six feet under.

Here are comments on various trusts—and what they can do.

The variable variety

One of the hottest items today is the variable trust. "It gives you more flexibility than anything in this field of planning," says top trust man Robert Ferguson, the highly regarded trust officer with Pittsburgh National Bank.

In New York, trust officials agree, and some see a possible

trend. The basic idea is to put a reasonable percentage of your securities into a revocable trust, with you and a bank serving as co-trustees. Many banks will now take smaller accounts; so you could put in, say, $25,000, and if the idea worked well, add more in future years.

The bank provides three stages of service: custody (your securities are kept safe, coupons are clipped, dividends collected, and so on); management (custody plus investment advice); and full management (the bank takes over and acts as the sole trustee).

You can switch services at will, electing "management" while traveling abroad, perhaps. In later years, you might pick "full management" to avoid making portfolio decisions. You could, of course, cancel the whole deal at any time; the trust is irrevocable only upon death.

The variable trust provides service, but no present tax savings. It's well worth a look, however.

Trusts that multiply

Dollar savings come in with the use of multiple trusts that split income into lower tax brackets. The idea has just received some solid backing. You can establish as many trusts for one person as you like. So in theory you can set up, say, several trusts for a child and thus cut the total income into several parts, each taxed separately in lower brackets.

Planners have avoided this in part because of the chance that the Internal Revenue Service would lump the trusts together and tax them at a single higher rate. Then came a Tax Court case of a man and wife who set up 20 trusts in separate accounts, separately handled, for a married son. The court told the IRS, in effect, that the income-splitting is legal.

Obviously, there's a common-sense limit to this sort of thing. Among other limitations, at some point, trust management fees could eat up any tax savings. But the concept is well worth checking with an adviser—though you should check closely.

You can, it seems, pound a trust into almost any shape, and

often still pick up side benefits. Another Tax Court case makes the point. Say that you and your wife make a gift to your children and have the property—both principal and income—held by them as trustees for the future benefit of your grandchildren. You still get an immediate double tax break: You split the income away from your own tax bracket, and you and your wife get advantage of your annual joint $6,000 gift tax exclusion, plus your joint $60,000 lifetime gift tax exemption.

Another recent case says that a trust beneficiary himself can assign income from the trust to someone else for 10 years or longer—and thus temporarily split the income away from his own tax bracket.

The Indian giver's trust

It takes a long time for any innovation to make the grade in the field of estate planning. But in the last two or three years it has become clear that the revocable "living" trust really has come into its own.

With a revocable trust, you transfer property to your family without using a will. This feature—avoiding probate—has picked up interest. It will save your heirs delay, red tape, and some money. But there are other, even sharper advantages to look into.

You save no income taxes because you can cancel the trust at any time—but the right to cancel, in itself, can be a prime advantage. "On balance," says James North, Chase Manhattan's top trust man, "the revocable trust is an exceptionally smart way to work an estate plan."

Under one method, you use a professional trustee (bank, attorney, etc.), and transfer to the trust some income-producing property. The trustee pays you the income, manages the assets. He charges an annual fee of less than one-half of 1% of portfolio market value—less than that charged by an investment service. (In some cases, the fee is as low as one-fifth of 1%).

When you die, the trustee automatically carries out the terms of the trust on behalf of your family. None of the red tape involved in the probating of your will delays distribution of your bequests. *Note especially:* During your lifetime, you can add property to the trust—or revoke at any time, or change managers. So, you can "test" trustees.

Another approach—mentioned above—is a boon to high-bracket executives who expect to add to their assets through retirement benefits and insurance. Here you set up the revocable trust, but let it remain unfunded. In case of your death, any future assets become payable to the trust. You name the trust as beneficiary of your personal life insurance payoff and company retirement benefits. Again, there's no question that probating your will might delay the operation.

You can, in your lifetime, make the revocable trust irrevocable. If you do this, you pick up income tax advantages: for instance, splitting off income and putting it into a child's lower tax bracket. In any case, the trust becomes irrevocable when you die. And if it operates through two generations—say during the lives of both your wife and your children—there can be some sizable estate tax savings.

That such a trust lets your heirs avoid probate is indeed a point. Probate can sometimes be a costly courthouse routine. You may have other reasons for avoiding probate: For instance, you may fear bequests could stir up a contest over your will; you may want your assets shielded by the privacy of a trust, which unlike a will isn't on public record. The net saving in money, though, is not likely to be all-important.

The 10-year trust: for the medium haul

Long-term estate plans and short-range monthly budgets get much attention. But what about the middle run? This is where the 10-year trust comes in. This idea, often neglected, is a money-saver that you should be aware of in any review of affairs.

It has some fine advantages. A 10-year trust permits you to:

▪ Split income temporarily for tax purposes.

▪ Get back the income-producing property after the trust expires.

- Act as trustee, and guide the investment of the principal.

It also has some highly practical applications (college financing, for instance), and can be worked to fit snugly with retirement-income plans.

And note: The drawbacks (inevitable with any trust device) won't snuff out the life of the idea the moment you step into an adviser's office.

Take a case couched in prosperous terms. You have a son going to college in about 10 years. Your taxable income is $37,-000 (45% top tax bracket). You set up a temporary 10-year trust for the boy, and put in enough to produce $1,000 a year in interest or dividends. The result: In 10 years, when he's ready for college, your boy—with the $1,000 per year invested at say 5%—has nearly $13,000, after taxes.

Meantime, since you're in the 45% bracket, you save $450 a year by not having to add the yearly $1,000 to your taxable income. You can figure, too, that for you to put aside the $13,000 over 10 years—in your tax bracket—you would need roughly twice as much income-producing property.

Finally, at the end of the 10-year term—or it can be longer—you can return the securities to your own portfolio. This, of course, may tie in with your retirement income.

The temporary or short-term trust is flexible. You can use it for such things as supporting an aged aunt, establishing an insurance program for a child, or creating a nest egg for a teenager who will one day need money to start up a business or profession.

The drawbacks? One is the possibility of having to pay a gift tax at the time you set up the trust. But the way around this usually is pretty clear since you and your wife together can give $60,000 free of gift tax, plus $6,000 a year to any one individual.

In some states, putting a child through college may be considered part of your legal obligation as a parent. In such a case, the income from your educational trust might be taxable to you, not the child. But there usually are clear, legal ways to avoid such obstacles. A competent trust adviser will see you around them.

There is a word of caution on trusts of all kinds. It applies particularly to the 10-year variety that looks so attractive at first glance: Don't be so anxious to garner tax savings that you lock up too many of your assets in a trust. All trusts—if they give you tax advantages—are binding, for whatever period they're set up. You must always judge carefully the benefit of tax savings against the risk that you may suddenly need the property that you have put out of your reach for 10 years.

The flexible "fixed-income"

Have you thought about the highly flexible "fixed-income" trust? Some advisers currently are recommending it. Here's the idea: Instead of the more usual trust that has income going to a man's wife for her lifetime, then to the children for a period of years, and finally outright to the children, the husband says to the trustee: "Pay a fixed sum to my wife each year—and if the income falls short of this liberal amount, then you may reach into the principal."

In effect, you tell the trustee to sell off some of the securities— if necessary—to obtain capital gains for your widow's use. If invading principal worries you, an adviser will likely point out that these days many persons, with the aid of good portfolio management, are able to dip into principal—and still see it grow.

A trust of this type obviously gives the trustee a great deal of freedom in investing. It might also—at least in some family situations—head off an argument among beneficiaries over investment policy.

New York's Irving Trust Co. points to yet another possible advantage. If the trust income is more than the fixed amount the widow is to be paid yearly, the excess can be put into principal. This is better than paying her more than she really needs —then having taxes bite it down, anyway.

The "sprinkling" of wealth

Estate advisers lately have been focusing on discretionary trusts—those that give wide latitude to the trustees.

They point to some clear advantages. For example, with a

"sprinkling" trust the trustee can distribute income and principal to members of the family at his discretion—depending on their needs at the time. Two major points:

- When both parents die, the trustee can divide family wealth among the children without making equal distributions. The children, whose own wealth may vary a lot, may be much better off than with the traditional even split. "We're getting away from the ironclad even split—and it makes sense," says Chase Manhattan Bank's James North.

- When a husband dies and there is more trust income than his widow needs, the extra income can be sprinkled among the children so that it drops down into the lowest tax brackets in the family. Income taxes are cut accordingly.

In discussing the idea with an adviser, check on the new law that boosts income taxes where money is accumulated in a trust. This needs extra planning.

Childless couple's trust

The childless couple—or the couple whose children are already quite well fixed—might consider a "charitable remainder trust." This estate planning idea, which benefits a widow by saving a sizable slice of federal estate tax, has come in for some favorable comment among the pros lately. And—you may be sure—from the fund raisers.

If a single man dies and leaves, say, $500,000, the federal estate tax comes to roughly $115,000. If he's married, 50% goes to his widow tax-free—under the marital deduction—and the tax drops to $45,000.

Now, figure in the charitable remainder trust. It works this way: The part of the estate that doesn't pass under the marital deduction is put into a trust—with the income going to the wife during her lifetime. When she dies, the principal goes to charity. The result is another huge slice from the tax. In the example of the married man above, the Treasury's bite goes down to around $5,000. Thus, the widow has substantially more income available for as long as she lives.

The plan has its limitations—hence a note of caution. For

instance, the trustee's power to "invade" principal for the wife's benefit must be restricted, and the amount going to charity firmly fixed. The idea, though, is solid and workable—if you get skilled advice.

An umbrella trust

The question of a single trust for two or more children—instead of frequently used separate trusts—is a point in planning you may want to review with your adviser. There are some pros and cons.

New York's Irving Trust Co. points to this example: Say you leave everything to your wife in trust for life, then to your three children. When you and she are gone, there's a net amount left of, say, $240,000. With an $80,000 trust for each of the three children, the annual trustee's fee runs roughly $1,000—whereas a single $240,000 trust costs about 25% less.

And note: Besides this saving, a larger single trust gives the trustee more room to move in selecting investments. The portfolio can be broader, better balanced. This can, of course, be vital.

But there are cases where separate trusts might serve well— for instance, where the age spread of the children is great, or where there are substantial differences in their economic status. The point is—and on this, all advisers agree—this kind of decision depends a lot on the family situation. It's a case of weighing pros and cons.

When a bank watches your nest egg

If you're setting up a trust—for the children's education, say, or your wife's support in later years—you might look into the common trust funds run by banks and trust companies. What you get, in effect, is something close to a mutual fund: You name the bank trustee, and the bank, in turn, mixes your funds with other private accounts for investment in a single portfolio of securities.

The trend is for the common trust funds to pick up bigger accounts than in the past, with some customers who formerly would have started individual portfolio accounts. The range today for the common fund is mostly $10,000 to $50,000, but some people go up to $100,000 and more.

One advantage, of course, is that your investments are spread far more widely than is practical with even a large individual account. Another is that cost is lower. At some big city banks, the minimum yearly fee for a common trust fund is $250 for accounts up to $50,000, against $375 and more for an individual trust.

Also, the common funds provide some attractive flexibility that was formerly available only with individual portfolios. For example, you often can name a co-trustee to serve with the bank, if you wish—when you want someone available for consultation who is closely acquainted with your family's needs.

You can create the trust today (a "living" trust) or set it up in your will to be activated later (a "testamentary" trust). If you decide on a living trust, you would likely make it irrevocable; but it could be revocable—which means, of course, lopping off some tax advantages.

The banks offer several types of common trust funds. If you set up the trust without specifying the type of investment you want, the bank is required by law to put you into what is called a legal investments fund. This means a highly conservative type —possibly about 60% bonds, 40% stocks.

But if you give the bank full discretion as to the type of fund, you'll be letting bank experts decide where you belong, in view of such factors as family income needs and size of principal. Here you'll wind up in one of four types of funds: the balanced fund—today usually about 60% common stocks, 40% bonds; the 100% common stock fund; the tax-exempt bond fund (fastest growing type today); or, finally, the taxable (corporate) bond and preferred stock mix.

When you establish the trust, you can name the type of fund you want. But this may or may not prove an advantage, depending on your property, income, and family situation.

As for the possibility of an individual portfolio account, in many cases the reasons for one are now more limited than in the past. The decision usually hinges mainly on taxes. Here's one point that should be considered: Before you can get into a common fund, any securities put into it must first be liquidated. This, of course, can mean high capital gains tax. With an individual trust, however, your stocks can be turned over directly without first being sold.

One question to check carefully: Find out how the performance of the bank's various funds shapes up. Some may, indeed, be lagging behind top mutual funds.

Summing it up

There are fine benefits—but also some tricks—that crop up in trusts. Affluence and the shape of the tax laws have combined over the last 10 years to make trusts about the most popular device in long-range personal financial planning. In any meeting you have with financial advisers, you'll find that trusts won't stay out of the conversation for long.

There's no doubt that the trust can be a workable and often rewarding idea; because it helps reduce taxes it has some gold-plated allurements. But you don't hear so often of some of the perils involved; they're rarely publicized.

Some people, because of hasty advice and over-eagerness to save taxes, put money in trust but foolishly insist on keeping too much control over the property. They may, for instance, want freedom to reshuffle the trust portfolio as they see fit. The result can easily be trouble with the Treasury and loss of possible tax savings.

Others are so anxious to garner the tax savings that they make binding trust arrangements—and later discover that they urgently need to use the property they've parted with. Still others create airtight tax-saving trusts for children, but fail to think of some possible non-tax results.

A father who, for example, sets up a college education trust for his child in some situations will learn that to get advantage of having trust income taxed to the child, the income must be paid to the child's bank account. This is fine—unless the child, later on, starts to spend the money carelessly. If the father then instructs the trustee to pay him the earnings—as "agent" for the child—the father may find himself taxed on the income.

To avoid complications when setting up a trust for a child, a father may learn that he must permit the trustee to turn over the trust principal, or at least the accumulated income, to the child—at age 21. This may be far from the father's idea of what is best for his family.

Life insurance trusts also can misfire. Here the husband puts his life policy in irrevocable trust. His wife gets income from the trust as needed after his death, and the remainder—upon her death—goes to the children. Thus the policy payoff is taken out of both the husband's and his wife's taxable estate—providing, in many cases, a substantial saving.

But in practice there may be hitches. The husband often discovers that he must pay heavy gift taxes. And ways around this can cause the trust property to be taxed in the wife's estate, after all. Here especially, there's the danger that the husband will later regret putting his money resources beyond his own reach.

A trust, of course, has great tax-saving potential. This, indeed, is allurement that is hard to bypass. But before you go ahead with a trust, check some of the alternate possibilities. For example, if a child is involved, at least look into the idea of establishing a "custodian account." In any case, get the advantage of top advice on trusts—the kind that comes from the estate planning department of a leading bank or trust company, or from a highly qualified estate lawyer.

Finding the right lawyer

Locating and hiring the right lawyer—for your personal and family affairs—may be a smart step to consider in any financial review. This is particularly true for the man who has come up fast or the executive who has moved to a new city and not yet made all his contacts.

And now, with income tax laws in a state of flux and estate and gift taxes up for reform, getting good legal advice becomes steadily more important. Make your contact now. Talk over with the lawyer your medium- and long-range plans—then let him advise you as the laws change. "Estate and gift plans, primarily, will need a thorough going over—maybe a full redo—in the 1970–72 period," says a top New York adviser. "A man of means can't ignore this."

Mainly you'll be seeking legal advice—estate work, realty deals, and so on. But today you can get more personal, semilegal advice than ever before. The general practice attorney handling personal affairs answers a wide variety of questions for clients, going way beyond legalities.

For example, a prominent Midwest lawyer notes that "businessmen transferred from out of town will ask me to suggest a stockbroker, or a real estate agent, even a car dealer. It's become part of my job." A New England attorney explains that he must advise on such things as juvenile problems in a family—even on intimate questions such as where to get psychiatric help.

One point seems certain: If your man is "out" whenever you seek some purely personal guidance, or if, when you see him, the discussion is hurried and matter-of-fact—you may have the wrong man.

When you contact a new lawyer, make sure your wife is along during your early conferences. But make it plain to her that, despite his liberality in counseling on a wide range of questions, the family attorney is in business, too. Mere chit-chat and verbal hand-holding on matters of little real consequence aren't part of the arrangement.

Today it's important to get to know the whole law firm, not just the individual who will be your anchor man. If your lawyer's firm is of at least medium size, you'll probably find it contains specialists in such fields as estates, taxes, real-estate, and negligence law. If it's a small firm, your man will bring in outside specialists (but you'll still pay just a single fee).

He will know estate taxes, but income tax work is probably the biggest limitation of the average family lawyer. You're often better off if you have a specialist plan your tax strategy and handle year-to-year work on your tax returns. Get hold of a CPA or tax lawyer (who may be a CPA).

Note: If a family lawyer takes on your April 15 taxes, his whole approach will often turn out to be highly conservative.

Legal fees for personal work have headed up, but not at the rate of, say, the costs for medical services. A simple will should cost no more than about $50 to $150. "It's a loss-leader for a lawyer," says a Manhattan pro. "He hopes to be compensated later on, as executor or attorney for the estate." A more complex will involving estate taxes, trusts, and so on, should come to about $250 to $500. An elaborate estate plan is in the $1,000 range.

Executorship commissions vary by state. They run 2 to 4% of the first $10,000, then 2 to about 3%. New rates in New York, as of this fall: 4% of the first $25,000, 3½% of the next $125,000, and 3% of the next $150,000.

A family lawyer—hired primarily to handle your will and other estate chores—will also take on the usual range of legal problems. Here's what you will be charged: A real-estate contract and title closing will often run 1% of purchase price—or about $600 on a $60,000 home. This jumps an extra $200 or $300 if an indpendent title search is included in the lawyer's fee.

Going to court can cost real money. An attorney's fee—figured on a time basis—runs $35 to $60 an hour, depending on your city. It can go up to as high as $100 an hour in an exceptional case. (Add to this about $20 to $25 an hour for a legal assistant.) And even a simple lawsuit can take 50 to 100 hours.

Some negligence lawyers will take a contingency fee; it should be about one-third of the recovery. But even here, you often pay the lawyer's out-of-pocket expenses, which can easily amount to hundreds of dollars.

Note: Your lawyer should keep you out of court, if possible, especially in this day of jammed dockets and long delays. Settlement by negotiation will cut your legal bill substantially. If your new lawyer isn't settlement-minded, you would be smart to find out why.

Careers and Compensation:
The Brass Ring

**Are you job-minded—or
job-hunting?**

In this day of mergers, consolidations, tender offers, failures (company failures, that is), tax changes, and shifts in compensation and career trends, you might want to recap in your own mind some of the prime points that relate to a man's advancement in a corporate organization. A book could be written on careers-compensation, of course. (Many have been.) Still, it's possible to wrap up in a few pages the thinking of top specialists with respect to such leading items as professional job-hunting help, the use of the "bio" and resume, the need for a job contract, and executive pay packages and how they are affected by the changing tax law.

Start with a brief review of sources of "professional" job-hunting help. The word "professional" is put in quotes because insofar as some operators are concerned, it's strictly a coined expression.

Getting help to land a new job

Some who make a business of redirecting talent, the so-called career consultants and executive counselors, have been under fire. Oftentimes, say their critics, these outfits offer little more than hand-holding—at fees as high as $500 to $2,000. "Practical career guidance and job leads are what people need and pay for," says a leading adviser. "They're apt to get hot air instead."

There are some reliable job-hunting services. But a man who decides to use this kind of help must pick cautiously. Look first at the *executive search firms*. They find and place men mostly in the $20,000 to $50,000 bracket.

These screening agents for their client companies follow two main approaches: (1) They go directly to an employed executive and offer him a possible spot with a client; and (2) they sift their files of resumes to find likely candidates. The search firm is always employed by the hiring company; it is obligated to its client, not to you. Still, dealing with such a firm can be a help.

Generally you mail a resume to the firm with a covering letter mentioning salary, which is best left off the resume. You may happen to fill the bill for a search under way; if not, the resume will be filed. The best idea is to send a resume to a half-dozen or more search firms. Any top firm will get your okay before proposing your name to a client.

Some reputable search firms: Boyden Associates; Canny-Bowen-Howard-Peck; George Haley; William H. Clark Associates; Antell, Wright & Nagel; Heidrick & Struggles; Spencer Stuart & Associates; Ward Howell. All have offices in New York, and some in other major cities. A few are even active in Western

Europe. Ward Howell, Heidrick & Struggles, and Spencer Stuart, for example, have offices in London.

Note: The search firm gets a fee equivalent to 20% to 25% of your first year's salary—but the company, not you, pays this fee. "A professional firm won't ask you to pay anything," says McKinsey & Co. consultant on compensation, Arch Patton.

Some top *management consultants* have special departments for executive recruiting. Among them are Fry Consultants and Booz, Allen & Hamilton. Cresap, McCormick & Paget and Boston-based Arthur D. Little, Inc., among others, do limited recruiting in connection with their consulting assignments. Some others, such as McKinsey & Co., try to avoid recruiting but frequently refer client companies to top-rank recruiters.

The newest group of recruiters are some of the big CPA firms that operate nationally. Among those on this list: Arthur Young & Co.,; Peat, Marwick & Mitchell; Price Waterhouse, Haskins & Sells; Ernst & Ernst. The big advantage here is that each firm serves a long list of big-name clients, so you get a good spread of possibilities. *And note:* Today the CPAs are handling non-financial jobs as well as financial, a sore point with conventional search firms.

Finally, there are reputable employment agencies that sometimes handle executive jobs (with the job-seeker paying the fee in some cases). But this approach usually hits under $20,000.

Much of the job "consulting" that has been criticized amounts to mass-mailing of resumes (sometimes too elaborate), plus psychological testing (sometimes of doubtful value). "You can put your own irons in the fire with short, crisp resumes—without anybody's help," says an adviser. And anybody who wants psychological testing might be best off at a city university that offers this service or will refer you to a reliable firm.

Putting your profile on paper

The executive who is changing companies—whether or not he employs professional help—usually must put himself on paper. This may mean a personal resume, or a short biography if he's a senior executive. Or he may decide on using several well-placed personal letters instead. Whatever the choice, this presentation on paper is one of the least-understood—but most important—aspects of changing jobs.

The biography or "bio"—a brief, low-key, personal history—has its merits. And there's the standard resume that openly "sells" and mainly details your business career. The finely tooled personal letter—directed to the president of a company—also has its place. The question: What form to use and how to use it.

The resume, of course, is a basic tool at the junior executive and middle-management level. It should start with a short but effective statement of career objective (often left out), followed by a section of personal and educational facts. Then the main part: A chronology (or maybe an essay treatment) of your job history. This account probably should name all employers, including your present one. The idea, of course, is to point up your capabilities.

A very short covering letter should go out with each resume, the letter always individually typed and tailored to the particular company. If you state salary requirements, do so in the letter, not the resume.

The resume, frankly, is largely the device of the man on his way up—who still feels the need to "sell" himself. But sometimes it is useful to a top executive with a smaller or medium-sized concern when he wants more aggressive exposure than a bio provides. One of the few reasons why a top manager of a larger company would need a conventional resume is to have a piece of paper to file with a professional executive recruiter. Such firms as Heidrick & Struggles, Ward Howell, Canny-Bowen-Howard-Peck, and Boyden Associates, plus some larger management consulting and accounting firms, rely at least partly on resumes. The resume, though, has some limitations.

A senior executive in a known company—assuming that his move will rest largely on personal business contacts—may prudently decide to use a biography. The reason is apparent: The bio—one page tops, compared with two for a resume—is a little like a Who's Who entry. In fact, it's done in pretty much the same style. Unlike the resume, it has no "career objective" section; and if it does list all your past companies (though it needn't), it won't expand on your various jobs and responsibilities to show what you can do. The bio says, in effect: "Here's a summation of my personal history." It makes no pitch.

When you use a bio you assume that the facts will speak for themselves. The bio reflects an attitude of success—a man who knows his status and needn't rely on the more promotional resume. It is straightforward and discreet. And it is used discreetly. Unlike the resume, the bio goes to only a few important business contacts; it is not mailed out to a list of people.

In a subtle way, though, the bio does some selling, of course. Its very air of self-assurance is *low-key* salesmanship—but this will come off only if matched by the man who (often casually) presents it.

The personal letter, individually written to the chief executive officer of a company, can be the preferred approach (assuming you're well past the junior executive level). This is the best appointment-maker you can find, says Carl R. Boll, author and placement chairman of the Harvard Business School Alumni Association. But, cautions Boll, send your letter to the top man in the company—never to the second line. Have a bio or short resume on hand when you are invited in for a talk.

Finally, all leading advisers in this field stress two points to keep in mind: Take time for careful preparation of a resume, bio, or letter; and above all, write it yourself and keep it brief. "A professionally written job usually has a false veneer," says one pro. A good book for boning up: *Executive Jobs Unlimited,* by Carl Boll, a savvy how to do it for people on the move (Macmillan).

Job contracts fill a need

In negotiating a new job proposition, you may want to consider asking for what may amount to a sizable concession on the company's part: an executive job contract.

A contract will come your way only at the officer level, except in some special-assignment cases, and the idea often applies where the company is something less than a giant in size and reputation. But instances of "special cases" are growing, and several trends in business today make the personal contract of considerably greater interest.

With top-quality executive talent scarce, companies increasingly are keeping eyes open for the seasoned manager who knows the ropes. Often this means hiring a man over age 45 or 50. But a man of say, 50 is likely to have a healthy build-up of fringe benefits with his old company. And as for relocating, he can afford some risk—but might not go too far. Since he's well established, he might want a contract that will protect him, not only in terms of salary and service, but also spell out fringe benefits with the new company.

Then there's a developing corporate trend to hold onto the consulting talents of top managers who retire from full-time duty. This situation is typical: You're age 60, plan to retire at 65 (maybe a bit earlier)—and have been asked to consider serving for an extra five years as a consultant on a part-time basis. You're in a logical spot to receive a contract that defines what "part-time consulting" will mean in your case, and spells out compensation.

True, phasing into full retirement this way may be an appealing idea. But no vital part of retirement income should be left to chance (like an unforeseeable company shake-up)—or to anybody else's decision. In such case, a firm contract may be a prudent move.

Foreign service provides another argument for a contract. You are 45, have 10 or 15 years with your company, and are offered a spot by another concern as head of its operation in Milan. If it's a big international outfit with a fixed policy covering executives going abroad, you just may be offered a contract; but if not (and this is far more likely) you're usually safe without one. With such a company, you couldn't buck standard procedure and get a contract, anyway—unless the Milan job was a top overseas position.

But if it's a small or medium-size concern—where such policy isn't too firmly fixed—you might be foolish to consider moving your residence and family abroad without the safeguard of a contract. The contract, incidentally, should clearly cover any company-paid moving costs.

Finally, a merger or acquisition can give even a highly qualified executive an uneasy fear of being squeezed out someday (see below). The fear is especially real where your company is bought out. If you're slated to "stay on" in a middle or even top management post, you might seek a personal contract. This way you cut down the danger of being left high and dry in a future reshuffle.

Other special cases where you might lean to a personal contract are the *family-business setup*—where you go in to manage but fear the capriciousness of the family owners; *the rescue mission*—where you go into a company that's in trouble, and fear the impatience of an anxious board of directors; and where *fringe-benefit plan* promises are so complex that they need to be put on paper.

Why not push for a personal service contract in every case? There are two main reasons. One, of course, is that with a contract you pretty well shut the office door behind you. Getting wedged into an uncomfortable situation, with no easy way out, can be difficult and frustrating. The second reason is largely psychological. By merely asking for a contract, you register a certain unspoken lack of confidence in the company—or, indeed, in yourself.

To be sure, the executive's personal service contract isn't really an iron vest: You can get fired under numerous circumstances (see your lawyer); and conversely, you can always quit and the company can't literally force you to stay on. What a contract boils down to is that the company can make it difficult for you to quit; and you make it tougher for the company to fire you.

**Keeping your cool
in a rough merger**

What about self-protection when you see a possible merger of your company on the horizon? Here, of course, a contract may help—but there are other considerations. Top advisers mince no words: The executive caught up in a merger can find himself eased out with little ceremony—and maybe at an age when relocation is a long, hard process.

Merger consultants, attorneys, and compensation specialists make this point: If a man is high-salaried and past 50 (and sees a merger coming) he's foolish not to take firm steps to protect his position. Says one leading consultant: "First, figure where you'll stand in the merged organization." Through competitors of the other company and industry sources, you can get an idea of the company's reputation and overall organization.

But go further than this: Through bankers and other contacts in industry, get a clear line on the man who is your counterpart. "If you're about 55 and at $45,000 and he's 40 and at $30,-000—you may have some hard thinking to do," says a McKinsey specialist. "If the reverse is true, you may be in good shape." Failure to investigate can cause a lot of agony.

No matter your age, you might want a "protective" contract for a guaranteed term of years. This idea is coming into greater use; it makes sense if your company will be taken over by a larger outfit. It gives you a degree of protection—and it legally binds the merged business.

But weigh the pros and cons, say the experts. Don't rely too heavily on any agreement that you manage to acquire as a safeguard. "The trouble is," says Chicago consultant John Struggles, "for you, it isn't ironclad; they can ease you out if they really want to."

In some cases, the reverse happens—you may be put under pressure to sign a term-of-years contract for the protection of the merged organization. This has been especially true lately in the case of the conglomerate that picks up unrelated businesses requiring diverse talents. The trouble with this, say the pros, is that you may find it hard—as an individual—to get out from under. Thus, advisers point out that generally you should sign such a contract for a term of no more than two or three years—especially if you're going into a newly merged organization.

The *tender offer* can be about as tough on the managers of a company as any major move in business. Say the pros: Don't delude yourself—this type of takeover is often aimed at promptly erasing top management. If it happens to your company, your quietly putting out feelers for a new job will be clearly understood by a prospective new employer.

As to any shares of stock you may own—prior to a tender offer—the best advice is to sit tight and be guided by the recommendation of your board of directors. If you sell out quickly, you may be accused of deserting the business at a point of crisis. If you hold a stock option, though, you might consider exercising it, depending on the stock price that will be produced by the takeover.

Once a merger has jelled—and an executive has survived the shaking out—the question usually is, how much more money? Generally, the cases show that a man with expanded duties—but who operates on the same managerial level—will get an increase on the order of 10 to 20%. A step up in grade (say vice-president to executive vice-president) usually will rate a boost of 20% and up. Anything less than these ranges of increases, say the advisers, and you have some questions to resolve. But much depends on special factors—and, of course, the general state of business.

Asking for a stock option following a merger (or in the course of one) may be smart. But some advisers warn against getting oversold on this (see below). The same applies to seeking a deferred pay deal that would start paying out upon retirement. If your tax bracket is, say, 50% or better, fine—but still weigh carefully what you could do today with cash in hand. "For the short run," says a consultant with Towers, Perrin, Forster & Crosby, "a cash bonus deal may be your smartest approach."

Along with getting your compensation fixed in the merged organization, pay special attention to getting a clear, precise definition of your title, duties, and authority. Fail to do this, say the pros, and you can wind up in a muddy situation—and in trouble.

What you may get from a hitch overseas

Overseas assignment is another facet of career advancement, and one that needs much planning and weighing pro and con. One point is sure: Today U.S. companies are keeping closer control than ever over their overseas operations. The trend will continue.

On the plus side, a man of 28 to 45 (the usual age range of overseas appointees) generally gets a boost in his career: higher pay, broader responsibilities. Major companies are sending their top-ranking younger men abroad, not employees they want to "bury." Says a Chase Manhattan Bank executive: "A man is smart to have some overseas time if he really wants to move up the ladder." About 80% of those Chase sends abroad are sent for career development. The same holds for a growing number of big and medium-size international outfits.

The usual hitch lasts from two to five years. And the man most apt to benefit from it is the middle manager. He will probable get control over a whole local operation. That lets him prove his general managerial ability. And if he is successful, he returns home with higher status. A younger man is smart to go for experience—even without more pay.

A far less attractive deal involves going overseas for an indeterminate period to train a national for a job abroad. This missionary may return home to discover that a former equal has stepped above him.

Usually, of course, a man over 50 goes abroad only to fill a high-ranking spot. Some big companies now provide added incentive; they allow foreign service men to retire early (often at 60) with varying retirement benefits. *But note:* The benefit setup should be checked carefully.

The big gamble, though, is not so much age and assignment. It's how well a man's wife and children will adjust to the relocation. There's likely to be at least moderate strain—and there are plenty of cases where relocation has broken up marriages. Even a move to Western Europe can be difficult. "People who have strong family ties back home are poor risks," says a Jersey Standard personnel executive.

Some self-examination is a must. But too often this is ignored by the man eager to push ahead. Says one old hand in the international field: "If you're just trying to get away from it all, forget about going abroad. Your problems will magnify."

As a rule, you won't get a contract for an overseas hitch (and it may be best not to push for one). But there are some things you will want to nail down. You should expect a foreign service premium of 15 to 25% above your base salary. This is what many of the larger outfits are paying. Note that the cost of living abroad can be higher than in the U.S. For example, in some cities it may cost up to $200 a month more to rent a comparable house in Europe than in the U.S. "Making a profit on a tour abroad doesn't work these days," says one pro, "except in a place like Nairobi."

Moving expenses should be paid, too. This may mean $5,000 to $6,000 (non-taxable) for moving your family to Western Europe.

Many companies will pay $800 to $1,000 per child per year for school expenses abroad. Some pay for one round trip a year for a college-age son or daughter studying in the U.S. Quite a few companies will even help you in your search for a school and pay exceptional costs such as high tutoring fees in remote areas. Press these points when you negotiate.

As to language study, if you have time you can take a 200-lesson, one-year evening course at schools such as Berlitz for $1,000 and up, depending on the language. If you're on short notice, the Berlitz "immersion" course is nine hours a day for two or three weeks—and a lot of it sticks if you go abroad soon after. Your company should, of course, pay the tab.

Boning up: Centers offering special courses and briefings include the Business Council for International Understanding at American University in Washington; International Study & Research Institute in New York; Thunderbird Graduate School of International Management, in Phoenix. Also, you might read *Executive Overseas,* by John Fayerweather (Syracuse Press); J. J. Servan-Schreiber's *The American Challenge* (Atheneum), and *Living Overseas,* by Louise Winfield (PAP). Check your public library.

New rules in corporate gamesmanship

What about overall career planning? Even a minimum of planning can help a man's corporate career take off. Call it strategy, advancement techniques, or just smart self-guidance. Using it at critical stages, say top advisers, can set the direction in which a man will travel—and maybe how far he'll go.

Top-ranking management consultants and executive recruiters maintain that too many executives simply let their careers happen, in a sense. Precisely what "planning" have they in mind? There are some surprisingly firm answers. There are critical moves to make at age 30, others to try at 50, and there's the smart "lateral shift" in a company at any age.

The struggle starts early. The "junior management" candidate—starting around age 25—can make one decisive mistake: He can fail to pick out long-range goals; maybe he doesn't even fix on any goal at all. "A man must keep loose, very flexible, at this stage," says John Stevenson, vice-president at Arthur D. Little. "But he has to find his career, too—and decide, in the first place, if he really wants to be a businessman."

This point is stressed by the pros, particularly these days when many younger men are at odds with themselves. If the basic decision to aim at corporate management comes hard, a young man is wise, they say, to do some practical testing. One way: Work in a small company for a year or two, and rack up as varied a range of duties and responsibilities as the boss will allow.

Once a budding executive has made his career decision, say the pros, he should promptly think in terms of broad experience, not job continuity. Today, the bigger, well-managed companies aren't nearly so leery of a job changer as they were even a few years ago. These outfits are, in fact, looking for smart, qualified younger men who have made some company-to-company moves.

They're looked on as the best prospects for top jobs. "This is important today," says Chicago consultant John Struggles.

Also important for the young executive: He should avoid the company that is too paternalistic—or, at least, be well aware of the paternalism. Further, he should not get himself on a fast-transfer list that means periodically moving around the country to do the same work, even if the pay gets a little greener each time. "The transfer list," says Struggles, "can bury a younger man."

The middle manager in his late 30s or 40s would be smart to keep well in mind another important trend in business: going back to college. By this age, warn the advisers, a man's formal education may have grown stale. If he's aiming for top management in a front-rank company, he is likely to need new viewpoints, whether he knows it or not. The graduate management programs at such universities as Harvard, Chicago, Wharton, and Stanford can add the fresh ideas and attitudes.

"This is getting more vital every day," says Robert Harman, vice-president at Booz, Allen & Hamilton. The advisers generally agree that "back-to-campus" will be a major top-job prerequisite in the 1970s. It will take effort. The casual two-week summer seminar just won't be enough. The biggest blunder, they add, will be to stay complacent about formal education, relying on experience and the ability to "handle" people. "A man will need to show that he's up on new ideas, and thinking of next year's ideas," says New York executive recruiter Ward Howell.

The executive who's just a step or so beneath top-brass status must, of course, follow a demanding strategy if he's to get in line for the spot he seeks. But, say the pros, he may ignore the right moves out of an unconscious fear that he may not really fit the job. The obvious moves? Get to know the whole business, not just one bailiwick. Get to know the board members well. Make no secret whatsoever of the quest for the top ranking position.

Here is where dedication to the company is a 24-hour affair, covering everything from work, to wife, to the book one reads.

"If he can't do this without straining to the point of a coronary," says consultant Struggles, "then he's better off where he is." The consensus: Some men—well suited to a vice-presidency—can make a botch of things at the peak of their careers by straining too hard for the top spot, then getting lost in its mass of responsibilities.

One pointed piece of strategy that the advisers say is worth a special note: It can be a great advantage in a large organization to accept or even seek a lateral move (maybe for little or no more money) that involves entirely new, different job responsibilities. To be top brass, it appears that varied experience is what shines.

Flak and flap: executive stock options

Here is a look at major "fringe benefits" in view of changes dictated by the tax reform act of 1969: Start with the qualified stock option, which has been stirring up a good deal of misunderstanding. The new tax reform law has nipped off some of the juiciest parts of the option, especially for a senior, high-salaried executive. But if you are still coming up the line in business—reaching new status in your company, or changing companies—there may be rich returns for you in an option deal.

Note: At this writing, stock prices are way down. This gives an added spin to the option idea. The odds may well be that a company's stock will head upward in the next few years. At least, it's a point to weigh—along with taxes.

Look at the basics. With a qualified option, you get the right to buy a fixed number of shares of your company at a price that's no less than the market value as of the date the option is granted. You must exercise your option within five years, and if you hold the shares for at least three years thereafter, the profit on your sale is taxed as a long-term capital gain.

But there are some hitches in the new tax law.

▪ When you buy the shares, the difference between the price you pay and the current market value is "tax preference" income. This type of income in excess of $30,000 reduces dollar-for-dollar the amount of your "earned income" that will be subject to the new lower 50% maximum rate. (The 50% rate goes into effect in 1972.) You could end up paying as much as 70% on this part of your salary. Tax preference income—if it's high enough—will come under a second formula in the new tax law. The formula: Figure your taxes otherwise due for the year and add on $30,000. Any preference income over this amount is taxable at a flat 10% rate.

■ When you sell the shares, your profit is still treated as long-term capital gain, but the 25% maximum rate applies to only the first $50,000 of the profit. Beyond that point, the tax goes up to 35% maximum, starting in 1972. Half of this capital gain is also treated as tax preference income, meaning another tax bite for people whose brackets are high enough.

So the new tax law chops away at the option's advantages for some top managers. But take the case of the man who's still moving up the line. Smith's salary is, say, $35,000. He gets an option to buy 1,000 shares at $30, waits two years, and buys when the market is at $45. No tax is due.

He holds the 1,000 shares for three years and sells at $60. Meantime, his salary is up to $50,000. Assuming it's his only capital gain for the year, his $30,000 profit is taxed under the 25% rule—maximum tax, $7,500. At this level, Smith runs into none of the drawbacks of the new tax law.

In option deals like this, there is considerable leeway before the new tax law's deeper bites sink in. Rule of thumb: You begin to hit these added taxes only when your taxable earned income for the year is above $52,000, and your tax preference income is above $30,000.

Note: The new law, incidentally, applies to all outstanding stock options.

Compensation: more plans

Besides the qualified stock option, there are a variety of new and revised compensation plans for executives. Some of these package ideas fit in neatly with the option. But most of them are valuable on their own.

A major trend: compensation plans that make you wait for the payoff, but that take advantage of the new 50% maximum tax rate on "earned income" that goes into effect in 1972. Says consultant Arch Patton of McKinsey & Co.: "The 50% rule is bringing in all sorts of things for the $50,000-and-up man." Other compensation specialists point out that the younger up-and-coming executive can latch on to some of these, too.

Non-qualified stock options look better. This type of option isn't limited to five years—it can extend for any period of time. It can be fixed at any price, too—50% of current market price of company stock, for example. When you exercise the option you pay ordinary income tax on your immediate profit, but the pros say that the 50% top rate will probably apply. If you hold the stock for just six months, you are taxed at the capital gains rate on any sales profit—or half your ordinary tax rate, up to the new 1972 maximum capital-gains rate of 35%.

With a non-qualified option, the company gets a tax deduction for the amount of your personal profit at the time of exercise; it isn't allowed a deduction on a qualified option. So, in effect, for the same cost the company can give you a non-qualified option covering more shares. *Note:* You can exercise a non-qualified option even if you have a qualified one outstanding.

With "phantom" stock schemes, the company credits you with a block of imaginary shares. You end up—if you're lucky—with a deferred cash bonus. For example: XYZ Corp. credits you with 500 shares currently at $100. You pay out no money. You wait, say, five years, and XYZ goes up to $175. You then get $75 in cash for each share, or $37,500. You pay ordinary income tax on this, but the 50% top rate will apply—if there's a risk of forfeiture in the plan. Here the usual "risk" provision is that you lose the bonus if you leave the company before the payoff date.

In the past, phantom stock has been tied in with retirement plans for executives. But now some companies have started to work the idea on a short-term basis—during a man's career years, say, from age 45 to 50.

The deferred stock bonus is another plan that's gaining wider use. Here you have a deal similar to phantom stock except that real shares are used. You are credited with XYZ shares at $100 and again you make no cash outlay. You wait a span of years, and see XYZ go to $175. You then get a payout of the actual shares, plus reinvested dividends. Your profit will be taxed at the high ordinary rate. But again, the 50% maximum will apply if there is a substantial risk of forfeiture. The pros point out that this is another retirement-bonus device that can apply to career years.

Annual cash bonuses, tied to performance, will also get more emphasis in executive pay packages, partly because of the coming 50% maximum tax rate—and because of demands for maximum performance in today's time of profit squeeze. Some top men in past years have even managed to pull in bonuses amounting to 100% or more of their regular salary. But if you'll be bargaining for a pay package, note that the trend now is more conservative. A survey by Peat Marwick Mitchell & Co., the accounting firm, indicated that many companies are setting top limits on bonuses at about 50% of salary.

Combinations: Companies will start to offer individuals more pay mixes—for example, qualified and non-qualified options, and qualified options and phantom stock. Usually you'll get one or the other, not both. In some cases, say Towers, Perrin, Forster & Crosby consultants, you'll take your pick—based on computer-model information comparing dollar results.

Still seeking the best of secretaries?

The right secretary can help your career along, too. Call this the lighter side of career planning. The point is, though, that for maximum performance—and maximum efficiency in your own operation—you need a private secretary with appeal, brains, tact, polish—and know-how.

Today, as the executive's job gets more complex, the gal who sits outside his office door needs to be just that much better qualified. A stenographer isn't enough. You need more than mere mechanical skills. You want someone, of course, who can handle everything smoothly, from private-office management and last-minute travel planning to declining invitations (and favors) without losing friends. And shouldn't she be someone who can help bridge the gap between you and subordinates, who will keep mum on confidential matters, and whose sense of loyalty isn't just a pretense?

The question: How do you find her? Management consultants, psychologists, personnel managers—and highly skilled Girl Fridays—suggest these rules, to start:

- Pick a secretary who will balance your own shortcomings. For instance, says New York psychologist Dr. Mortimer Feinberg, if you make a lot of speeches but find writing them agony, hire someone with the skill to take bare ideas and put them in the form you want. Katherine Gibbs, incidentally, reports that more of its well-placed grads are spending an increasing amount of time writing executive's speeches.

- Pick a secretary who is pleasant, but not obsequious. The latter can mean inner frustration—and trouble, says a consultant with Psychological Corporation. It also means she won't have the nerve to tell you when you're wrong, or to screen you from the idle talkers, favor-seekers, and problem children who might otherwise jam your office.

- Pick a secretary who shows at the first interview that she's vitally interested in the job. If she's passive, says a Columbia Business School psychologist, she lacks the quality you want most: enthusiam.

However depressing it may be, the evidence says clearly that the cute girl in her early twenties, though bright as a dollar, just can't make it as an executive secretary—not working for top brass in a sizable corporation. The best age bracket for the job is 30 to 45. The 30-year-old is still ripe for training, a big plus. But the 45-year-old is good, too, provided she isn't set in her ways: She's likely to place a lot more value on landing—and keeping—a good job.

If she's single, fine—but try to steer clear of the old-maid type. If she's married, make sure that her husband is steadily employed—but there's a twist here: You'll probably be better off if his job is below the management or professional level. At the same time, don't hire a secretary if she'll be earning as much or more than her husband. This can mean trouble, and a phone call may keep you out of it. If she has children under 16, be sure that they have steady daytime home supervision. This is a must.

Social note: Experience has shown that the social type with a country club background can do a superior job—*if* her special talents are put to use. For example, if she's going to help organize business social functions, play hostess at VIP parties, and such, fine; otherwise pick a girl you won't meet at the country club.

Ideally, you want somebody with at least two years of college, plus the usual secretarial training. Among executive secretaries, college is the trend. Don't reject a girl as being "overqualified" because she's a college graduate (unless she has an advanced degree).

The girl you hire should also score well above average in your secretarial-skills and language-usage tests. But note: Beware of personality tests, which can be faked by a job-seeker.

Mechanical skills? Ignore words-per-minute scores (or claims). A simple typing test will show if she is reasonably fast. The trouble here is that business school standards vary, so reported scores mean little. Anyhow, more important than typing is transcription speed—with those speedy shorthand notes accurately translated. And you may not want to judge mechanical skills at all. If you have higher-level chores in mind, have the pre-job testing done on a higher-level basis.

You'll get maximum performance from a bright secretary if you let her know a good deal about yourself. This is practical and inspires loyalty. She should know such obvious things as where you keep your safe-deposit keys, tax returns, and such, plus some things not so obvious, like the addresses of your lawyer, tax adviser, broker, doctor, relatives, friends. And if you can't remember your wife's dress size—she can.

PART TWO

Family

SEVEN

Community Activities:

Life as a Volunteer

The average executive or business owner is often tied up tighter *after* five o'clock than before. He leaves the familiarity of his office and walks into a maze of avocational activities that strain his staying power to the utmost. Fund raising, local politics, college volunteer work, teaching and being taught, serving tours of duty at the country club and the church—you name it. It's a mixture of sweat, strain, and satisfaction that gouges the nervous system. Here are a few thoughts—and tips—on how to survive after five.

The political drive: after five

Take politics. If you're itching to take a hand in any big political campaign, the tip is to start early. If it's national, don't wait for the primaries to get settled. Get in. There is no effort where early participation counts for more than in a wing-ding political drive.

Some doors, you'll find, are almost always wide open, and as a businessman in town with good connections, you should have little trouble getting into the swing. In a political campaign, you can do more than make a few phone calls. "Nobody expects to tell a businessman or professional to go see his ward chairman to pick up some routine job or to go canvass a building," says former Democratic National Chairman John Bailey.

But an executive who's a novice at politics shouldn't assume that he can pick up one of the glamour jobs in a national campaign, such as convention delegate or local candidate.

From the viewpoint of a politician such as a party county chairman, you may well be capable, aggressive, useful—but you're still an amateur. Running a corporate board meeting, the political pros point out, is a far cry from staging a rally. So it's usually a case of settling for a campaign job that's in tune with your own background.

Helping a candidate—before or after convention time—is where you can get in some satisfying licks. You can work either through your party's regular county organization or for an "independent" group. Today the independent "citizens' group" that backs an individual candidate gets a bigger play than ever before. For you, the prime advantage is that you can work for a candidate without formally aligning with the party. This independent approach is appealing to more and more voters.

In any case, the role you land probably will depend on your experience and on your connections. For a citizens' group, especially, you may find yourself discreetly boosting your man at luncheons; or you may be asked to contact quietly a fairly sizable list of possible campaign contributors (despite the no-tax-deduction rule).

If you have the inclination—and are well known in town—you may land in a front-line spot. You could be a public sponsor of a candidate or group, or the regular chairman of a series of public meetings.

Chairing meetings, particularly, puts you under pressure. If you go this route, say the pros, you should figure at least two evenings a week out speaking, and usually four or five hours a week boning up on the issues. Bobbling an issue as a chairman not only hurts your candidate, the pros warn, it probably also will erase any chance of yours as a future candidate. Obviously, your platform manner can make or break you, if you have any notion about running for office yourself some day.

But more than poise, you need knowledge. "To run for public office," says former Republican National Chairman Ray Bliss, "a man has to know the issues and be willing to work at it day and night. You have to be willing to put up with many inconveniences you wouldn't put up with in business."

The point, of course, is that if you're aiming for public office in the future, you might use some basic experience in a current campaign as your starting point. *Note especially:* A businessman who is serious about this—and who is looking ahead—might be smart to volunteer his services through the office of the state governor. Serving on a task-force study panel, for example, can be fruitful, politically and otherwise. Also, it's generally a role not sought after by the professional politicians.

A word of caution: As a businessman—and a novice in politics— don't try to throw your weight around if you get active in a campaign. Do this and you court a quick brush-off.

Town politics: moonlighting

Shift political direction—from national campaign to local politics. Does election time make you wonder what it's like to serve as a suburban town official? If so, remember: Such jobs are not sinecures. They can make you sweat. Businessmen playing key political roles in bedroom communities from Greenwich to Lake Forest to Beverly Hills have to moonlight—often.

With one of the more important jobs in town—mayor, councilman (or commissioner), school board, or planning board— figure two to four evenings a week attending mettings (private and public), with the usual board meeting lasting a good two to three hours. "Home at 11:30 is typical, and 1 A.M. isn't unusual," says a senior vice-president of a big New York bank who recently served as mayor of Ridgewood, N.J., population 30,000.

A key job also demands five to six hours of homework each week. It varies, of course. Some assignments—the library or health board, for instance—aren't so demanding; the pressures of school board service can differ widely. But underestimating the time and energy for this type of public service has tripped many a business executive.

This means, too, that you should be careful to clear your participation with the top man in your company, or with the board. True, most big companies now encourage local political activity by their executives. Nevertheless, getting clearance is a must.

"If your wife doesn't go along 100%, don't even consider running for a major town office," says a New York architect, former mayor of his commuter town. Besides the regular duties of the job—and this applies especially to the tasks of mayor and councilman—you and your wife will be attending everything from the police dinner dance to church coffee sessions. Old hands agree that if you have any new ideas you want to push, then appearing in public frequently—for exposure—is a must.

Emotional strain? Small-town politics can be a hot kitchen. Such issues as where to put a school or even a streetlight can become burning questions, and may make enemies for you. You can't do the job by being a perpetual "nice guy," say old hands. Adds one: "Ample homework on the issues is one way to beat off the critics."

As a businessman, you're also apt to be quickly and frequently frustrated over the town-hall way of doing business. For instance, the time needed to pass the simplest ordinance can turn you gray. A suburban politician who heads his own sizable company adds a warning: "You need damned good physical health to follow the routine."

Requests for favors can plague you whether you're mayor, playground commissioner, or school board member. The point, of course, is to sidestep most of them. Not only townspeople but town employees will be watching you. The best advice is to let it be crystal clear at the outset that you won't grant favors, even if it means offending the father whose son is in trouble with the town police or the dowager who wants her leaves picked up every Friday. "One favor gets you one vote and loses 100," is a smart political slogan.

Reversing the coin, don't let town employees do even small favors for you or your family. Make it plain to your wife and children that they are not to ask for them—or expect them. Even a small favor—such as privileged parking for your wife—can cause you all kinds of headaches. Also be aware that even the smallest hint of conflict of interest between your business and the town can damn you. Clear this point in advance.

Get rid of any notion, too, that the school board is a serene pasture. You are under political fire constantly, considering that—in most high-income suburban towns—the schools eat up 60% to 70% of the local budget.

The job is demanding and can be charged with emotion. Today, especially, school board duty is a hot seat because of growing pressure from parents (and children) for admission to quality colleges, because of changing practices in education (such as those recommended by Harvard's Dr. James B. Conant), and especially because of the teen-age drug problem.

Once you take on a public service job in your town, you will forever be tagged as a "doer"; you can expect a constant demand for your services. Says one voice of experience: "You have to learn to say 'no'—or they'll never let you off the hook."

Taking your problems to Washington

Take yet another facet of off-hours political life. Pose this query: Have you a company problem—or a personal one—that you would like to take to Washington? Today, the new emphasis on getting business and businessmen closer to government gives you a greater chance than ever to make your voice heard. The question is: What are the ground rules?

There's one basic reminder: Putting a problem before your representative or senator is not only proper, it's often highly effective. "You would be surprised how much we really need more direct contacts from businessmen back home," says Leslie Arends, ranking GOP member of the House committee on ethics. "We can use the expertise and the ideas."

Most congressmen will go to great pains to push the right buttons on your behalf. What your congressman can or will do varies a lot. But his attitude, you'll find, usually will turn out to be surprisingly nonpartisan.

He's apt to be especially helpful in simply speeding up a decision in a case where you've been kept hanging by a federal agency. A prod from your congressman often will help move your case off the back burner. Or, if you're pushing for a new project, he at least can sort out the maze of government offices for you and get you to the right man at the right time.

If pending legislation may put you or your company in a bind, don't hesitate to send a personal letter or telegram to your man. A letter signed by a small group of businessmen can be highly effective. But skip "form" letters; organized signature-collecting often goes ignored by congressmen. Who really knows how many such signatures are valid?

Your congressman can help you get your viewpoint before a Congressional committee. He may pave the way with a letter of introduction or a phone call. He can vouch for your standing, and may even suggest to the right people that you be invited to testify.

In any situation, if you want to have a quiet, private talk with your congressman, you might use a good hometown political contact. Let him set up an office meeting or even a luncheon at home or in Washington.

In dealing with a federal agency, especially a regulatory one such as the Interstate Commerce Commission or the Federal Trade Commission, you are skating on thin ice if you make the wrong approach. It's proper to ask your congressman to help with introductions; and he may even go with you and help present your case.

But it's more likely that he will want to stay in the background. He'll probably suggest that you lean more heavily on a corporate or trade association representative. If you lack a good contact, he'll help you line up a Washington consultant who knows the ropes. Tip: If you get this kind of lead, you'll be wise to follow it. Don't press a congressman if he backs away from involvement in regulatory matters.

Note especially that government contract problems have you hemmed in with rules that rarely bend, even under pressure. If your company has been unfairly frozen out of some important government work, you can always approach your congressman. He may ask the agency for a prompt report on your case, and this may open the door for you. But in this type of transaction — in dealing with a federal agency — keep all contacts strictly in writing, on the record. This can be vital.

You can, of course, ask your senator or representative for small favors: helping to speed a passport approval, getting quick delivery of a new business-related report or survey. But there are some requests — help with an IRS tax ruling, for example, or making a point with a state or city official — where a congressman's intercession might backfire. Let him be the judge. You're not being brushed off if he turns down this type of request.

Stating your case to congressmen

Speaking of dealing with congressmen, do you have something to tell a Congressional committee? Plan well in advance if you want to score some points on any pending legislation.

To testify before a Senate or House committee, first write to the chairman telling why you want to air your views. You'll likely get a letter suggesting that you merely file a written statement to go on the record (and this can sometimes be just as effective if it's a technical matter).

But you may be allowed to appear in person — top executives often are, and frequently specialists will be asked to appear to support general testimony.

If you're going in person, prepare a clear brief of your testimony, as short as possible, and forward it to the committee a few days in advance. Take with you about 100 copies for the press—and be sure to include a terse summary (one or two pages). *Tip:* Pep up the summary with a catchy sentence or two that stress the main point. This might help give you press coverage back home.

Boring the committee members is an obvious but often overlooked blunder. So avoid reading tedious, lengthy testimony. Keep your statement crisp—perhaps using a few notes. If you use charts, tables, or statistics as part of your presentation, just have them put on the record—don't go over them step by step. And skip what other witnesses have already said (you can easily get transcripts). Note: You'll have a chance to see your own transcript before it's printed, to correct errors. But don't try to change the substance.

You'll appear more expert if you go solo to the witness table. But seat your lawyer or public relations man close by, for quick consultation. If you have a friend on the committee—maybe a sympathetic member from your home state—it's not considered out of order to talk to him beforehand and frankly suggest a question that he might put to you. Or if you expect hostile questions from the others, he may help you out if he's briefed.

Have your company's Washington representative or your trade association fill you in on the committee members and their views on the subject. And try to show how your proposal will help various committee members back in their own home districts or states.

Most questioning will be friendly, sometimes designed as much for consumption back home as to elicit information. But the chairman's questions, which come first, are usually fed to him by counsel and are more probing. Even if you get some hostile, repetitious, or downright silly questions, maintain a stance of dignity and restraint. You can't possibly win an argument—and if you try, the entire committee may turn against you.

Don't be disturbed by members arriving or leaving during your testimony. Senators, particularly, may be attending several different committee hearings and other sessions the same day. If your hearing is televised (sometimes in the Senate, never in the House), the members will stay put. Reminder: In this case, or if you think you might be interviewed by TV reporters after the hearing, wear a pale blue shirt.

If you are called to testify in an investigation—such as the House Judiciary Committee's continuing hearings—the routine becomes trickier. Stick to written testimony that has been carefully screened by company counsel, as well as by a Washington lawyer who knows the ropes. Also, in this case have a lawyer with you at the table and confer with him before answering any dangerous or leading questions. Remember that the written record—not your show of personal confidence—might be the basis of a suit or other action that would work against your position. Bring along any other company officials who may be able to support your testimony. One or two may sit at the table with you, the others just behind.

For more tips, see Donald C. Bacon's *Congress and You,* a book designed to help the newcomer on the Washington scene (American Association of University Women, 2401 Virginia Avenue, N.W., Washington).

Private roles in the urban crisis

Another vast area for after-five activity is the urban crisis— the ghetto cleanup drive. The urban crisis clearly has become the concern of corporations. But individually and on their own time, more and more businessmen and professionals are taking a part in efforts to better race relations and cool the temper of the times. Today, this work goes on with the benefit of few of the headlines that follow every move of radical groups—but it does go on. It's being done quietly and effectively.

The work goes well beyond writing out a check to one or another worthy organization. These businessmen are giving their own time, their own effort. And those who have had some experience say that the time and the effort can mean a lot more than money.

An executive's business knowhow—and his influence in the community—often produce far more results than a cash donation. But there needs to be a word of caution for the novice.

Says a prominent New York businessman: "This work takes time, patience, and staying power."

Some executives are working on race relations problems in their own suburban towns. In one city suburb, for example, an executive recently organized a group of fellow commuters for several community projects. They're raising money to send a group of bright but underprivileged high-school students to college. But they're going beyond that. Like other such groups, they're also getting tutorial help for high-school students whose family backgrounds and home surroundings make study especially difficult.

In many cases, businessmen are posing questions concerning local ghetto conditions at town council meetings. A Cincinnati executive comments: "In our suburb it's a case of whether the 'poor section' is getting the same treatment from the town officials as the affluent. And if you put your personal attitude on the line about such things, especially if you're known in town, it means more than sending a letter to the mayor."

Building up person-to-person contacts between black and whites is the object of some other businessmen's groups. Here, the church often can help. One executive, a member of a prosperous Ridgewood (N.J.) congregation that has "adopted" a church in a nearby ghetto neighborhood, suggests that a clergyman open the path to personal contacts. "Let him pave the way for visiting back and forth," he says. "Take it slowly."

The essential advice from him and from other executives is: *Don't strain,* don't force relationships, and remember, above all, that one patronizing gesture can wreck any number of good intentions.

A Westchester County businessman admits that one of his recent efforts bred resentment. He went to the homes of several black parents to ask if their boys had been given a fair try-out for the town's Little League baseball team. "What I did must have seemed awfully phoney," he says. "I should simply have checked this out with the league director."

A generally agreed-upon rule of thumb is that a businessman who wants to help in a ghetto neighborhood should do something that uses his experience—not his emotional feelings about community betterment. Service on a local "task force" for a ghetto project that needs administrative knowhow is one activity where qualified businessmen are widely needed. Projects of this kind are expanding in cities across the nation—but more energy and practical help is required.

Assisting black businessmen is a prime activity—for example, advising shopkeepers, giving pointers on purchasing, accounting, inventory control, and other matters. White-black businessmen's discussion groups is another idea spreading in several cities. In Boston, executives have been helping black businessmen get much needed loans and cut red tape.

But a Cleveland executive adds this note of caution: "If it's to be a business group, be sure that black businessmen are in on the policymaking."

Executives' wives are helping in this community work, too. Volunteering to tutor underprivileged children in ghetto schools is a growing activity, as is daytime child-care duty to help working mothers. Teen-agers (16 or older) are volunteering to provide ghetto children with organized sports.

It's better, say some experienced people, to carry out such youth programs in the ghetto itself. Says one executive: "A good basketball court in a poor neighborhood helps build some community spirit. And for a ghetto boy, it means more than a few days away at summer camp."

Today, behind the ugly headlines, this work is going ahead.

What fund-raising campaigners face

Fund-raising is an after-five effort that often has bedroom communities bouncing at the springs. Fall starts the fund-raising season, and if you'll be active you may find that some obligations have changed since your last stint as a money-raiser.

For one thing, many big campaigns have spread out on the calendar in the past few years. College drives that once took one to two years now require two to five; community drives often run to a full twelve months—and tie down the people who take on the important jobs.

Note: One vital matter adds heavily now to the fundraiser's chore—the uncertainties about the new tax law's treatment of charitable deductions. Many people who make big donations are confused. They're likely to be wary of committing themselves to gifts—they'll want explanations and reasons.

If you have been collared to serve as a fund drive chairman or to be on the steering or executive committee for a college or community drive, you may end up in a position that can make extremely heavy demands on your patience. A chairman faces three principal jobs at the outset. He must give leadership and emotional punch to the campaign. He's also expected to use his contacts in business and his persuasive powers—plus his reputation—to gather top-rank volunteers. Beyond this, he will usually have to work closely with the "leadership gifts" chairman in an effort to pull in some large gifts from wealthy individuals and companies. These help to promote bigger routine donations.

Note that in a college drive, the chairman and other workers may have particularly rough going with some donors who are upset over student unrest on the campus. Those with key roles in college drives, though, say that most donors come through—after a good deal of persuasion.

Typically, any drive chairman will put in as much as a half-day a week if the campaign is long-range. If it's a fast-paced community drive lasting, say, through the fall season, a chairman may devote one full day a week. Executive or steering committee members in a sizable drive—usually a group of five to fifteen people—may find that they spend as much time and energy as the chairman. They decide policy, pick out area chairmen or captains, perhaps hire a professional fund-raising consultant, and see that the consultant gets the right kind of cooperation. They'll also often take charge of special campaign subcommittees.

Intermediate jobs are frequently underestimated, too. The regional chairman in a national drive and the city-section captain in a community drive have roughly comparable posts. Each heads a team of workers who, in turn, supervise small groups of volunteers. On average, each can look for about a half-day of work a week during most of the campaign.

If you're pressed for time, you may want nothing more than the job of an ordinary volunteer. Here the routine hasn't changed much recently. Usually, you're given—or asked to select—a list of five to ten names. Covering these, even in a difficult drive, should cost you no more than five to ten hours, over a span of time. The span varies: It may be just a week for a fast community drive. It can be a month or more for a college drive where the stress is frequently on planned giving instead of straight cash donations.

Remember that face-to-face contact most readily brings in the cash. And keep your approach personal when you seek out potential donors. Set up all appointments yourself—don't have your secretary do it. If you fail to get the nod on a first call, don't simply leave a pledge card or later write a letter. Unless you go back in person, you can't expect to chalk up a strong result. In any case, tackle the more likely prospects first. This way you gain sales talk for later calls—and boost your own enthusiasm.

A reliable fund-raising consulting firm will usually work on a monthly fee basis, with the fee tied to the man-hours put in by the men assigned to your drive. Top outfits won't work for a commission or percentage. More than 30 such firms operate nationally, and 25 of them are members of the American Association of Fund-Raising Counsel, 500 Fifth Avenue, New York, N.Y. 10036.

Tough course ahead for college trustees

Another type of campus-related volunteer work is service on a college's board of trustees. It can be a hard tour of duty. In this time of campus unrest and revolt, the college trustee can no longer work behind a closed boardroom door. He's on the firing line—and often in the local headlines.

The tempo has been picking up for some time. Now the trustee's role has become intense. It adds up to work, time, emotional tension. "A trustee can't be removed, remote, or casual any longer," says Dr. James Killian, longtime chairman of MIT. His colleagues echo the view.

A trustee's job today isn't only harder, it's a target for open hostility on many campuses, from city to small town. So if you get invited to join a board, review the prospect. Take a look at the campus.

You're likely to be challenged by students, faculty, and practically everybody in town from the mayor to the father of an irate college boy. Some boards have even been challenged on their traditional duties. At some colleges, for example, students have started to participate in the search for a new president, and on many campuses students and faculty are sitting in as observers and critics at trustee meetings—unheard of a few years back.

For a businessman or professional it adds up to this: If you can't afford to get deeply involved on the campus because of your activities, forget it.

A trustee signs on for a term that may range from three to nine years (even life), on a board averaging 10 to 24 members. The trend is to drop men at age 70 or 72 and to take on more people in their late 30s, 40s, and 50s. Top-ranking businessmen are in demand; but you'll also see more women and minority group members joining boards on many campuses. Formal, full-board meetings take place just once or twice a month. But during today's periods of stress on campus, meetings are sometimes more frequent and last longer. The two-hour meeting on campus after lunch can turn into an all-day affair—and it can happen weekly and even daily during a crisis.

There's also more homework. Three or four hours to bone up before a meeting is average. The reading covers more than just college reports, university financial statements, and the like. Today, especially in large urban colleges, the trustee finds himself wrapped up in all sorts of affairs: city planning problems, ghetto problems, and the like—all of them intense, demanding. Today the college newspaper is must reading for a trustee. As one experienced trustee explains: "It gives me a fix on what the students are thinking."

There is also a social side. Besides the serious work of managing finances, choosing administrators, and acting as a buffer between the campus and the public ("You can't get through a cocktail party without at least one hot argument over campus affairs," says a trustee), there's a lighter, but time-consuming side, as well. The job includes attending such affairs as the president's annual reception, the June graduation, and annual athletic banquets.

Most boards of trustees operate on a committee system, which gives a new member a chance to concentrate on work that best suits his experience. Logical spots for a businessman are the committees on finance and investments. But far more exhausting are such chores as "student affairs" and "academic affairs," where conflict these days is greatest. These jobs—ranging from helping to quell a riot to hiring a new dean—call for men willing to stick their necks out.

On top of all this, the trustee is forever faced with an old stand-by: fund-raising. If the college embarks on a major drive, all trustees are called on, regardless of their specialized committee assignments. Some trustees estimate that 50% of the time they devote to campus affairs is spent on fund-raising work. With education costs soaring and colleges forced to expand, these problems are mounting, too.

Yet it all adds up to challenge with its own rewards: stimulating work and accomplishment in a difficult field of public service. If you do consider a trusteeship, some preliminary reading will help. Jacques Barzun's *The American University* (Harper & Row) and *The Academic Revolution,* by Jencks and Riesman (Doubleday), are recommended.

Businessmen back on the campus

Some businessmen are plunging even deeper into campus affairs. They are becoming teachers—at business schools, especially. From scores of different industries, hundreds of executive and professional types have turned to teaching in the last few years. Some merely lecture one night a week. But others hold down full professorships at graduate schools. Some put in their time at local night colleges. But others are on the faculties teaching management and related courses at Harvard, Columbia, Carnegie Tech, the University of Chicago, and Stanford. And the list of colleges goes on—from Boston College to Dennison (Ohio) to Pomona on the West Coast.

These examples merely highlight and do not fully cover the still small, but certainly significant and increasing, flow of men from full-time executive jobs to full-time positions on the campus. What causes a man to make such a seemingly sharp switch in his career? Obviously, personal motivations, such as an individual's desire to make a thoughtful contribution in his field or his long-standing wish to be a teacher explain much of this movement from office to classroom.

But three other elements are making it easier for an executive to change from the practice of management to the teaching of its theories. There's a lot more compatibility between business and the classroom now than in past years. Classroom theory and business practice are closer. Moreover, the vast majority of executives hold degrees, and even if the degrees aren't PhDs, they help toward entry on a faculty.

College faculty members—particularly those in the business schools, of course—are no longer so remote from industry and the workings of the economy. Working executives and full-time business school professors often rub shoulders these days as members of the same corporate boards of directors.

College faculty salaries have climbed, too—and that's significant. Certainly they're still a long way below the usual salary of a corporate vice-president. But they're not the poor pittances they once were, and they match the money that many semi-retired businessmen might expect to make as business consultants. At most top colleges, an assistant professor gets $10,000 to $12,000 or more, an associate about $14,000 or so, and a full professor $16,000 to $20,000—frequently as much as $25,000.

Nor is the business school teacher kept isolated nowadays from some of the sweeter fruits of business. Many spend from 40 to 50 days a year as industrial consultants—earning, on the average, from $200 to $500 a day.

Most of the businessmen who have lately joined a college

faculty full-time are between 45 and 50 years old. Some have made the move at 55, even at 60. And it's true that the academic career is relatively "ageless." Retirement age at Harvard, for example, is 66; at Columbia it's 68. And often a college won't adhere strictly to its official retirement age.

But don't get the idea that a man who turns to college teaching at 50—after working hard in business to make himself financially secure—can expect to breeze along in an easy, non-competitive atmosphere. True, the academic life brings more time for travel and study. But there's persistent pressure for academic standing—particularly for every faculty member to get his PhD, and to get his work published. And politics on the campus can be played just as bitterly as in the office.

Of course, experience in business doesn't automatically fit a man to teach business courses. Many executives lack the craftsmanship needed for quality teaching and find it difficult to maintain the required attitude of constant sympathy for sharply differing opinions. Those who do best fall in two groups: the teacher at heart (who may well have had the PhD before entering business), and the college-minded businessman who has kept well abreast of academic trends and campus affairs.

One wise approach to a campus career—aside from the long process of earning a PhD, which takes a middle-aged man three to four years full-time and up to 10 years part-time—is to find a berth as a two-hour-a-week teacher. You can test your dedication conducting a one-session class. But don't underestimate the time involved in this. At a quality business school that uses some part-time faculty men—like Chicago, Northwestern, Wharton, or New York University—you can figure on at least three to four hours a week for non-classroom duties, plus reading time.

Breaking 90 in club management

The froth of after-five service is doing a hitch as a club officer. It's non-vital duty, but it can churn a fast ulcer. Look at the country club.

It's not just an early-season failure to break 90 that has country club officers muttering to themselves in the locker room.

These days, clubs are facing pressures they rarely confronted a few years ago. Old-timers who've seen their clubs evolve from male retreats into family amusement parks—as well as such top club consultants as Harris, Kerr, Forster, and Horwath & Horwath—sound this precaution: Before you agree to serve as club president—or even as chairman of the greens committee—be sure you know what you're getting into. And that's a lame understatement.

Unless your club is exceptional, be prepared to do a lot of moonlighting. Take personnel problems: Finding and holding staff—from bartenders and waiters to the club manager—is a worsening headache for club officers. Today, you may consider it a coup to locate an A-1 manager at $25,000. But then be prepared to sweat out another search when he quits a year later to take a $30,000 spot at a bigger club. And union negotiations are another personnel consideration. In some places even the caddies are organized.

Or look at taxes. Lately Internal Revenue has been putting the vise on private clubs, taxing them on income from such events as golf tournaments, banquets, deb parties. In 1970, a crackdown here has had club people moaning. As club treasurer, you'd be the man on the spot.

You'll also find that squabbling over local real-estate taxes—and even club liquor licenses—is part of the routine. "As president of the club, I'm mixed up in local politics more than when I was on the school board," says a New Jersey suburbanite.

Speaking of real estate: Clubs get increasingly handsome offers from housing developers for parts of their land—and this usually brings bitter divisions among the members. As an officer, you're right in the middle—again—and forced to take sides. Also, before you agree to sign on as an officer, find out if the club is planning new activities: paddle tennis courts, basement bowling alleys, a bigger swimming pool, a renovated clubhouse. This means more soul-searching about what kind of a club it's going to be, decisions over special assessments, and frankly, a lot of in-fighting among members and officers.

If you do serve, how much time will it take? On average, a

good club president spends at least a half-day each weekend plus maybe two evenings a week working at the club—and must attend major club events and represent the club in dealing with the community. Same holds for the club treasurer. (Don't sign on unless you're a financial man in business.)

Chairmen of such major committees as greens, house, and membership all have heavy loads. Note that the "house" chairman may have especially long hours—he's generally the man who supervises the club manager. And as for the membership committee, don't take this unless you're prepared for delicate—and occasionally unpleasant—situations.

Then there's the "family" side of club activities—whether you're president, chairman of the swimming pool committee, or teen-agers' activities chairman. Repercussions of a Saturday night poolside dance for the high-school set have been known to make strong men weep.

A secret of success as a club officer is knowing how to treat the professional manager. Rule no. 1: be cordial, but not personal. And never, never bypass him in issuing orders to the staff. Businessmen who know better at the office often make that mistake at their club.

How can you tell if the financial operation of the club is up to par? Club accountants, such as Howath & Howath, explain that the club should break even on the basis of overall operations. This is true even though the food department will almost always lose money. If the books show a sustained loss over two or three years, take a close look at (1) the manager, (2) the activities schedule, and (3) the dues schedule. Maybe you should be paying a stiff special assessment.

Mr. Chairman, ladies and gentlemen

If you're going to be up to your ears in volunteer and related activities, you are likely to fall now and again into the role of public speaker. So—how do you rate at the speakers' table? If "saying a few words"—or putting over a full-length address—

is pretty much hit-or-miss in terms of effectiveness, you're not alone. And more than ever, businessmen are seeking professional help to polish their public speaking. Most of them come out way ahead.

But a word of caution at the outset: Some teachers still push the old "speaking coach" approach. Here the idea is that if you practice and master "platform techniques," you'll be effective. Top pros (such as network radio and TV people) will tell you that this is mainly nonsense. Same holds for a new method that has you imitating the style of a professional after-dinner man. These methods will bring out the ham in you—nothing more.

What counts most, say the experts, is to remember that each man—introvert or extrovert—has his own particular form of effectiveness. Your best chance of survival on a platform is to "be yourself." This is not to say that you don't perform—you do. But you develop and use your own best talents as a speaker, without reliance on gimmickry.

Being yourself is more and more the theme of the short public speaking courses now offered to businessmen by such people as Glen Mills and Calvin Downs of Chicago, Howard Navins of Boston, and Arthur Sager, who teaches mainly in New York—and by professors at such colleges as Purdue where the speech department is outstanding. The Dale Carnegie people also have "Executive Class" sessions for management brass.

For example, Arthur Sager stresses informality. He is a New Englander who has trained executives in such companies as Sylvania Electric, Corning Glass, and Monsanto. His course (one night a week for seven weeks) is often held in a private club, with cocktails and dinner a regular part of the routine. The course is limited to about 15. "They learn to think on their feet, in a natural way," says Sager. Each student gets a stiff critique—more from his peers than from Sager.

But for all the informality, there are some mechanics to be mastered. The sine qua non of good public speaking is careful preparation. Even for a brief talk, make a precise outline on paper. Plan on a sharp, provocative opening (a common fault is to make this part too long). Then build up your points—use factual examples; avoid generalities. And finally, a strong, fast conclusion.

If you can, speak from short, logical notes — not from an entire script. A full reading of a speech is usually dull. If you must read, underline key words and phrases and use them as a guide. (This is especially necessary if you work with a speechwriter.) At all costs, avoid memorizing a speech word for word. Delivery is dull as stone, and if you get lost, you're in real trouble.

In your delivery, avoid rapid speech (what sounds a bit slow to you is probably just right); poor enunciation (mumbling, swallowing words); flatness (you've got to show some enthusiasm — and a smile won't hurt). You can forget about gestures. Let them come naturally, or not at all. A word on timing: In planning your talk, always shave something off your allotted time. If asked to speak 20 minutes, take 15. And never, never talk more than 30 minutes if you can help it.

Finally, learn something about audience psychology. This comes down to sparking an emotional response in your audience — largely by trying to talk to listeners as individuals, not just as members of a group. A listener must be able to identify with what you say, and there are some ways to accomplish this:

- Inject as much human interest as possible (don't reel off statistics).
- Keep a light touch (but avoid joke-telling unless you're good at it).
- Respect the audience's intelligence (don't talk down).

Little things count for a lot. Like catching the eye of the man in the third row, and speaking directly to him. This gives what you say a sound of intimacy (you'll feel more relaxed speaking to one person than to a multitude). And your interest can kindle his enthusiasm, which can be contagious and quickly spread throughout the hall.

Arthur W. Sager's book, *Speak Your Way to Success* (McGraw-Hill), is really a good deal more profound than the title suggests. It's a sensible guide to the businessman who has to spend many evenings on a speaker's platform. It's not phony, overdone, or over-promising. Among other things, Sager stresses this point: Underplay when you speak—be yourself, not somebody else.

Going on TV? Watch the red eye

And how's your TV rating? Do you come on like Walter Cronkite—or freeze solid when the camera's little red eye turns on?

More businessmen are on TV these days. It could be a network panel show or, more likely, a local news spot or interview. (TV wants more business news and opinion.) And there's educational TV, and closed-circuit programming at sales conventions. You can expect closed-circuit telecasting to become much bigger in the 1970s. The trouble is, businessmen's ratings often aren't what they ought to be. TV professionals point out that you can't use your tried-and-true "live" audience technique. Subtlety is the key to smooth television performing, and it's needed more urgently than in straight public speaking. You must "be natural," say the pros, but at the same time, underplay. It's a matter of raising an eyebrow instead of an arm.

When you speak before a live audience—with TV covering— there's a twofold rule, whether it's a 3-minute sales pitch or a 30-minute address:

- If the people in front of you are your main target, you talk to them and forget about the cameras. The rule of restraint still goes, but you let the camera director pick you up as best he can.

- If you're aiming at the TV audience, you "work" to the camera. Best idea is to think of it as somebody sitting six feet away, and simply talk as in private conversation. So, don't stare unwaveringly into the lens—and don't turn away and talk to the live audience either.

Note: The camera-as-person idea works well in a bare studio. But to keep yourself and your speech from going flat—with no audience reaction—let your delivery be a bit more persuasive. But just a bit. Don't overdo it.

If you have a script, don't try to hide your use of it from the TV viewer. Your glances will be a dead giveaway anyhow, and you may wind up with a tense, unnatural performance. Again, never memorize your talk. Just underline key words as a guide, and avoid the novice's "bald-spot" delivery. That is, bending to read, with the result that the camera picks up the top of your head instead of your face. For this ailment, a little practice with a mirror works wonders.

You'll time a speech, of course; but when you're on camera, let the director handle the timing. He'll signal for speed-up or slow-down.

As for mechanical prompters, the best rule is to use them. Some people shy away from a prompter, and that's a mistake. Your speech flows past at eye-level on a screen that appears transparent to the audience. The advantage is you can pace yourself—even pause for side comments—because you're followed by a technician offstage. But if at all possible, do a dry run with the equipment first.

Best rule for voice—no matter what kind of TV show you're on—is to remember that the pause is the simplest and subtlest way to emphasize a point. It's far better than straining your vocal chords. Generally, you use normal tone and let the director handle volume. Anyway, since you're working with a picture, you needn't "project" so much vocally. A special point on panel shows: Avoid the amateur's habit of waving an arm in front of your body or face. (Your wife will say she missed you.)

For TV, wear solid, medium-shade suits, dark ties, pastel blue shirts for black-and-white, and any off-white shirt for the color cameras. The best make-up is a suntan. Otherwise, let them apply pancake make-up at the studio, especially for color TV. Without it, you'll look unshaven.

If you want some TV coaching, your best bet is a private tutor. At a graduate school of speech or journalism, like Northwestern or the University of Southern California, for example, faculty members often do such chores on the side. Three or four one-hour sessions, working with a closed-circuit set-up, might run $200 to $300. You might even buy your own videotape recorder ($1,000 to $2,000)—or suggest that your company buy one. They're proving useful in training salesmen as well as public speakers. What you do is record both sound and sight, and then play it back on a TV screen.

**The delicate art of dealing
with the press**

If you get grooved into the after-five swing, you can't go too far
without rubbing elbows with the press. Whether you wind up
Indian wrestling or not will depend on your technique. Press
people—let's face it—are a temperamental lot, and even the
most skilled VIPs in business and politics have their ups and
downs in dealing with them. In any case, you're far from alone
if—as spokesman for your church, country club, political group,
or your company—you feel the need for more effective contacts
with reporters, interviewers, and editors.

Here are some suggestions: First, remember that since a newsman's commodity is news, your story should have timeliness and
interest. The first is usually easy. You get your story to the press
as early as you can—and generally you can count on newsmen
not to break any release date. The exception is where you have
an especially hot story and one that might be confirmed from
other sources ahead of your own planned announcement. Here
you might consider holding the story yourself until the moment
you want to see it in print.

The interest element is harder. The question, of course, is
interesting to whom—you and your group, or the public? Best
idea is simply to present the information, then let the press decide whether it is worth a column or a paragraph. The danger
is that if you manage to get a weak story accepted, you put the
press on guard in the future; you may well have a tough time
with your next story, even if it's a good one.

Frankly, if you find that a news outlet will readily overplay a
lame story, you can be sure that its readers—or listeners—are
aware of the habit, and that they discount such items accordingly.

Trying to have a story killed or played down by the press,
TV, or radio—no matter how noble your intentions—is apt to
prove costly. This goes deeply against the grain of newsmen,
even though they may well have personal sympathy for your
position. Unfortunately, even if you're trying to save a found-

ling hospital from destruction, your motives may be misconstrued—with the danger that if the item does get in, the very thing you want played down may be stressed. As for the deliberate news "leak"—where an item is given solely to a friendly reporter to pass along anonymously—consider this advice: Pick your newsman with great care because you'll be more or less at his mercy; and keep your story clear-cut and simple—to guard against all-too-easy distortion.

A frequent mistake is to rate your story's value too high, and drag members of the fourth estate to a press conference that isn't justified. A simple press release to the papers and other media is better if the story can be put on paper, mailed, and still be timely and complete. Phone calls can do the job for fast-breaking news—but here there's greater danger of facts getting twisted or emphasis being misplaced.

Should a single reporter inquire, let him have the information on an exclusive basis if you can. But if others call later for the same information, give them the story, too. But don't pull the rug from beneath an enterprising reporter by putting out a fast general press release.

Avoid off-the-record statements. Don't give information, then say "But don't use this." Often, though, it's quite proper to give some facts but to specify that you don't want your name used. You generally are better off if you do not see the final version of a story before it appears. Professional reporters and editors are better judges of what to write and how to write than you are. Anyway, most of them will turn down a request to see final copy.

In dealing with reporters, be candid, informal, and as generous as possible with your time. Your attitude is likely to be reflected in the story. *A final suggestion:* Try not to be either too cautious or too outspoken in contacts with the press. This way, you avoid getting a limp, lifeless story—and you avoid mangled facts, misquotes, and retractions.

Children: Problems, Decisions

The rebels around your home

For you, as a parent, what meaning lies in the tragic stories about teen-agers: the runaway cases, the senseless car crashes, the school failures, and the marijuana and "hard-drug" parties?

All have a point in common: They are distorted and destructive expressions of what otherwise would be normal teen-age emotional tensions. Teen-age rebellion against parents and the adult world has been around a long time; it's when it grows excessive and bitter that it becomes a menace to the family. Specialists in child psychology and guidance say this: You, as a parent, must expect the rebellion, be able to channel it—and know what to do if it gets out of hand.

Look first at the sensational cases. "We're going to see more runaways, more frightening drug abuses," says Harvard psychiatrist Graham Blaine, Jr. "One reason is, the teen-ager now has a sanctuary, a place to go—the Greenwich Villages around the country." And, indeed the town pizza parlors and town parks. Their locales may change; the "hippies" may go by another name. But teen-age motivations—and their desperate conduct—will not change.

What are the motivations that underlie violent instead of "normal" rebellion? The specialists sum it up: feelings of insecurity and inadequacy; anxiety over evidence of excessive violence in American life; maybe most important, a misguided quest for things not found at home, such as enough love, respect, or guidance. "There's a desperate search under way," says Dr. Richard Sallick of the National Institute of Mental Health.

What about drugs? By far the most common one used by teen-agers is marijuana, which is available around many—if not most—high schools and prep schools. Why smoke marijuana when alcohol is so easy to come by, and the effects are similar? "The kids don't want to copy the adults," says Scarsdale (N.Y.) psychiatrist Gerard Fountain. "Besides, they want the risk that goes with flaunting the law."

Some slight reassurance: A marijuana cigarette (or "joint") is thought by many experts to be no more harmful than a martini. So, a bit of experimentation, though dangerous, may not be dire—so long as it doesn't become excessive. (See below.) LSD, less available than marijuana, may produce very serious and long-lasting effects.

Outlandish (not just different) clothing shows excessive teen-age revolt—it isn't just fun and games. Dress and behavior that seem to border on the effeminate may show more of the same, plus possible confusion over sex. But note: This confusion generally is outgrown by the late teens.

Unexplained flunking in school may be part of the same

emotional pattern. "When a bright boy fails in school," says Dr. Fountain, "he may be doing the same thing, in a sense, that another boy does by smoking pot."

What can a parent do? First, say the specialists, understand that the teen-ager must assert himself, and it means competition with his parents. If he fails at this, he will never grow up. The rebellion is almost bound to be distorted if staunchly resisted. But this doesn't mean a father should sit at dinner and be willing to look at a boy who is unkempt, ill-dressed, with hair to his shoulders. The father must react and set firm, though reasonable, standards.

And note: If a father habitually lets infractions go ignored, then the boy—seeking guidance—will resort to more and more drastic conduct. A father needs to keep things in a delicate balance. He needs flexibility and a sense of humor.

Go a step further. Start communications early and keep them flowing. This means two-way talk with the youngster, without lecturing, if possible, and without any self-righteousness about the established order. It also means not underestimating a bright teen-ager who is apt to be far more adult than his father was at, say, age 14. A Columbia psychologist adds: "Don't give lip service to talking with the kids. Mean it, and be willing to listen— and willing to learn something from them."

Prolonged problems at school or at home may signal the need for professional help. But generally, say the experts, "symptoms" in youngsters are hard to separate from normal growing pains. Don't, like some parents, read too much into the teen-ager's "symptoms."

If you do decide to seek outside help, first contact the school psychologist or psychiatrist. Don't be too surprised if he suggests, first, some changes at home, and don't be alarmed if he suggests a private therapist for the youngster. This may not mean serious trouble. In many cases, therapy for six months to a year provides the answer.

Books: A good starter on this subject is Graham Blaine, Jr.'s, *The Parent's Guide to Adolescence* (Little, Brown).

If your teen-ager uses pot

Keep cool, if you suddenly discover that your youngster is smoking marijuana. Parents who overreact in panic or outrage will only induce hostility, scorn, guilt, or excessive rebellion—which may lead to even more drug-taking.

As yet, there is no medical evidence that "pot" is physically harmful—unlike such drugs as amphetamines, barbiturates and heroin. Equally shaky is the common assertion that pot-users step up to narcotics. Dr. Sidney Cohen, a drug expert with the National Institute of Mental Health, says that "95% or more who take pot don't go on to heroin." Some do try such drugs as amphetamines.

Estimates of those who have tried pot range from 5 million to 20 million (with the habit steadily increasing on the college campus and in school yards). Yet about 65% are "tryers," says Cohen, "who may smoke one to ten times a year." Another 25% are "social pot users," who smoke once or twice monthly. Only 5 to 10% are "potheads" who take it daily and are often "stoned." This group, whose lives revolve around the drug, is of grave concern.

What prompts youngsters to use marijuana? Many try the drug out of natural curiosity or from pressure to conform to their peers. Then, too, the prospect of "a high" can be attractive. In most of these cases, the youngsters will probably remain "sometime" users. Pot can spell real trouble, however, for the teen-ager who overuses it to relieve tension, escape boredom and depression, or avoid such adolescent problems as coping with school work or relating to the opposite sex. If he finds balm in pot, he may eventually experiment with more potent drugs.

Medical research on marijuana is sadly sparse. A recent study in Boston, however, found only minimal physical effects of smoking pot (reddened eyes, slightly increased heart beat). "Marijuana appears to be a unique drug in that it doesn't do much to the body," says Dr. Andrew Weil, co-author of the study.

Another unexpected finding: Experienced pot smokers can maintain "effective" performance even when high. First-time users, however, suffer some impairment of mental function and physical coordination (a good reason for them to keep off the highways). Regular users seemed to show no such ill effects after their accustomed doses of the drug. Experts also point out that pot is nonaddictive and causes no hangover.

For all that, the doctors do worry about the effects of pot. At very high doses (10 "joints") some researchers have reported hallucinations, delusions, and vast swings in mood from euphoria to severe depression. There's the question, too, of what unknown long-term effects the drug might have. And psychiatrists worry about the use of pot as an escape from problem-solving at a time when the adolescent should be learning to deal with reality. The maturing process of the "pothead" is, in effect, arrested.

Experts offer these guidelines for parents confronted with the problem:

- Avoid extracting a pledge from your child that he will stay off drugs. You may be asking the impossible, and wind up creating a sure-fire guilt situation.

- Examine your own habits, especially drinking. A parent who coddles his end-of-the-day martini will find his drug strictures sound very hollow.

- Be frank and honest. Remember, youngsters are quite well-informed on drugs today. So read up on the subject, and avoid unreasonable assertions.

- Spell out the penalties. Kids know that possession of pot is a crime, but you can make clear the chances of a fine, a possible police record, even jail.

- Above all, accept the possibility that you may not be able to talk your child out of it right away. But keep up the dialogue and don't reject a child in anger as a way of forcing the solution you want.

If your child is taking pot—or other drugs—to excess, it's a good bet that he or she needs medical help. Consult your family doctor or a psychiatrist who specializes in treating adolescents. The school or college psychiatrist or psychologist usually will keep the drug-taking in confidence.

Added danger: Along with all of this, it's now pointed out by a specialist with the National Institute of Mental Health that in some people, even small doses of pot can cause dangerous reactions. Memory, for instance, can be distorted. A parent can explain this uncertainty to a teen-ager. And note, too, that there's the added chance that pot may be adulterated with hard drugs or toxics. Adulteration appears to be a growing menace. Some say that pushers "hook" kids this way.

Reading up: You'll find that *The Drug Dilemma* by Dr. Sidney Cohen is up-to-date, factual, extremely well-written (McGraw-Hill).

If your teen-ager uses alcohol — to excess

Why teen-agers drink, how much, when, where — and with what effects — are carefully explored in an excellent study by researchers Margaret Bacon and M. B. Jones. *Teen-age Drinking* (Crowell) pulls no punches — and a lot of them are aimed at parents with dated misconceptions.

The obvious point is made: By and large, a teen-ager's drinking habits are patterned after what he sees his parents do. But from here on, the advice is less obvious. Some samples:

- Drugs: Don't relate the drinking experimentation of your teen-ager to the use of drugs. Most teen-agers do, in fact, drink to some degree; but the two habits are quite different, and drinking rarely leads to drugs.

- Driving: Discard any dogged insistence you may have that drinking is a prime cause of teen-age auto accidents; teen-agers are generally well aware of the driving-drinking problem, often more so than parents.

- Sex: Discard the notion, too, that teen-age drinking is a sure sign of maladjustment. As for sex, evidence shows that most teen-agers are, again, well aware of the alcohol-sex relationship.

Some evidence indicates that modest drinking actually may reduce experimentation in sex.

Finally, the authors—whose conclusions are based on a number of well documented studies—ask the question: Why are so
many parents so ready to believe the worst about teen-agers?

Put the brakes on teen-age crackups early

Headlights shining up the driveway, the reassuring slam of the
car door—your young driver made it home. But some don't.
If you lose sleep over teen-age driving, you're like most parents.
There are more cars, more teen-agers. The death rate per 100,-
000 motorists under 20 is twice what it is for 40-year-olds; ditto
the number of injuries per 100 accidents. And while boys are the
offenders, most recent data suggest that the girls' driving records are slipping. So don't just lay down the law to the boy. Work
on his sister, too.

Scare them a little. Tell how suddenly, explosively, a killing
or maiming accident can happen. How insurance companies
rate young people. How a jury's accident award can hit the
family of an erring young driver. And tell them your concern
is not just a case of the older generation oppressing the young.
It isn't generation gap, it's based on hard statistics.

Start before the garage door is open—with driver training.
The driver training in many high schools is weaker than it
should be; don't rely on it too much. But insist that the youth
take the course, then build on the foundation in practice sessions with you.

Ideally, a fledgling driver needs six months of practice before
going out on his own. (This may be well-nigh impossible to
enforce—but it's a bargaining point.) And once launched, the
new driver needs two years of careful observation—with occasional pointers, reprimands (but not needling). *Note:* You can do
all this only if you know your own driving faults. "Don't pass
on your bad habits," warns Dr. Leon Brody of the Center for
Safety Education at New York University.

As for the practice sessions: Keep them short (15 to 20 minutes). Keep them simple at the outset; start with low traffic density and work up to fast freeway driving. Keep seat belts on—indeed, make a fetish of it. Keep your cool, because the boy or girl will be tensed up hoping to please you.

Don't buy a high-school youngster a car—if you can possibly avoid it. The experts say it provides too much freedom for 16, 17, and 18-year-olds. And if you pay for the car, your boy or girl may place too little value on it—and perhaps on safe driving responsibilities. The same thing goes for the "hot rod" or "heap" bought with the boy's own savings. Old cars and hot-rod psychology are hazards. And don't compromise by buying a motorcycle or fast motor bike. A cyclist's odds on being killed on the road are 20 times those faced by the auto driver.

To be sure, each youth is different. In some cases, motoring maturity comes early. You can tell by observing driving skills, attitudes toward rules of the road—and toward authority in general. So temper your prohibitions with judgment—and with sympathy. Dr. Lawrence Schlesinger, a safety expert at George Washington University, says: "Don't forget that, to the boy, the car is vitally important. To him it's the introduction to adulthood. It's more than just fun."

Schlesinger goes on to talk about rules: "He'll test your standards of driving discipline—your rules. But at the same time, he really wants the rules." Lay out a reasonable code of auto behavior—in advance, and with a clear understanding of the punishment that might arise. Fix a curfew for nighttime driving; have him phone if he's detained by a flat (teen-agers have cracked up rushing home to beat the deadline).

Have it understood that his first moving violation grounds him for, say, 15 or 20 days. If there's a second, take away the key until you have evidence that he accepts the responsibility that goes with driving a car. What should you do if he has an accident? Don't panic and apply heavy punishment until you have carefully investigated. Conversely, don't be tempted to pay the fine or whatever and promptly "give him another chance." The boy or girl must realize the consequences of his driving.

Remember: A young person's driving—good or bad—is an

expression of his attitude toward himself and others, and toward authority. The chronic troublemaker—and his parents—may need outside help, from a clergyman, school counselor, psychologist, psychiatrist.

Here's how insurance companies treat young drivers: When your teen-age son starts driving the family car, your premium will roughly double. For his sister, the boost is 50%. Girls lost their adult driver status several years ago. However, once they hit 21 their premium is the same as yours. Boys carry a surcharge until they're 30, though it drops slightly each year.

If a boy has a car in his own name, the premium will be triple the adult rate (if someone will underwrite him; your own connections can help). At the same time, the insurance men give discounts for evidence of responsibility at the wheel. Completion of a school-sponsored driving course sometimes wins a premium. A number of companies give discounts to students with B averages or class rankings in the top 20%.

Heading off a college drop-out

The wintertime holiday season often gives parents their first chance at a close, at-home reading of how their freshman is doing in college. Unfortunately, the holidays sometimes bring the first whiff of trouble. The fact is that the college "drop-out" is an increasing problem for many families—and for colleges struggling to cope with bumper crops of students. And more often than you'd expect, according to top educators, the trouble arises from the swift change of environment rather than from any inability to handle the academic work.

Typically, a boy steps out of high school or prep school and onto a college campus, where he is suddenly confronted with considerably more independence than he's ever known. He goes from a disciplined environment to nondiscipline. All of a sudden he must make his own decisions—and he can't lean on his parents. Some kids will flounder, and even the best freshman advisers—or prodding parents—can't save them all. The result is a drop-out.

The point is this: Wise parents will start emotional preparation for college in the high-school years—and before. The father has a special role to play. According to Eugene S. Wilson, dean of admissions at Amherst, the basic trouble is that the father, typically a business executive, often finds it hard to encourage his youngster to make his own decisions. "Too many boys come to my office still holding onto their fathers' coattails," Wilson says. "The boy, not Dad, should map out his own college admissions program, for example. But a lot of fathers can't let go." Wilson counsels parents to let a child make some mistakes before college. "Then he won't have to live through this part of growing up at the expense of his higher education." Among other things, the college applicant should long since have managed his own bank account.

Finally, if your family does have a college drop-out, don't make home his haven. Put him on his own—with a job, if the military doesn't grab him, and let him find his own way back to the campus. "He'll get back if he has the basic stuff," says Wilson. Many do, and then college has real meaning.

If the drop-out results from a drastic problem—such as the use of drugs—the parent can only seek outside guidance, and attempt to follow it in a spirit of calm and patience.

What's in the new draft rules

About the clearest explanation yet of the current military draft—and the bases used by local draft boards for awarding deferments and exemptions—is to be found in two new booklets published by the Scientific Manpower Commission. *Draft Act 1970* outlines regulations and procedures under the law, of interest to all draftable men. *Draft Facts for Graduates and Graduate Students* discusses in clear terms such things as occupational deferments, and—for those drafted—getting a slot in the military that will utilize the inductee's collegiate training (SMC, 2101 Constitution Avenue, N.W., Washington, D.C. 20418).

Points made by the commission: (1) The lottery doesn't change the rules on deferments or exemptions; for graduates and graduate students, it means that the period of prime draft vulnerability is just one year. (2) Occupational deferments follow no pattern—some boards grant no deferments on this ground, others have been quite generous and have granted almost all requests. (3) The basic rules probably won't change until after 1970.

Problems less dire concern parents whose youngsters are small fry, pre–teen-agers—or smiling little schoolboys or schoolgirls. Here a few are reviewed:

Sports: football . . .

With more football players churning up turf, the experts are pointing to this fact: One out of four high-school team members will suffer a serious injury sometime during the fall season. Some points for parents: No body type has proved safe from serious injury. It's a matter of strength, agility, good coaching, equipment—and attitude. A boy who is not enthusiastic (maybe pushed by his father's school record) will tend to restrain himself and hold back on the field. This is one reason boys get hurt, says Dr. Allan Ryan of the American College of Sports Medicine.

Good coaching in blocking and tackling—and effective refereeing of games—will prevent many injuries. A doctor should be present during games and available at practice. Finger injuries are the most common; next come injuries to the knees, shoulders, and ankles. Most serious injuries involve the neck and head, and these account for 75% of all football fatalities. Some specialists, like Dr. Jerry Patment, University of California, suggest that boys with longer-than-average necks be disqualified from playing.

Smoking: You can tell your boy that what the coach says about smoking is quite true. The habit will "cut the wind" and interfere with performance on the field. Science can now prove this, says an AMA committee on sports medicine. Smokers tend to falter under maximum strain. *Note:* Sports medics are warning of the dangers of a football blocking and tackling technique called "spearing"—or head-butting—which they say is all too prevalent on high-school teams.

The point to all of this, of course, is that a smart parent will investigate the school's athletic program, before giving a 14-year-old boy a complete green light to compete on the squad.

. . . Baseball and golf

Have you a Little League pitcher in the family? A new medical study offers some advice for boys in the 9-to-14-year age group. Since pitching can cause permanent and serious arm injury at this age, practice should be closely restricted; a boy should pitch no more than three innings a game (not five or six)—and curve ball throwing should be eliminated.

If you've a boy active in Little League, see Al Rosen's *Baseball and Your Boy;* it's fine pre-season reading (World).

Meantime, for golfers age 8 and up, *Better Golf for Boys,* by the editors of *Golf Digest,* is a well-done and much-needed book (Dodd, Mead).

Time to think about summer camp

January–February is the time to think about a summer camp for your youngster. The best camps fill up in March—and if you're new to the game, you have some homework to do. The task: to pick from over 4,000 well-rated resident camps in the U.S. and Canada the one that best suits the child's personality and needs. It's harder still if you're looking for a camp with a school program that gives academic credit.

These "school camps" are few now—but growing. Usually they're set up with four hours of morning class, two evening study hours, and the time between for camp activities. Thus, six to eight weeks at a camp like Wassookeag in Dexter, Me. (coed), or Allegro in Pittsfield, Mass. (girls), virtually assures credit in two, possibly three, subjects.

Another trend: camp extensions of boys' private schools. Examples are the Hill School's camp in Wolfeboro (N.H.), and Tabor Academy's in Marion (Mass.). A few camps are specially geared to gifted students, others to children who are handicapped—emotionally and physically. Two excellent references:

Porter Sargent's *Guide to Summer Camps & Summer Schools* (11 Beacon Street, Boston) and *Summer Studies in Private Schools & Camps* (Bunting & Lyon, Wallingford, Conn.). These books are available in many suburban libraries. And, of course, you'll check with your child's school gudance counselor.

But in most cases the task is simply to find a good, safe camp that will give the youngster a summer of fun—and some accomplishment. Best starting place here is the American Camping Association's *Directory of Accredited Camps,* listing hundreds of private and nonprofit camps (Bradford Woods, Martinsville, Ind.), and the Association of Private Camps' listing of about 300 in the Northeast (55 W. 42nd Street, New York, N.Y.). Listing in one of these directories assures at least minimum safety and health standards—such things as a doctor or registered nurse on the campgrounds at all times, a minimum age of 19 for all counselors, and a minimum counselor ratio of one to eight or 10 campers.

But there are subtle, important differences in atmosphere and philosophy that don't show up in a catalogue—or price tag. Some camps are permissive, and let the child pick and choose his own activities (fine for some kids). Others are highly structured, with every day scheduled, hour by hour. Ideally, start planning a year ahead, and visit camps in session. In any case, talk with a camp's director, and parents of campers.

Cost isn't an indicator of quality, but you'll find that $700 is at the low end for eight weeks in a good private camp today. Indeed, at most camps, eight-week tuition now runs $700 to $1,200. Then there are extra fees: transportation costs for side trips, insurance, laundry, horseback riding, and—sometimes— uniforms.

If you plan a family trip for part of the summer, you might look into four-week sessions (cost is more than half the full summer rate). But remember that the better camps don't encourage split seasons; if only a few campers change at midsummer, you may risk having an unhappy child.

Another point of caution: Never "send" a child to camp. Wait until he wants to go and is enthusiastic about it. (The smart parent can, of course, kindle a child's interest.) And although camp age is generally six to 16, wait until age eight or nine if you have any doubts about your six-year-old's readiness.

You'll find, too, that "specialized" camps—those that give special emphasis to one field, such as science, language, music, drama, art, riding, tennis—are best suited to the "veteran" camper, not the young first-time camper. They're fine, however, for the teen-ager.

For a younger child, the so-called "traditional" camp is your best bet—one with a balanced program of land and water sports, creative or artistic activities. Days are balanced between group and individual activity, interspersed with quiet rest periods in the afternoon and evening. Thus the young camper learns to get along—and develops skills.

Kids' world: For parents who want their kids safely away in a good summer camp, *Parents' Guide to Summer Camps* (Harper and Row), by Shapiro and Jarmul, is quite helpful. It shows a tuition range of about $600 to $1,100 for eight weeks—but it is already outdated by inflation.

How to find your way through toyland

A money gift for a child is easy—you sign your name. But walking into a bulging toy store before a birthday or Christmas can be an exercise in confusion—especially if you're just a friend of the family. Here are some ideas on picking presents for a child, starting with a sound rule of thumb: The most successful, popular toy requires participation from the child. Children delight in working things out for themselves—using their limitless imaginations. So say child psychologists.

If a toy has only a single limited use, it will provide no challenge to the child. He'll quickly lose interest, for example, in a missile-launching rocket that takes just pushing a button, despite the excitement when the box is opened. But assembling a model auto kit (or airplane or boat) gives the satisfaction of achievement.

If you're a true novice at gift-buying for youngsters, note that a perfect example of a toy with no end of possibilities is a building block set—from simple, large blocks for toddlers to elaborate 100-piece sets. Toys that lead to fantasy and "pretend" play are also classic: dollhouses, play kitchens or grocery stores, doctor's and nurse's kits.

Another key to smart gift selection is, of course, knowing the stage of development the child has reached. A toy that's beyond a child's capabilities will only frustrate him. Here are some guidelines:

The toddler—age 18 months to three years—is trying out newly discovered muscles and finding out how things work. Curiosity impels him to take things apart, so toys should be simple, sturdy (with parts that are too large to swallow). He likes to ride and climb on things—like a tricycle, kiddie car, wagon, truck, or an animal. He also loves anything that makes a noise—like drums and tambourines, wind-up phonographs, toys with bells inside. Other ideas: sandbox and sand toys, simple gym sets, a slide, swing, or teeterboard, pegboard sets, putty, fingerpaints.

From three to six years, children spend much time acting out grown-up roles. Costumes and miniature equipment to play cowboys, Indians, policeman, doctor, nurse are fine for most kids. Puppets, scaled-down kitchen equipment, and miniature tool sets are also good. At this age, too, the child ventures beyond home into the neighborhood. He wants a bigger tricycle or a two-wheeler with training wheels. *Note especially:* There is no set age for a two-wheeler—and it's important that an adult's fear of accidents not be transferred to the child.

By age seven boys and girls begin to have different play interests. Most boys are greatly interested in racing cars, construction and science sets, work benches, and real tools. Now is the start of serious model building—planes, cars, boats. Girls' interest in housekeeping continues but now the toys are more sophisticated—like a sewing machine that really works.

From seven to nine, youngsters are interested in many board games (even chess). Boys want sports equipment that really works in a competitive game—and girls want elaborate doll wardrobes and realistic doll houses.

Real hobbies develop during the years 10 to 12. Chemistry, photography, leather work, block printing, and handicraft sets for painting, sculpting, and ceramics are now past the "toy" stage. Real telescopes, microscopes, planetariums, and model kits in great detail—all these open new worlds.

Because of the violence they represent, many people are apprehensive about giving boys toy guns, Army tanks, play daggers, and such. But many leading child psychologists maintain that these are necessary tools in a child's development. Far from contributing to juvenile delinquency in later years, they provide a way for working off destructive feelings, which are quite normal.

The four-year-old hammering on his pounding board or the eight-year-old playing war with guns is discharging destructive drives. From this fantasy play he gradually learns to channel his aggression into socially acceptable and constructive behavior. A child who doesn't have an outlet for these drives may actually be more potentially disturbed.

Children's gifts that grow up with them

As for writing out a check, or the like, a gift that goes beyond the usual mishmash of toys might brighten the eyes of a youngster in the family—by the time he's 20, that is. It could be a share of stock, a bond, a $100 bill—or something more elaborate that requires a bit of planning. The planned gift is worth looking into if you have a sizable amount in mind. Tax savings come into play.

A trust, for instance, gives you a lot of leeway for projects such as college financing. Simplified case: Say that your child will enter college in 10 years. You're in the 45% top tax bracket— the $36,000 to $38,000 taxable-income range. You establish a 10-year trust for the child and put in enough securities to pay about $1,000 a year in dividends or interest. Ten years from now, the $1,000-a-year—at 5% compounded quarterly—comes to about $15,000 in the child's account, and he gets the income almost tax-free. You save $450 a year in taxes since you have split away $1,000 of taxable income, and your saving is a bit more if you figure in a surcharge. For you to put away the same $15,000 over 10 years—after taxes—would take about double the amount of income-producing investments. And the beauty of it is that in 10 years you can return the trust property to your own portfolio.

If you want to avoid the formalities of a trust, consider setting up a simple custodian account. You sidestep appointing and dealing with a trustee and avoid periodic accountings and miscellaneous costs. Assuming you're giving securities, you go to your broker's office and register the gift items in your name—or in someone else's—as "custodian for the benefit" of the youngster. As custodian, you can sell the original securities, reinvest the proceeds, and invest the annual income as you see fit.

You still save taxes by splitting off family income into the child's low tax bracket. There are, though, two possible drawbacks: When the child reaches 21, the property becomes his; and if you are personally named as custodian and die before the child is 21, the property is part of your estate for tax purposes. *But note:* You can name a family member as custodian.

There is also, of course, the simple savings account for a child. If you bank $1 today at 5% compounded quarterly, it builds to $1.64 in 10 years—and doubles in 13 years. A bank will work out a savings schedule for anybody who wants to plan something sizable, such as college financing. For example, for a five-year-old, you need to put $68 a month into a 5% quarterly compounded account to have a $15,000 kitty when the child enters college at age 18. He can then draw out $2,041 in eight equal semiannual installments during four college years (the payout totaling $16,328). A similar account—with the same payout—for a child aged 10 takes $127 a month for eight years, and for a teen-ager of 15, $386 a month for three years.

Another idea is to start a child on the road to his own life insurance program, beginning at a low premium. You ease things for him in later years. Straight life costs about $8 a year per $1,000 at age 5, around $9 at age 10, and $10 at age 15 — assuming at least $10,000 in coverage. This jumps to $16 at age 30 when your child, maybe as a young parent, might need to buy.

You can get some added values by attaching options to a child's life policy. Take a simple example: Say that you buy a $10,000 policy for a boy aged 10 for $90 a year. Adding an option charge of $9 a year will give the boy the right to buy more coverage, in $10,000 jumps, at option dates in the future, regardless of his state of health. Under a typical plan, his possible coverage is $70,000.

Birthday, Christmas, or graduation gifts for the children in your family can mark the start of long-range gift planning that's tied in with saving estate taxes. If you give $60,000 to your children (the amount of a married couple's lifetime gift tax exemption), and your taxable estate turns out to be more than $100,000, your family will save at least $15,000 in taxes. These savings mount fast as bigger money becomes involved. A $100,000 taxable estate is hit with about $20,000 in estate taxes, but this jumps to nearly $62,000 if the estate reaches $250,000. It's $133,000 for a $500,000 estate.

Besides your husband-wife $60,000 lifetime exemption from gift tax, you and your wife can give $6,000 a year to each member of your family tax-free. But, this annual exclusion can't be carried forward. At year's end it is lost for good.

Schools and Colleges:
Pointers for Parents

The modern parent, when he makes a business move to a new city, views the quality of the new school system as being on a level of importance with stock options, bonus, mortgage rates— you name it. The whole family is up tight about schools, schools, schools, from the time a child crawls until he gets a BBA. Following are some tranquilizers to help parents.

Sizing up a suburban school system

If you're moving to a new metropolitan area, you'll want to take a close look into local schools. This is usually high in a parent's mind when it comes to picking a suburban town. And even established residents in a town with youngsters coming along should size up educational prospects. And, say the educators, it should be done when the youngsters are still in the elementary grades.

In any case, the pros warn, don't rely too heavily on the casual opinion of a friend in town. "'It's a fine school system' can be terribly misleading," says a Harvard educator. "Your friend may be thinking of his high tax rate"—and high taxes don't necessarily make a workable school system for anybody's youngster.

To find out if a high school measures up, go directly to the principal's office; he may, in turn, refer you to the chief guidance counselor. If it's a first-rate school, you'll get candid answers to your questions. And here are some of the areas you might probe.

At the outset, be on the lookout for new ideas, new academic programs, experimentation in the high school. These are healthy signs. They mark a progressive direction behind the school. A rigid, formalized program is apt to be lagging behind the times.

And note: Size counts for a lot. If the senior class has only 100 or so students, much valuable specialization—found in larger, well run high schools today—will be missing. A senior class of about 300 to 500 is ideal in a school of quality, and this means a three-year senior high school.

A top-rank high school will have one guidance counselor for each 250 to 300 students; in the senior class, one counselor will be responsible for no more than 100 students. A good counselor will have toured many college admissions offices, and have a down-to-earth understanding of how to help get the best college placement possible.

For the academic top 20%, the school should offer five years of mathematics, including computer math; four years of a single foreign language (with Russian often added to the usual list); and at least three years of science plus, ideally, an added course in, say, geology, advanced biology, or astronomy.

Today, in progressive schools, there's a new emphasis on advanced courses in the humanities; for example, a study of

American history in terms of the arts and literature. Also current is a 12th-grade course in U.S. government and social problems of the day, with open, free discussion of the issues.

A quality school system should have advanced summer courses for bright students who want to push ahead, and "advanced placement"—for limited freshman college credits—should be available. A new trend is to give top students the chance to attend neighboring colleges, sometimes in freshman classes, or in special high-school groups.

On the other side of the coin, there should be summer classes open to slow learners. "These should be designed to encourage ability—not just force passing grades," says a leading educator. Slow readers, especially, should get special remedial instruction beginning in the ninth grade.

Routine yardsticks: Class size should be a maximum 25 to 30 in high school; if it's over 30, it's an indication of weakness and crowding. There should be six or seven 45-to-50-minute classes a day. Teachers shouldn't be overloaded; for instance, an English teacher should have no more than four classes a day— a heavier load indicates staff inadequacy.

Most high schools have tabulated their college-admissions record, and will gladly show you the chart. *But note:* The percentage of grads that goes on to college means little—in an upper-income suburban town, this will range 80% and up. Quality is the key. How many grads last year entered known top-rank colleges? And—most important—how many grads later became college grads, in a given year?

Look also at the school's National Merit Scholarship record. How many "letters of recommendation" in the last senior class? You can easily compare high schools on this point. Finally, check on the College Board scores record. A mean score of 500 or over for verbal and math is good.

But use your judgment in comparing schools, and don't downgrade a school too hastily. If a high school measures up on all but one or two points, it's likely first-rate; only if it's weak in several areas should you have serious doubts.

If the high school in town is good, chances are the junior

highs are, too. On the junior high level (grades 7, 8, and 9), there should be special provision both for bright children and slow learners.

For example, there should be accelerated math in the eighth and ninth grades—which makes it possible for students to carry a fifth math course in high school—and, conversely, continued instruction in basic reading skills, if needed.

Two elementary-grade standards: There should be a classroom-size library with a full-time librarian and, again, a maximum of 25 in a class.

Now shift scenes and look briefly at a reasonable formula for evaluating a private secondary school. Some points are quite similar to those suggested for inquiring into a public high school. First a note on admissions in the 1970–72 era, starting with Manhattan.

What a parent faces in finding a private school

If you want to get your youngster into a private school in New York City, remember that the pressures are fierce. You will need to pull all the strings you have. To get the child admitted you should start a campaign—rounding up information and personal contacts—a good year to two years in advance.

In most of the other big cities, the demand isn't so intense. Admissions are tight in Washington, Chicago, and San Francisco, but elsewhere there shouldn't be too much difficulty in placing a youngster for next September's term (1971–72).

Wherever you are, finding the right private school will require careful screening of the schools, planning for admission, plus a sizable outlay of cash. You'll find that two basic trends are current in top quality day schools and boarding schools alike:

■ They no longer have mutually exclusive "traditional" or "liberal" labels. Today, the best ones have hit a balance between the conservative, formalistic approach to education and the highly flexible approach that stresses elective subjects and limitless "broadening" experience for students. Don't depend on past reputation alone to fix the character of schools today. They have changed a lot in the last five years. Note, too, that many top schools now may be coeducational—the private schools are here following the lead of the colleges.

▪ There's a lot more community consciousness among the private schools. The strictly "WASP" approach is dying out, and you'll find varied racial and religious backgrounds among students at most of the top schools. Along with this, private school students are getting more and more involved in community service projects—working in hospitals, tutoring disadvantaged children, and so on. The shut-in, sanctorial atmosphere has largely faded away—except in a few diehard, snobbish schools.

The curriculum is one sure guide to quality. For example, a good private secondary school should offer four years or more of study in such languages as French, German, and Spanish, and maybe a year of Russian or Chinese.

In science, you should expect the basics, but look also for electives in such subjects as advanced physics, oceanography, astronomy. Some front-rank schools now have courses in environmental science. One way to judge a strong math program: It should offer a full-credit course in computer science—and, like the quality public high school, five years of math.

Senior students should be able to get five or six advance placement courses for college credit, and top students should be able to take college courses in summer.

Check the school's library. If it's musty and seldom used, there's something seriously wrong with the school's program. The library should be an active study center—with films, tapes, and perhaps electronic information-retrieval equipment. This doesn't mean that it has to be housed in a fancy new building. In fact, the physical layout at many private day schools is quite modest, and a parent should not be put off in the least on this account.

Ideally, 50% of the school staff should have advanced degrees. But stability in the faculty can be more important than having a sprinkling of PhDs. If a school replaces as much as 20% of its faculty each year, you'd be wise to find out why. Classes should have 10 to 20 students (or 30 to 40 in lecture sessions), and the student-faculty ratio should be 10 to 1 (though up to 15 to 1 is acceptable).

Again, no school will score 100% when judged by all these standards. But if too many points fail to check out, start screening another school.

Apart from looking over the curriculum and the faculty, take a measure of the headmaster. His personality and viewpoints tend to give the school its atmosphere and direction. An informal chat with him will give you some insights.

Costs at private schools vary widely within cities and among them. For day students, the range now goes from $1,000 to $2,200 a year—plus fees for extras. The parents of boarding students pay fees on the college level (see below).

Picking out a prep school

What about the small circle of big-name boy's prep schools? Parents and boys alike should broaden their views on what constitutes a good prep school, according to top private school advisors and admissions officers at leading colleges. The "name" preps—such as Andover, Exeter, Lawrenceville, and Hotchkiss—are today running parallel to the Ivy League: They're usually crowded and not fertile ground for easy admission.

A survey of college preparatory schools by advisers Bunting & Lyon, Wallingford (Conn.), suggests that you bear in mind two conclusions:

▪ Only boys who score in the top third on the Secondary School Admissions Tests (SSAT)—and qualify in other ways as well—can reasonably count on entering one of the 25 or so nationally known preps.

▪ There is a good deal less crowding than might be expected

at a fairly wide range of top-quality, but lesser known, preps around the country. Today, these prep schools—especially those located in remote towns and villages—have a sizable number of openings for youngsters. (One reason: The kids want to stay in the city where the action is.) This means that a location for next term is still quite possible for many a boy who has been turned down by a Choate or a Deerfield.

Another point for many parents, of course, is to become better acquainted with some of the lesser known preps that are highly respected by campus men—but that aren't in the top 25. Here's a partial list:

New England: Westminster, Simsbury (Conn.); Wooster, Danbury (Conn.); Hebron, Hebron (Me.); Brooks, North Andover (Mass.); Berkshire, Sheffield (Mass.); Governor Dummer, South Byfield (Mass.); Lenox, Lenox (Mass.); Suffield, Suffield (Mass.); Tabor, Marion (Mass.); Wilbraham, Wilbraham (Mass.); Holderness, Plymouth (N.H.); Vermont, Saxtons River (Vt.)

Eastern: Millbrook, Millbrook (N.Y.); Northwood, Lake Placid (N.Y.); Blair, Blairstown (N.J.); George, Bucks County (Pa.); St. Andrew's (Del.)

Southern: Asheville, Asheville (N.C.); Woodberry Forest (Va.)

Midwestern: Western Reserve, Hudson (Ohio); Culver Military, Culver (Ind.); Lake Forest, Lake Forest, (Ill.); Shattuck, Faribault, (Minn.)

Western: Fountain Valley, Colorado Springs (Colo.); Orme, Mayer (Ariz.); Cate, Carpinteria (Calif.); Thacher, Ojai (Calif.)

Overall, you can figure that around 75 to 100 preps rate on an academic level that compares favorably with the top 25 names. One good way to pick an alternate school, if needed, is to get a list of four or five likely names from the admissions officer at your first-choice school. But this will narrow you down, and in some cases it's wise to seek a professional adviser—especially where you want a school that stresses tutoring or "special help" of some kind.

These advisory services are recommended by prep headmasters and college admissions officers: Bunting & Lyon, Wallingford (Conn.); Porter Sargent, Boston; Robert Parsons, Boston; and Ruth E. Bishop, New York. The first two publish large, comprehensive directories of all the preps, and these books can be ordered through regular book stores.

Bunting & Lyon, for example, charges about $200 up for prep school consultation with boy and parents. Others listed are in this range. But some advisers promote certain schools—on a commission basis. It's very wise to check on this point before you become in any way involved.

Note: Just as you can sometimes pick up tickets to a hit Broadway show by stopping at the box office at 8:30, so a boy can be admitted to a top-name prep at the last minute—maybe because the admissions officer sees a spark that the grades don't show. So, before following any alternate route always check first with your top choices.

You'll find, perhaps to your surprise, that it's often easier for a boy to gain admission to one of the "better" schools than to a good college. One reason is the marked improvement in the last few years in the better suburban public high schools. Note, too, that many prep schools today are no longer so rigid as they have been in the past in demanding that pupils attend for four years.

There's a trend now toward the three-year course, covering 10th, 11th, and 12th grades. It results partly from the fact that public junior high schools take a youngster through the ninth grade. Sending a boy to private prep school for three years instead of four also cuts the parent's prep school cost by 25%—a big point when you consider annual school costs in the $2,500 plus range.

It's even possible—in some instances—to send a boy to a prep school for one year, after he has graduated from high school. Few schools regularly follow this practice, but it can be arranged, especially where a boy has achieved good grades but is too young emotionally or socially for college.

Special preps

A limited number of college preparatory schools specialize in the student with various emotional problems. Some examples: Anderson School (co-ed) at Staatsburg-on-Hudson, N.Y. (tuition $5,400); Devereux (co-ed) at Devon (Pa.), and with branches elsewhere ($7,200 to $10,200); Grove (boys) at Madison (Conn.); and Oxford Academy (boys) at Pleasantville (N.J.), with even higher costs.

The Tax Court now says the medical-related part of tuition is tax-deductible. But this point should be discussed with a tax adviser.

The high cost of the private school

Tuition costs have been going up a steady 5 to 10% a year for the past 10 years. Now the range is from $2,500 to as high as nearly $4,000 for boarding students, less for day students. You can expect some tuitions to go even higher, though the small-town preps and girls' boarding schools are apt to level off after 1970.

For a boarding student, the basic tuition charge covers true tuition, room and board, and often laundry and routine medical services. But count on an extra 10% for books, supplies, special fees, and another 10% extra for clothing and spending money. One more expense that must be figured: A boy (or girl) will visit home at least twice during the academic year—and this means you'll pay for at least six train or plane fares each year.

One secondary school expert estimates that the average cost of keeping a student in a private boarding school is now about $3,750 a year—and that's an average. Obviously it can go higher, and at some girls' schools the cost can hit $5,000. (Did you ever think of what they charge for dancing, riding, and such?)

Note that not just the high-power Eastern schools are up in cost. The big fees range at top level, coast to coast. Here's a cross-section of private schools, showing 1970 charges and the relationship between boarding and day student charges:

School	Boarding students	Day students	School	Boarding students	Day students
Berwick	$3,200	$1,250	Masters	$3,800	$1,900
Browning ..	....	1,800	Monson	2,900	1,215
Choate	3,600	1,500	Orme	3,350	
Dalton	....	2,275	Peddle	3,250	1,700
DeVeaux ...	3,150	1,350	Taft	3,200	1,600
Foxcroft	3,600		Vermont	3,200	1,400
Gould	2,900		Western Reserve .	2,550	1,300
Hewlett	3,200	1,250	Wilbraham	3,100	1,450
Hoosac	2,950		Emma Willard ...	3,850	
Lake Forest .	3,350	1,900	Williston	3,175	1,725

As you read this, many of the above dollar amounts will already have gone the way of the fat, demanding cash drawer. But don't blame the schools—they offer quality, not quantity.

Teen-agers can travel and study abroad

If education is to be a "total" experience, there's no reason it shouldn't reach from one end of the year to the other—*without* skipping summertime—and from New York to Tokyo, and places between. Thus, the query: Does your high school or college youngster lack firm summer plans?

Student tours and study programs abroad—in Europe, Latin America, even Japan—are open. The new trend: greater stress on study, less on sightseeing. And this will surely be the mood in the 1970–75 era.

The scope of activity is wider than ever. The National Student Association, for example, sponsors several tours for older teen-agers. One, a 45-day tour, concentrates on politics and economics in nine European countries, with briefings by Common Market, NATO, UN and EFTA officials, among others. NSA also sponsors 52-day French and Spanish study tours, including a month's university language study.

Fees range about $750 and up (plus overseas travel cost). For information on these tours, and others for younger age groups, see NSA's guidebook *Work, Study, Travel Abroad* (available at many local public libraries).

Experiment in International Living, Putney (Vt.),—the group that long has promoted the idea of living with a local family in a foreign setting—lately has expanded into language-study programs, carrying college credits. Italian, French, Spanish, German are among the languages taught at three-week camps in Vermont—prior to the student's stay with a foreign family abroad, followed by a month's tour. Rates are $1,000 and up for Europe, up to $1,500 for Japan, including transportation. Again, there are more modest programs for juniors, ages 13 to 15.

Similar student tours are conducted by two newer organizations: Classrooms Abroad (Box 4171, University Station, Minneapolis); and Continental Study Projects (527 Madison Avenue, New York, N.Y. 10022).

The agents: There are, of course, student tours offered by travel agents (at varying prices). However, these are mostly for sightseeing, with travel cost part of the "package" price. University Travel (Cambridge, Mass.) and Arista (New York) are among the specialists.

Summer study overseas sponsored by U.S. colleges lets your youngster pick up academic credit. The Council on Student Travel (777 United Nations Plaza, New York, N.Y. 10017), for example, lists many such programs. The scope is wide—from Michigan State's 8-week language programs in Paris, Cologne, Madrid, to Loyola's Spanish course in Lima, Peru.

Or a student can sign up on his own for a summer program at a foreign university. Pan American's *New Horizons in Education* lists many of these (Simon & Schuster). Generally, the minimum age is 16 or 17; morning study sessions are devoted to language, afternoons to field trips. Advanced language students attend lectures on literature, history, art.

The Institute of International Education (offices in New York, Washington, Chicago, Houston, Denver, San Francisco) provides guidance.

The youngster with a yen for adventure (and a limited budget) can join a small American Youth Hostel group for a cycling, hiking and camping tour of Europe. For details, write to AYH (20 W. 17th Street, New York, N.Y. 10011).

Or if he's going to travel on his own, the National Student Association's *Official Student Guide to Europe* lists hotels, hostels, restaurants, trains, airlines, etc., that give discounts to a youth holding an International Student Identity Card (available at many colleges).

A top-notch collection of "inside" tips for students traveling abroad is found in *The Student Guide to Europe* (Harvard Student Agencies, Cambridge, Mass., available at many public libraries).

Colleges

The college campus today is a disaster area in the minds of many middle-aged parents. This is nonsense—part nonsense, at least. What is true is that colleges, from Harvard to Arkansas Normal, are tense, turmoiled, and changing rapidly. They demand patience and understanding—and yet the old basics stay pretty much the same when it comes down to such mundane problems as admissions and costs. Here are some points to review, as calmly as possible.

It will be harder than ever for a boy—even a bright boy—to get into a quality college next year, or *any* year in the 1970s! The class seeking admission next fall will be the biggest yet.

There's one compensation: An increasing number of colleges are upgrading themselves and offering an undergraduate education equal to the Ivy League in almost every respect but reputation. In the future they will be taking more and more of the students who'd have gone, a generation ago, to one of the big names in the Northeast.

Admissions problems and trends have undergone a thorough airing at annual conferences at Williston Academy, Easthampton, Mass. Over 100 representatives of quality colleges have attended those sessions. Two main conclusions stand out:

■ Academic standards in private colleges all over the U.S. are moving up. This is particularly true of colleges in the Midwest, West, and South. Schools in these areas with a new generation of successful alumni and often big private foundation money behind them, are broadening their curricula, greatly improving facilities, capturing top-rate teachers and staff.

- Admissions standards—at front-ranking colleges—are on the rise. In the Northeast, many say they've become impossible. Even the first-rank secondary schools are digging hard, searching out campuses in other areas where admissions officers are more receptive.

Educators have some sharp advice for you, as a parent: High school boys are tense enough these days without a father's pushing for big-name admission. Let the boy hit his natural stride, they say—he may make Harvard. But don't kid him, or yourself, on this score. And if you're an old grad of a leading college, don't make any assumptions about preferred treatment. Your old grad status is apt to cut little ice.

In any case, you'll be broadening your boy's sights—and his chances—if you see that some of the campus choices take him to smaller, lesser known colleges. Obvious, you say? *No*—far too many parents lose all sense of realism where college admission is concerned. Some fathers hold onto the Ivy League idea as though FDR still lived in the White House.

Just what are the top colleges looking for? Good grades are a must, of course; but today the quality colleges are seeking wider abilities. Creative talent, leadership, and active interest in com-social problems are being stressed. The "late blooming" boy— who shows evidence of some unusual ability, particularly where original thinking is involved—is often admitted in place of a less-colorful straight-A student.

The admissions interview is vital, and your boy should stand on his own at this point. Let him make his own blunders—many a good boy has been frozen out of his first-choice college by too much father-protection. Today, some high schools are even conducting classes on the interview.

Knowledge of two current trends could improve your boy's chances:

- Early decision: Some colleges will accept well-qualified

boys in their final year in high school instead of waiting until the traditional acceptance date. But under this procedure usually the boy may apply to only one college. It should be his first choice, because other colleges might score it against him if they find out that, after getting an early decision, he is applying to them, too.

Most boys who don't try for an early decision—or who don't get an acceptance—apply to at least three colleges around the middle of their senior year: one top quality, one middle, one "sure." It's also wise to vary college types and locations. In a toss-up, many colleges will lean to the applicant from a distant part of the country, although pure-and-simple geographical spread isn't as emphasized as a few years back. Today the greater stress is, of course, on a broad "spread" in the sense of diverse family, social, economic, and racial backgrounds.

▪ Advanced placement: Over 1,300 secondary schools are presently offering advanced courses to 11th and 12th graders, enabling them to enter college with some of the freshman work completed. Harvard boys now enter with advanced standing, in many cases, and the practice is now standard at many top-rank colleges. You may want to consider another high school, if your local school is outside the program.

If advanced-placement courses are offered in your boy's school, and he fails to take at least one, his chances of being accepted by a top-flight college these days may be slim.

In any case, you can ignore the recent talk about bungling and confusion in the handling of college admissions. This is mostly nonsense, from Rutgers west to Pomona. What you can't ignore, though, is the population pressure that is hitting college admissions offices today. This is dead serious.

The greatest overcrowding of would-be freshmen—now and in the foreseeable future—is at the leading "name" colleges in the Northeast. The eight-member Ivy League, for example, accepts just over 15,000 students to fill about 10,000 places each year, but rejects more than 25,000 others (presumably youngsters already screened). But as you get away from the Northeast, this pressure lessens.

The truth is, a number of superior schools in the Midwest and

South—and to some extent, in the West—would seem far better bets for admission in the next few years than almost any ranking college in the East. And, unless your youngster is riding securely in the top 20% of his class, he may find it wise to have alternate plans. MIT, for instance, even figures on the top 10% of a graduating high-school class.

In your mind, the Ivy League probably goes well beyond the eight members of the formal league and includes at least 20 or so other front-rank names, from New England to the West Coast. But perhaps you should add liberally to this list and go farther West.

Actually, out of more than 1,500 four-year colleges in the country, at least 50 rate top academic standing on a near-par with the highest Ivy standards. Here you get a wide range of names and locations—Duke (N.C.), Kenyon (Ohio), University of Michigan, University of Chicago, Lawrence (Wis.), Carleton (Minn.), Tulane (La.), Rice (Tex.), University of Colorado, California Tech, Pomona (Calif.), and Stanford (Calif.), to name a few. And, say educators, you can safely tack on another 50 names and still stay on a high level.

Harvard, Yale, Princeton, and the likes of MIT still put a boy a step ahead, of course. This seems still the case today when it comes to getting favorably located in the professions, such as law. But, on the other hand, if your boy is two or more years away from college, remember that you may be kidding yourself and him if you let him think he has a top college "made" when he hasn't. The point is, if there's any doubt in your mind, now is the time to get him better prepared to broaden his (and your) ideas about other good schools.

A frequent parental mistake is to implant seeds of anxiety in a youngster by making him feel that getting placed in a good college is almost a matter of emergency. He gets quite enough of this in school, say educators, and your pressing the theme might do him more harm than good. Instead, simply encourage him to hit his best natural stride of accomplishment. Briefly, here are some practical points you'll want to stress in talking it over:

- Prep schools: Shifting to a superior private college preparatory school may be a good idea, especially if your local high school is weak or if your boy shows signs of needing a more disciplined working routine — if you can afford it. The best colleges aren't favoring prep boys, and in many cases, they actually are giving an inch of preference to the outstanding boy from the obscure public high school.

- Rating colleges: First, you should read a book such as Cass and Birnbaum's *American Colleges* (Harper and Row). All leading colleges in the country are covered as thoroughly as in any guidebook. The next step is to see that the boy follows through in contact with his high-school college adviser. He also should see the admissions official of at least one of the colleges he has in mind. Finally, visit several campuses each summer, especially if it looks as if your boy will be entering a lesser-known college. Some smaller schools not only rate high academically, but have campuses and physical facilities that may surprise you — Oberlin (Ohio), Reed (Ore.), and Vanderbilt (Tenn.), for example.

- Applications: In applying to at least three colleges — one shooting high, one middle, and one "sure" — your boy should vary both school types and locations. This is most important, say admissions people.

If Junior isn't set for college

In mid-summer, the youngster who's through high school but lacks a college berth for September is probably:
- In the lower 50% of his high-school class.
- Too ambitious, having aimed too high without having made a "safe" application.

In any event, there's practical last-minute help available from some special college admissions clearinghouses. Best known among educators: The Admissions Center at the National Association of College Admissions Counselors, 801 Davis Street, Evanston, Ill. The Center reports vacancies at several hundred colleges, mostly small and mostly private.

These are generally solid (not obscure) colleges, though not "name" institutions. Most are in the Midwest, Southwest, and on the West Coast.

A youth who planned poorly, but has a reasonably good high-school record, may hear from five or ten of them. Those in the lower 50% of their class have about a 50–50 chance of getting placed. Write to the Center for applications; the Center will contact the colleges.

Another reputable center of the same sort is the College Admissions Center, 461 Park Avenue South, New York, N.Y. 10016.

A visit to the college campus

If you have youngsters in senior high school, it may be time to think about seeing some colleges first hand. With competition for admission to top colleges keener than ever, the personal interview can be one of the most important factors. The admissions office likes to weigh an impression of the applicant's personality in the balance with scholastic records and test scores.

Some admissions people frankly say they won't consider anyone who hasn't been interviewed. And if you live within convenient driving distance of the campus and don't bother to make a visit, the obvious interpretation is that you're not really too interested.

In any case, the college visit can help your youngster decide whether he likes the atmosphere—and really wants to apply to spend four significant years there. And for you, of course, this decision means a substantial emotional and financial investment; you want it right.

How can the prospective student get the most benefit from a visit? And how do you, as a parent, fit in? To begin with, the ideal timing is in 11th grade—when a student has some idea what he wants in a college, and has enough of a school record to be meaningful. Senior year is often too late.

It's always better to go when college is in session—preferably in the fall or late spring. Admissions offices usually close their doors to visitors from January to April to process applications.

Avoid holidays and weekends. On some campuses, there are special weekends or days to introduce high schoolers to college life. But the drawback is that these usually include no interview, and provide little chance to investigate the academic side.

Three weeks or so ahead of the planned trip, have your youngster write requesting an interview. Colleges usually save every scrap of correspondence from an applicant—including the postcard asking for a catalogue—and it's important that each letter be a model of correct spelling, punctuation, and grammar. *And note especially:* Parents should never do the corresponding.

Your boy or girl will win points for enterprise if the letter is addressed to the admissions officer by name—and makes specific requests. Apart from the standard interview and tour, for instance, a letter might ask for a meeting with a professor in a field of interest, or with a certain sports coach. It's sometimes also possible to sit in on classes and eat or sleep in a dormitory.

Some homework should precede the actual interview. Nothing galls admissions directors more than being peppered with questions that are plainly answered in the catalogue. Intelligent questions show that the youngster has done some hard thinking about his record and his future.

For example, ask questions such as these: What level of faculty teaches freshman courses—senior staff or junior instructors? How many hours does the average freshman spend in study a week? How many students share equipment in a lab? Are library books readily accessible to the students? What are some of the newer library services?

If possible, the campus tour should precede the interview. Bring along a school transcript, scholastic average, rank in class, test results, latest grades. Almost always, the candidate is interviewed alone—though sometimes parents are asked to join for the last few minutes. Admissions people can learn a lot from the interaction of the youngster and his parents—whether a boy is independent enough to stand on his own. Parents can help most by saying nothing unless called on.

Toward the end of an interview, a boy has every right to ask about his chances of admission. Often he will get a frank appraisal—and occasionally even an informal assurance.

While there's no substitute for a campus visit, more and more colleges arrange interviews for applicants who live far away. Often this is handled by an alumni committee—and don't downgrade the alumni: This type of interview can be almost as important as one on the campus, and the same preparation is necessary.

One final note: After it's all over, be sure your youngster sends off a note to thank the college officer who interviewed him and arranged the visit.

Digging deep to pay those college bills

Come September, you may need muscle at the loan window if you're short of ready cash to pay your youngster's college bills. Tight money has made bankers much less interested in low-interest, long-term education loans. Rates for shorter-term collateral or regular installment loans are sky-high. And depending on your investments, it may be a bad time to sell securities to raise cash. You'd be wise to call on your banker well in advance—just in case.

If your sone or daughter plans to live away at a private college, you'll need something like $4,000 just for tuition and room and board each year. And you can figure that your youngster's additional expenses—including transportation—will run to at least another $1,000 a year.

What are your alternatives for raising cash? You might start with government-guaranteed student loans. These—made to the student—have a 7% simple interest maximum, and are sometimes available through commercial and savings banks and savings and loan associations. The student can borrow up to $1,500 a year to a maximum of $7,500. He begins repaying the loan after graduation, and has 10 years to pay it off.

Some large banks, especially in the Northeast, are still making these low-interest loans, though many are not broadcasting it and most are now limiting loans to renewals or to the offspring of VIP customers. Some banks now require that you have an account with them for at least a year before they will make such a loan.

Another idea to check with your banker is an insured education loan. It is disbursed once or twice a year over a four-year period. Typically, you can borrow up to $15,000 at 9 to 10% (including life insurance charges) and take up to eight years to repay. You retire the loan in monthly installments, which begin almost immediately. Again, banks are reserving these plans for their best customers.

If this isn't available, you can, of course, borrow on securities. Banks are now lending up to 70% of the value of stocks or bonds. Effective interest charges in New York, for instance, range about 9 to 12% depending on the size and length of the loan.

Finance companies are in the college loan business, too. They charge higher rates than banks, but the money is more available. Among the largest, check Tuition Plan, Inc., a subsidiary of CIT Financial Corp. This pay-as-you-go plan calls for monthly installments. Disbursements are spread over four years, and you pay back in six. The simple interest charge is roughly 15% a year.

Education Funds, Inc., Providence (R.I.), has a revolving credit program with up to 60 months to repay. Simple interest rate is 15% on balances of up to $500, and about 9% above that.

Don't forget the loan value that may lie in your life insurance policy. You can borrow up to 95% of cash value at only 5 or 6% interest. This can add up. A man of 45, say, with a $50,000 non-dividend-paying policy bought 15 years ago, will have $10,050 in cash value today.

Refinancing your house mortgage is a last resort for cash, but you'll be paying rates of 8% and more—if, indeed, you can get the funds.

Ask the college about deferred payments if you're in a temporary cash bind. Some schools let you pay a minimum of one-third down per quarter, and space out two additional payments later in the quarter.

Your youngster might also look into student employment to pay off some of his living expenses—a practice that is, incidentally, followed by many youngsters in high income families. In the Northeast, the average hourly student employment rate is $2.50. Computer programming or tutoring often commands rates of $5 an hour. Example: A youngster who tutors can make $1,500 or more during the academic year. And he can often earn up to $3,500 or more as a part-time worker in business or industry.

Educators sometimes pose this question: If a boy (or girl) of age 18 or 20 isn't ready to pitch in and help with college costs—is he *really* ready for college at all? Even at Ivy League colleges, especially those in cities like Boston and New York, a high percentage of students work part-time.

How much you'll pay for college

Chances are you'll be paying more next year than this for a youngster's college education—and this could turn out to be the understatement of the 1970s. For parents, anyway. A survey of top private colleges and universities shows costs up about $200 a year—this covers room and board, fees, and other "direct" college costs. It doesn't include extras, such as transportation, private allowance, and such.

Here's how tuition and room and board stack up for a cross-section of private colleges—not allowing for boosts after 1970:

School	*Total costs*
Amherst	$3,500
Antioch	3,200
Bryn Mawr	3,200
Cal Tech	3,300
Columbia	3,500
Dartmouth	3,500
Harvard	3,700
Johns Hopkins	3,300
Kenyon	3,200
MIT	3,200
Notre Dame	3,000
Northwestern	3,300
Oberlin	3,500
Princeton	3,600
SMU	2,700
Stanford	3,300
Swarthmore	3,500
Tulane	3,200
USC	3,200
Yale	3,700

Note that the above figures are rounded; in many cases, the current costs—as you read this—may be $100 to $200 more.

Total tab: Figure generally that your total yearly bill for a youngster in college will be roughly double basic tuition, assuming he or she lives away from home. At Harvard, for instance, the tuition comes to about $2,500, and the total bill something in the neighborhood of $5,000 (even more). Note, too, that the big "name" colleges often charge little more than less-known regional colleges.

As for scholarship aid, you can pretty well count on *no* relief if you're a businessman. Such aid almost always cuts off entirely where family net income (allowing for taxes, number of children, and other factors) is $15,000 to $20,000.

State colleges and universities are no longer as inexpensive in relation to private institutions.

If you're thinking of a regional college within a state system (New York, Ohio, California, among others, have extensive systems), then it's true you're in a cost bracket far below private colleges. But most leading state universities—those that rate high academically and otherwise—are far from cheap, particularly for nonresidents. Generally, the cost for residents of the state is about 50% less than at private colleges, but only 25% less for out-of-state students—if they can get admitted.

Books on education: a fine sifting

There is no field more overwritten than "education." It gets to be a physical chore just to quickly scan such books on the shelves of a suburban library. The books range from front-rank to rear, and they go from intriguing to the crashing-bore stage without blinking an eye. Here are a few titles that might be worth your looking into, depending on interest; it's purely a personal pick, nothing more.

James B. Conant's *The Comprehensive High School* is a skilled updating of Conant's celebrated survey report. It is helpful to a parent interested in his community's schools (McGraw-Hill).

If you are thinking of private schools, see Bunting and Lyon's latest edition of their yearbook, *Private Independent Schools;*

or the more specialized *Summer Studies in Private Independent Schools* by the same authors (write to Bunting and Lyon, North Main Street, Wallingford, Conn.).

Parents with a slow learner in the family ("whose talents are slow to show," says an educator) might want to see *The Underachiever* by Porter Sargent; this is a guide to several hundred special programs in private schools and clinics—including individual tutoring, remedial reading, and the like (Porter Sargent, 11 Beacon Street, Boston).

How Children Fail, by researcher and teacher John Holt, is a frank examination of under-performance and its causes; as a parent you may not relish some of the book's conclusions (Pitman).

If you have teen-agers you likely know all too well the strains that repeated IQ-type school testing can produce in an otherwise healthy youngster. This topic is debated in Gene Hawes' *Educational Testing for the Millions* (McGraw-Hill)—it explains the myriad tests and tells what you and your kids can do about them.

The "new math" that once engulfed elementary schools and alarmed parents—and that now has slipped a bit as a subject for loudish PTA meetings—is detailed in Evelyn Sharp's *Parent's Guide to the New Mathematics* (Dutton). Foggy symbolism and poor instruction methods have been part of the new math problem, says the author, and if you're a frustrated homework supervisor, you may benefit.

If your son or daughter has a college admissions problem, *American Colleges 1970–71,* by Cass and Birnbaum, is probably the best guidebook you can get; leading—and less known— private and public universities and colleges are given clear, detailed treatment (Harper and Row). The same authors have also produced the *Comparative Guide to Two-Year Colleges and Four-Year Specialized Schools and Programs.*

Speaking of tuitions, *How to Earn (A lot of) Money in College* has some smart tips, and may be in your public library stacks (Harvard Student Agencies, Cambridge).

The Ivy League Guidebook, by Andrew Tobias, Arnold Bortz, and Caspar Weinberger, is an inside guide to campus activities and attitudes. It's candid, revealing. Harvard, say the authors, has 50 to 100 members of the New Left and hundreds of sympathizers (Macmillan).

With post-grads crowding the campus (more than 80% of Harvard grads go on to further study), a valuable source of information in a little-covered field is the new *Guide to American Graduate Schools,* by Livesey and Robbins (Viking). Besides admission requirements, details on studies, etc., the book gives you a clear idea of the costs that lie beyond the bachelor's degree. The authors note, especially, that scholarships and fellowships (which help to some extent) are awarded mostly in the arts and sciences—with professional school expenses (law, medicine, and such) self-financed.

For a summary of what student militants think is wrong with universities and their ties to the business world, see James Ridgeway's *The Closed Corporation: American Universities in Crisis* (Random House).

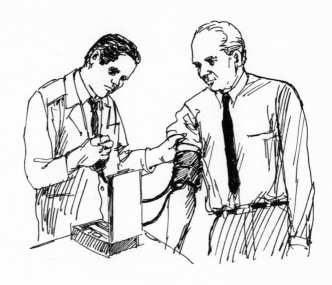

Health: Reducing It to Rules

For the average deskbound businessman—or, indeed, for any adult over 40—good health and ways to acquire and maintain it appear to start with diet and exercise. Why diet?

Watch that waistline

In a statement on avoiding heart attacks, the American Heart Association covers the usual ground (cholesterol, blood pressure, etc.) but makes a hard point on losing weight that goes beyond past statements: A middle-aged man who is 30% overweight has a 100% greater chance of a heart attack than a man whose weight is normal. There are no hard-and-fast rules, but 15% overweight, for example, is considered well outside safe territory.

And you can add to this the constant warnings of medical specialists in virtually all fields, from the internists who talk of obesity as a related cause of diabetes to the psychiatrists who think of extra fat as a sign of neurosis.

The first real step, if you're serious about your waistline, is to rethink your basic attitudes about food and discover why you eat too much. "You have to face yourself on this," says Dr. C. Glen King, a noted New York specialist, "or you'll probably be battling your weight for years."

Most men over 40 with a weight problem are (1) eating as they did at 25 or 30 despite less need for calories, or (2) eating excessively to dampen tension and anxiety—or maybe both. The specialists say this: Coping with the emotional side is hardest. It requires some self-analysis, a lot of discipline, and sometimes help that goes beyond simple dieting. But this step can best head off serious trouble later on.

Physically, say the experts, weight loss should come down to a balanced calorie diet. The fewer gimmicks you use, the better.

Quite apart from a need for more exercise, a man of, say, age 50 needs less food than he did at 30. Metabolism decreases about $\frac{1}{2}$ of 1% a year, so that a lapse of 20 years should mean consuming 10% fewer calories. This factor—added to an exercise slowdown —explains a lot of diet control problems, especially among middle-aged businessmen.

If you're this kind of candidate, some self-help is safe if you aim at a slow change on the scales. For this, add up your daily calorie intake and start eating about 500 less; then go down gradually to the 1,500 to 2,000 range. Around 2,000 is good if you exercise daily.

Generally, a deskbound man needs around 15 calories to maintain one pound of proper weight. So a man weighing 175 needs about 2,600 a day. The idea, of course, is to figure your diet formula and become what the specialists call "calorie-conscious." It sounds dull, but it pays off.

What about the diet foods? Artificially sweetened items, especially coffee sweetener, are bad for a dieter because they perpetuate the taste for sweets, and make the routine harder. The experts stress this. Yet it can make quite a difference: 6 tsp. less sugar a day is 150 calories, or 15 lb. in a year—and people tend to use the no-calorie sweeteners just half the time; so figure a good 7 lb. or more a year if you're a coffee drinker.

Drink-a-meal diets are safe and effective, but won't help you keep from regaining weight; and cocktails do you few dietary favors. Even whiskey-and-water is rough: 100 calories per oz. of 100 proof. "A lot of men have three stiff martinis a day and get 600 calories without knowing it," says Dr. King. Don't quit them, just count them.

The dangers that lurk in fad diets

Beware of the latest in diet fads—whatever it may be. Typical routines are the crash programs that promise you can lose weight fast without depriving yourself of "man-type" meals. The regimens go by various names: drinking man's diet, low carbohydrate diet, Air Force diet, Mayo Clinic diet. But all are basically similar—and all have been described by the experts as "nutritional nonsense, with hazards attached." In fact, both the Air Force and Mayo Clinic have disclaimed the programs attributed to them.

With minor variations, the diets boil down to a drastic cutback on carbohydrates—fruit, breads, cereals, noodles, root vegetables—and carte blanche on everything else, including meat, rich sauces, salad dressings, cheese, and alcoholic beverages, with no ceiling on calories.

Followed to the letter, this sort of menu automatically puts you on a high-protein, high-fat diet. This means danger for anyone who needs to worry about cholesterol—because of circulatory or arterial disease, a heart condition, diabetes, or kidney disease.

Besides, the program gives you only an illusion of fat loss—as much as five pounds a week. Actually, this is due to the body throwing off fluids as it adjusts to the new diet. Normal water balance—and weight—return when you go back to a balanced menu. The only way to achieve permanent weight loss is to cut down on total calories, not just carbohydrates.

Another danger is possible damage to the liver, which must

strain to convert protein and fat into the carbohydrates your body needs. If you keep up the diet too long, the body eventually will be flooded with toxic byproducts of this conversion. Finally, the diets can also produce a vitamin C deficiency.

The point is that the three major nutrients—carbohydrates, fats, and proteins—are so essential to the body's complex chemical processes that you can't skimp on one group without drastic readjustments. The ideal balance is 50% carbohydrates, 15% protein, 35% fat (if you're cholesterol-conscious, supplant most animal fats with vegetable fats), with 5% leeway up or down. Such a mix can be applied to a rock-bottom 900-calorie-a-day reducing diet just as well as to a normal diet in the 2,000-plus range.

Of course, the current fads call for continuing—or even increasing—your intake of calories. But the truth is that if you're overweight, you're most likely already taking in more calories than you're using. Surplus turns to fat.

The diet that lets you starve

Another potentially dangerous crash diet is the starvation routine—just plain no eating for a span of days while you're in a hospital under a doctor's care. The results for an obese person can be dramatic. But before you try to go this route—or suggest it to a family member—see your own doctor. The medics are split wide open on the subject, pro and con.

A dozen or more hospitals with nutrition centers in the U.S.— plus a number of individual physicians—are putting patients on the starvation routine, says the American Medical Association's Director of Food Science. At Pennsylvania Hospital, Philadelphia, for example, overweight cases have regularly been handled on a 10-day to two-week basis.

A patient gets plain coffee or tea, plus no-calorie soda and broth if needed. Weight loss is usually about 15 to 30 lb. The patient then goes home to eat a prescribed diet of 900 to 1,100 calories a day, with monthly call-back visits to the hospital (cost: up to $950).

The routine isn't always so severe. For instance, at Duke University Medical Center, low-calorie rice dishes have been used on the daily menu.

The negative view of the starvation technique is sharp. It's quite true, say some specialists, that overweight people will lose weight—and probably in hefty amounts. But even with medical supervision, results may be bad. "Fasting can turn out to be a fiasco, physically and psychologically," says Dr. John Mayer, professor of nutrition at Harvard Medical School. It's justified in a few exceptional cases. But it can cause gout, says Mayer, and maybe worse. "Losing two pounds a week is enough," he adds.

Finally, say the antistarvation critics, there's a psychological argument: The method does little to reeducate a person about his eating habits.

Do pills fit into your diet?

What do you need to know about diet pills? Where do drugs fit into over-all diet control—if anyplace? You can get a surprisingly clear answer from leading specialists.

"Some of the drugs can be used safely and profitably in the early stages of a diet—despite the headlines," says Dr. Philip White, director of the American Medical Association's Department of Foods and Nutrition. Other specialists agree. And they note:

- Diet and exercise go arm-in-arm, and the hardest part, by far, is diet—especially for a businessman over 40 who's tied down to a desk.

- Low-calorie regimens can, in fact, be so hard for some sedentary types that diet pills—at least some of them—are often prescribed as a crutch. It depends on which ones are used, and why and how, White adds.

Cardiac glycosides like digitalis (for treating heart disease) should never be used for obesity, and when combined with thyroid, use is irresponsible. Hormones-thyroid, diuretics, and laxatives should be avoided.

Mild sedatives and tranquilizers are more acceptable. They

can be used, in some cases, to help a dieter overcome diet-induced tensions.

Appetite suppressants (though ignored by some physicians) are regarded as useful; amphetamines—the "pep pills"—can be employed for a few weeks to help a dieter get through a hard routine.

But a dieter is asking for trouble if he acts on his own and gets an old prescription refilled. Long-term use of amphetamines is dangerous. Says White: "If your physician prescribes pills and you feel uneasy about it—ask him what they are and what they do."

So pills do have a place. But in all the talk about "diet pills," one basic point has gone largely ignored: The experts agree that even if a drug is perfectly safe, it serves only a short-range purpose. The same holds for crash diets. They help you to take off weight—but not to keep it off. They're temporary.

Reading up: If you're serious about losing weight but weary of dietary nonsense, read *The Thin Book by a Formerly Fat Psychiatrist,* by Dr. Theodore Rubin. It offers no fads or quick mixes—but some probing insights about mental attitudes vs. the overweight problem (Trident).

A few minutes that can keep you alive

Why don't more men exercise? There are plenty of places where middle-aged businessmen can work out—from Al Roon's exercise emporium in New York to the Detroit AC to the Presidents Health Club in Dallas to their own homes and offices.

The problem, say the medics, is that not enough men are willing to take the time or trouble. This shows up on the obituary pages, they add. Yet the time and trouble involved are not all that great. Says Manhattan's Dr. Richard Winter, who specializes in giving executives their yearly checkups: "A 15- to 30-minute daily routine can keep a man alive." In a word, that is why a man should exercise—to stay alive.

Medical evidence clearly shows that a regimen of daily exercise—if it's the right kind— will go a long way toward warding off a heart attack or stroke. What's more, a victim of either will have a better chance of pulling through—with minimum damage —if he's active and exercise-prone. In a study of 300 heart attack cases, 49% of those classed "least active" died within a month— but only 17% of those who were "most active."

Active men also have lower blood pressure, a lower cholesterol level, and can control their weight more easily than the sedentary. There are emotional benefits, too, especially for the hard-driving, intense type who lugs home a heavy briefcase on weekends.

The kind of exercise you need is a continuous-action or endurance routine that makes you strain and steps up your heart action. "It has to get you huffing and puffing to do the job," says Winter.

A 15- to 30-min. round of simple jogging, interspersed with brisk walking, is enough. Or you can run in place indoors. Bicycling is good, too—if it isn't an easy ride on level ground. Whatever the exercise, it should be rhythmical and reasonably strenuous.

And note: Unless you jump suddenly into a fast pace, you won't drop dead while going through your routine. About 50% of all heart attacks occur during sleep; 2% while active.

The point is that this type of exercise—if you do it regularly— has the effect of building a stronger heart muscle, with a more forceful, efficient pumping action. Also, the heart develops new channels (arterioles) that help to nourish it in an emergency. You end up with what the medics call "cardiac reserve"; if a coronary does occur, the heart is able to stave off the blow.

Lowered blood pressure, among other things, reduces the chance of a stroke; and lowered blood cholesterol, the chance of a coronary. One study of hypertensive men shows a 22-point drop in systolic pressure (pumping force) following a five-month physical fitness routine.

On top of all this, the glandular system is toned up by exercise.

And since the glands are a prime control of the aging process, a daily workout can help postpone old age—or lead a man into it more gracefully.

The effect on emotional health? Daily rhythmical exercise—jogging, swimming, bicycling, brisk walking—is a great reliever of tension. This isn't only psychological (though that may be all-important). The exercise dilates the blood vessels which are constricted when a man is under tension. The result is relaxation of a kind that you can't get by sitting and reading a novel. *Note:* Isometrics help build muscle, but won't help you relax.

The best way to approach exercise, say the specialists, is to make it a habit. Pick a specific time of day, and stick to it. A 15- to 30-min. break before lunch is a workable health-club routine. (Your afternoon productivity is spruced up, say executives who have tried it.)

But note: In picking a city health club, don't be impressed by a lot of shiny equipment. Saunas and steam baths, for instance, are no real help. Look for an indoor track, a pool, a stationary bicycle. The staff should be able to help you set up a step-by-step routine.

If you exercise at the office or at home, all you need is a 7- by 7-ft. space (though this means running in place). A manual exercise bicycle ($80 and up) and hydraulic rowing machine ($300) are items to consider buying.

Before starting on an exercise program, play it safe and have your doctor give you a clean bill of health. If you want to do some reading up, see *Vigor for Men Over 30,* by Guild, Cowan and Baker (Macmillan): A-1 coverage of exercise by top authors in the field.

If you do it on your own, take it in easy doses until you're in shape.

Walking your way to better health

Want to combine exercise with sport—a sport that you can take up at 40 or 50? Or even 60? Without a lot of lessons to take, rules to follow? Become a hiker. It's really little more than stepped-up walking—but the rewards amount to more than simply physical conditioning.

You "get back to nature"—far from the phones—and enjoy a remarkable amount of psychic income. And if you're the gregarious type, there's a good crowd of hikers to be met in organized clubs around the country. Some of them will be fellow deskbound businessmen—and women.

Medical specialists agree that you literally can walk your way to better physical and psychological health. Dr. Harry Johnson, a New Yorker who specializes in scanning the health records of executives, says this: "Three brisk 20-minute walks a day, plus a five-mile hike each weekend, will put you in shape. If you're past 50 and have to fight against slowing down, you're foolish not to give this idea a try."

The first tip about hiking is to forget about buying lots of equipment at the outset. All you need is a good, comfortable pair of ankle-high boots and a simple knapsack for toting your lunch and foul-weather gear. (Later on, there are some fancy accessories you might want.) Woolen socks are best, and it's a good idea to try wearing a lighter pair of regular-weight socks under them. The socks rub together as you walk and take up the friction of your foot rubbing against the boot.

To start—especially with new boots on—take a few slow turns around the neighborhood in the evening. After that, how far you can hike depends on your condition (and zeal). If you have been strictly a taxi rider, one mile is plenty the first few times out.

A fast hiker will go a steady four miles an hour on level terrain, two in hill country. But don't worry about speed. You'll pick it up. Maintaining a steady, rhythmic pace is the idea—without frequent stops and starts. And remember that, as a beginner, it will take you 10 minutes or so to get warmed up and hit your best stride. In this sport, it's rhythm that counts. Develop rhythm and you'll soon find yourself going on for six, eight, ten miles, even more.

You needn't go on safari. There are probably some good hiking trails near your home. In most areas, local chapters of such groups as the Appalachian Mountain Club and Sierra Club have helped to lay out trails.

This sort of thing is more highly organized than you might imagine. A call to, say, your state or county park commission or conservation department will turn up information. Or call the local Scoutmaster. Or, for a list of many hiking clubs and trails around the country, see *Trails for America*, a 155-page Interior Dept. book (Supt. of Documents, U.S. Printing Office, Washington, D.C. 20402).

You can, of course, go solo. Or do your hiking with family, a few friends, or the Boy Scouts if you have a teen-ager. But an organized hiking club has advantages. A good club offers more than just trail information and guided trips for the novice— there will be dinner meetings, talks and films, and such. After you get past day trips and the gentle field and country road stage, you may decide that you need more than hiking boots. If you're interested in overnight trips, for example, pack frames cost $20 up; on it you strap the canvas pack ($10) and perhaps a goosedown sleeping bag ($60). If you want binoculars, a 7x35 wide-angle type is best ($50).

Top suppliers of highest-grade gear include: Alpine Hut, 4725 30th Ave., N.E., Seattle, Wash.; Gerry Mountain Sports, Inc., Boulder Industrial Park, Boulder, Col.; Thomas Black & Sons, Inc., Boulder Industrial Park, Boulder, Col.; Thomas Black & Sons, Ogdensburg, N.Y.; and L.L. Bean, Freeport, Me. Plus, of course, Abercrombie & Fitch.

Cycling spins off pounds

Or, you might try riding a bicycle. With steady pedaling, you can keep just as physically fit. You'll find cycling less monotonous than jogging, and easier to stick with. You can keep in shape with three or four sessions a week, each half an hour to an hour. Age need not deter you. And cycle makers are now showing lightweight models made to order for the middle-aged physique.

How long does it take to get in shape? If you start sensibly (on flat surfaces) and keep at it regularly, says Western Reserve's

Dr. Herman Hellerstein, "in less than six weeks, you can be going on 25-mile bike rides." Added inducement: At 5 mph on a flat surface (equal to a brisk walk), you burn up an extra 4.5 calories a minute.

If you haven't been in a bicycle store lately, you may be surprised by the variety: sleekly designed unicycles, tandems, triplets, tricycles, mini-bikes, high-risers (for kids), and dérailleurs (multi-speed bikes).

Your best bet, however, is to start off with a three-speed, lightweight (36 to 46 lb.) touring bicycle. It will take you comfortably around town. With thin (1⅜ in.) tires, these bikes are easier to handle than the heavier, coaster-brake bikes with balloon tires that you rode as a youngster. By changing the gear ratio, you can also take hills more easily or increase speed without overexerting yourself.

Note: Be sure to get a bike with hand brakes—they act on both wheels and work immediately. The coaster brake (operated by pushing back on the pedals) is slower, stops only the back wheel, and may cause skidding.

Top names are Raleigh and Schwinn. Raleigh, an English bike, is slightly lighter and easier to maneuver. Schwinn's are sturdier and can take more abuse. Other makers: Columbia, Huffman, Murray Ohio, Stelber ($70 up).

For the man with long-distance riding in mind, the 5- to 10-speed dérailleur bike is a must. Features include dropped handlebars and thinner seats, enabling you to ride in a less tiring, hunched-forward position ($80 to $120). If you're determined to get really serious, you may eventually want a custom-built bike. You can get them weighing as little as 22 lb. This lets you cover long distances—50 miles a day—with less effort ($200).

If you want a bike you can stash in a car, boat, or small plane, see the folding bikes. Some of the imported models are hinged to fold in half merely by pulling a lever. But their 16-in. or 20-in. wheels make them uncomfortable for riding any distance. Names to check: Graziella (which has larger folding bikes also), Amica, Atala, Falter, Schwinn, Stelber.

Safety note: Though not all states require it, the Bicycle Institute of America recommends that if you plan to ride at night, get a headlight visible for 500 ft. and a rear reflector that can be seen for 300 ft.

When jogging might bring big trouble

If you're considering taking up jogging, you should be aware that a daily routine of it will ward off heart attacks and strokes. But for a man in the neighborhood of 45 or 50, even younger, there could be trouble. Harvard's Dr. Warren Guild, leading specialist in sports medicine, sounds these warnings:

- Have a full physical exam before you take on any serious exercise program (too many men have ignored this completely). *Added tip:* Be sure you get an elctrocardiogram following 15 minutes of brisk walking.

- Have a talk with your doctor—besides the routine checkup. Especially, don't be ashamed (as many are) to reveal shortness of breath or even mild chest pains. You can't bury possible trouble, says Guild.

- Do-it-yourself jogging tests are dangerous. They can actually fell a man who is out of condition.

People who carry around extra poundage—or, of course, those who rarely if ever indulge in exercise—should be particularly careful. For such a person, working up to 30 minutes of daily jogging should take four to six months—not four to six weeks.

First, says Guild, simply walk briskly several times a week for two weeks; follow this with a 30-minute routine of slow jogging—interspersed with ample walking—then gradually work up to 30 minutes of daily jogging. Too many men, says Guild, have been moving much too fast on this.

Getting the most out of your annual physical

Another life-saver is the annual physical exam, and the wonder is that so many sensible people ignore it. It's one thing to skip the dentist; it's another to miss seeing your internist. Anybody who procrastinates could be living dangerously:

■ New electronics may have outdated even your last checkup —for instance, at big clinics electrocardiograms are now computer-read for greater accuracy.

■ New chemotherapy appears just as fast—such as the cholesterol-lowering drugs that have made heart patients rest easier.

A fast-growing trend is the clinic in which several physicians pool resources: space, staff, high-cost equipment. So you may have a decision: whether to get your annual physical exam at a clinic or from an individual internist or general practitioner.

"We may lack some bedside technique," says New York's Dr. Richard Winter, director of Executive Health Examiners. "But we give a man the advantage of the views and advice of a half-dozen specialists." Thus, the "name" clinics—among them Mayo in Rochester (Minn.), Lahey in Boston, Oschner in New Orleans, Palo Alto near San Francisco—point to the plusses resulting from talent-pooling.

On the other side the doctor who works alone develops close relationships with patients, and there's more follow-through after an examination. "We can chart a man's health more than once a year," says one top internist. "We can say, 'call back in six weeks'—it means a great deal."

Start with a full routine if you've neglected the annual exam. Besides the usual items, keep these in mind:

The exercise-tolerance electrocardiogram that records while you're in motion is important, say some specialists. If you get a reclining-position ECG, you may want to ask your doctor about the exercise test.

The vital-capacity test of pulmonary function measures lung breathing capacity and can detect danger signals if you're a heavy smoker. (The machine used is going into more and more internists' offices.)

Rectal exam with a sigmoidoscope is the surest way to spot cancer of the colon. Early detection boosts survival chances from 34% to 68%.

The gastrointestinal x-rays (GI series) are important. "If you are past 50," says a top specialist, "have it once, then every three years."

Your blood cholesterol should test 150 to 250 "mgs %"; anything over 260 puts you in the danger area. Ask for your reading on this.

Often undervalued by the layman is the doctor's manual and visual examination of the entire body in which he checks everything from eyes to neurological reflexes. It's more important than any one mechanical test.

How much time is needed for a thorough exam? Apart from x-rays, electrocardiogram, and lab tests, you should spend at least 45 minutes with the doctor (assuming he does the rectal exam). Also, you should get a detailed summation of your general condition—and this ought to last at least 10 to 15 minutes. *Note:* Some of the big clinics also give a routine psychological exam.

A well-run clinic probably will point a man toward further help if he displays undue tension, anxiety, or unwarranted fear about his health. The private physician may be less inclined to do this.

The heart vs. the emotions

Are you working under heavy emotional pressure? If you are, the evidence is getting stronger that you are inviting a heart attack. Heart attacks (coronary occlusions) and related ailments account for nearly half of all deaths attributable to heart failure. This 50% represents more than the total deaths from cancer.

There's still some splitting of opinion among doctors as to the role played by on-the-job tension. But more and more doctors are being won over to the view that it's a paramount factor, especially as it pertains to businessmen in their 40s and 50s who (1) drive themselves hard at the office and (2) fail to break the emotional tension on evenings and weekends.

Several major types of heart "disease" aren't diseases at all, in the usual sense. Among these is the "coronary," which is an event rather than a disease. What happens is this: A clot of blood plugs the coronary artery, denying blood to the heart.

This plugging, or occlusion, of the artery is most likely in a condition of atherosclerosis, a thickening of the artery walls and a consequent narrowing of the passage for blood. The artery walls are thickened by fatty deposits from the cholesterol component of the blood.

This deadly buildup of fat inside the artery can be either caused or at least strongly influenced by purely emotional factors, many doctors now say. They don't deny that such things as improper diet, obesity, and lack of exercise play a part. But a leading specialist, Dr. Stewart Wolf of Oklahoma City, has drawn this classic picture of the coronary-prone personality:

"A man who is highly competitive in his attitudes, if not in his behavior; concerned with self-sufficiency and with doing things on his own, usually the hard way. Looking for new worlds to conquer, he takes less than usual satisfaction from achievement and, especially, has no time for . . . satisfaction between chores."

The basis for this kind of thinking goes far beyond educated guesswork. For example, a study by two San Francisco specialists compared two groups of men—83 aggressive executives and another 83 men who were deemed opposite in drive and personality. Physical factors, such as diet, were the same in both groups. Result: The aggressive group showed higher levels of blood cholesterol, faster blood-clotting time, and six to eight times as much heart disease.

A study at a U.S. Public Health Service hospital in New York turned up similar evidence. Here, 100 ailing and 100 healthy adults, all age 40 or less, were closely screened and compared. The finding: Job stress "appeared to be far more significant in the coronary picture" than such factors as family history of heart disease, high-fat diet, obesity, amount of tobacco consumed, or amount of daily exericse.

What about the effect of emotional strain on people who have already suffered a coronary? A Columbia University researcher says there's no rule of thumb on the question of whether a heart-attack victim should return to work. It's an individual matter. But the emotional stress of the patient's job is one "indispensable" element to consider.

On the negative side, some doctors say simply that the evidence backing the emotional viewpoint isn't at all conclusive. Nearly all, though, admit that there's no reason to gamble. Thus, the middle-aged executive is advised to do more than just maintain proper weight and get a healthy amount of daily exercise. Today—more than ever before—he's being prompted to master the art of emotional relaxation—through sports, hobbies, carefree travel, reading, and the arts.

Stroke: grim prospects, and hopes

Of all the medical disasters that can befall an active, productive businessman, a paralyzing stroke is among the worst. The statistics are grim: Some 30% of stroke victims die in the first week following the attack; only three or four out of every 10 who do survive that first dangerous period ever recover sufficiently to return to work.

Yet strokes rarely come without some warning. Many could be prevented if the early signs were recognized and the underlying causes treated swiftly and effectively. Some of the danger signs may seem so minor as to go unnoticed: momentary dizziness, brief blurring of vision, temporary numbness in a foot or hand. These provide reason enough for consulting a doctor.

In older men danger signs may be more noticeable but still brushed aside. Brief lapses of memory may constitute a warning of stroke danger, even though a man in his 50s or 60s may put them down to nothing more serious than "getting older."

If the underlying cause is the narrowing of an artery, the physician may prescribe anticoagulant drugs or even surgery, if blockage is confined to the neck. In some cases, treatment will alleviate the danger.

The main cause of strokes (and of heart attacks) is atherosclerosis, the clogging or hardening of arteries. In a stroke, the blood supply and oxygen are cut off from the brain, causing damage to brain tissue. The extent of a stroke victim's recovery depends very much on the area of the brain that's affected and the length of time that it is deprived of blood and oxygen.

285 Health: Reducing It to Rules

There's no rule as to precisely what causes atherosclerosis. High blood pressure, heavy smoking, high blood cholesterol, overweight, limited physical activity, and inability to cope with stress all play a part. Each tends to build up fatty deposits in the arteries, which eventually may block the flow of blood to the brain. Heavy cigarette smokers, some studies show, develop obstructive arterial disease at an earlier age and to a more severe degree than light smokers. Physical inactivity leads to sluggish blood flow. Brisk walking or swimming help keep heart and arteries healthy — so long as they are done regularly and frequently. One hour a day is best, say many doctors.

Specialists claim that short periods of exercise at intervals are not sufficient — and may be dangerous. Above all, they warn against irregular bursts of activity in fact-action competitive sports such as tennis, handball, or squash. These can be hazardous for anyone not in top condition.

A diet that cuts daily caloric and fat intake now gets strong medical support as a way to lower blood cholesterol and thus cut the danger of stroke and heart attack.

Physical examinations at least once a year can help spot conditions that may lead to a stroke — conditions that may show up as early as the teens. Arterial disease develops slowly, and tests for blood pressure, cholesterol level, and blood sugar can locate trouble before it becomes dangerous. So can x-rays of the heart and blood vessels and electrocardiograms.

Hypertension

High blood pressure (hypertension) is widely misunderstood by laymen, according to a published summary by New York's Dr. Harry Johnson, a specialist in executive health examinations. He makes these points:

Excessive emotional tension is not — as a lot of middle-aged men believe — a root cause of high blood pressure. If a man is under stress his blood pressure may rise, but this is only temporary.

"Essential hypertension" — 90% of all high blood pressure

cases—is organic and physical in its nature. The cause is unknown. (True, it's often related to overweight, but obesity isn't a basic cause.)

Another misconception involves the systolic (higher) pressure reading. For example, "100 plus your age" isn't necessarily normal. Actually, 100 to 140 is the normal range—but the closer to 100, the better. An elevated diastolic pressure (the lower reading)—above 90—is more significant. Finally, headaches, nosebleeds, flushed face, and such rarely indicate high blood pressure. Only a series of readings will reveal it.

Cancer: an optimistic view

Today, you can be calmer about cancer. How much calmer? There may not yet be ground for out-and-out optimism. But not many years ago, only 25% of cancer cases were cured—meaning that the patient survived another five years without recurrence of cancer symptoms. Today the rate of cure is over $33\frac{1}{3}\%$.

In some special areas, the outlook is brighter. For example, cancer of the stomach, with a cure rate of under 10%, has been declining steadily in recent years (possibly because of general dietary changes). Cancer of the skin is now curable 90% of the time. And uterine cancer in women is nearly 100% curable if it is diagnosed early.

Much progress also has been made in the treatment of cancer of the intestine, endocrine glands, and prostate gland. In the case of prostate cancer, which usually hits older men, the cure rate is only reasonably good, but in 80% of the cases, life can be prolonged, often for a number of years. (Incidentally, enlargement of the prostate is common in men over 50, and in four out of five cases is not due to cancer.)

The point is, say the experts, that the entire picture is improving steadily, almost month to month. Research—especially into treatment by chemicals and into viruses as a cause of cancer—appears to be on the verge of great strides. The ultimate object: to prevent cancer at its source.

What can you do to get the benefits of all this progress? The experts have this advice: The 33⅓-plus cure rate could be over 50% today if people would take full advantage of what science has to offer. This means a yearly physical checkup, among other things—especially for members of your family over 35.

Cancerphobia—unreasoning fear of the disease—keeps people away from early diagnosis and is a killer in itself, the experts emphasize. You can point out to any reluctant member of your family that at least 50% of all cancers can easily be detected by your family physician in the course of an ordinary office visit. Not only that, but signs pointing to the need for further examination can be spotted—and maybe most important, early warning signs of possible future cancer can be recognized. Thanks to new testing tools and techniques it's now much easier to see these warnings.

Early diagnosis is the key to cure in a great many cases, largely because of cancer's unique ability to spread throughout the body (metastasis). For example, New York's Strang Cancer Clinic for years gave regular checkups to adults without apparent cancer symptoms. This program assured early detection; as a result, 85% of intestinal cancer cases discovered in the group were cured —better than double the national cure rate. There are comparable examples relating to most forms of cancer.

Symptoms of cancer—from the layman's viewpoint—narrow down to seven: Any unusual bleeding or discharge, a lump or thickening in the breast or elsewhere, a sore that won't heal, a change in bowel or bladder habits, hoarseness or cough, indigestion or difficulty in swallowing, and a change in a wart or mole. A symptom that lasts longer than two weeks should take you to your physician.

A word on lung cancer: All the propaganda on this and its relation to cigarette smoking may be grimly justified by the fact that this ailment now is the leading cause of cancer death in men. The number of male deaths has multiplied six times in the past 20 years.

If you have any worries about lung cancer, don't fail to have a periodic chest x-ray—some doctors say twice yearly, if you're over 45. On the other hand, you can be philosophical. Even if you're the worst possible "risk"—because of your smoking habits, age, etc.—the odds of your ever contracting lung cancer are only 1 in 10.

The ulcer: home free, 90% of the time

A businessman over 40—if he's the hard-driving, intense type and hasn't yet made it to the top—can be a prime candidate for a peptic ulcer. "It's an executive suite ailment that seems to hit hardest at vice-presidents who work under pressure," says Dr. Richard Winter, director of New York's Executive Health Examiners. "Presidents give ulcers—and an ulcer giver isn't so apt to get one himself."

But high-pressure jobs on just about any level can pave the way for an ulcer. This is especially so if the victim is overly conscientious, a perfectionist, and the kind who willingly shoulders every available ounce of responsibility. If you have such characteristics—an "ulcer profile"—you have an estimated 20% chance of getting one. But there's still one chance in 10 without that profile.

One message is clear: To prevent an ulcer, learn to relax.

Stress lays the groundwork. But the specialists also point out that physical susceptibility is likely to be a factor, too. The ulcer victim may have a system that produces a larger-than-average amount of digestive acid. "You're a candidate if you get a sour stomach whenever you eat spicy foods," says a top Manhattan internist. "And if you regularly get quick relief from milk, see your doctor."

People with type O blood may be ulcer-prone, too, and so a tendency toward ulcers might be inherited. Some drugs—aspirin, cortisone, and those used for high blood pressure—can increase stomach acids and lead to ulcers.

Ulcer odds are highest for a man 40 to 60. Under 60, it's usually duodenal; after 60 it's more apt to be a stomach ulcer, and possibly more serious.

A slow-burning stomach pain just beneath the breastbone is the crucial sign of an ulcer. It starts an hour after eating and gets worse at night when acid is most free to work on the stomach lining. Food brings relief, without fail.

A combination of diet, medication, and more relaxation usually is the answer. Traditional ideas on diet have changed. Spicy foods, alcoholic beverages (even beer), coffee, tea—and smoking—are out, as before. But, says a Mayo clinic specialist, "The old dreadfully bland diet really isn't necessary."

Antacids are still part of the treatment. And tranquilizers such as Librium and Valium, or minute doses of phenobarbital, are important in ulcer regimens. In stubborn cases, some newer drugs such as Daricon are used to block the vagus nerve, which stimulates the flow of stomach acid.

For a patient, the problem is to stick to the routine after early relief is obtained—many don't. This is one reason that 30% of all ulcers return within five years. Another is that the underlying emotional problems too frequently go neglected.

If an ulcer causes an obstruction, deeply perforates the stomach lining, or erodes a blood vessel and causes bleeding, surgery can be the answer. Ulcer surgery is well within the "highly successful" category, and new methods have eased the burden on the patient.

Self-medication for stomach distress can be dangerous—especially if there's an ulcer causing the trouble. The danger: self-dosing can cover up serious complications, including cancer. The odds aren't bad. About 90% of all ulcers are the nonmalignant duodenal type, the rest are stomach ulcers. The trouble is, an estimated 15% to 20% of stomach ulcers are cancerous—so it's foolish to avoid a checkup.

Diabetes

There's disquieting news from the U.S. Public Health Service: Diabetes is increasing. It's a greater health problem than is generally recognized. PHS says that more than 4 million Americans are diabetics. Worse, half of them don't know they have the disease—though it's the third leading cause of blindness and a major villain in heart disease.

Why the buildup in diabetes? It's because Americans are eating too well. Overweight now is tagged as second only to heredity in triggering diabetes.

Diabetes can sneak up on a person. In 80% of cases, the classic symptoms—excessive thirst, frequent urination, mysterious weight loss, weakness, constant fatigue—don't appear until after age 40. Up to this age, the disease often remains hidden; some as-yet-unknown compensating mechanism in the body apparently controls it.

Then, when a person becomes overweight, the latent condition often erupts into full-fledged diabetes. Other things also can upset the balance—an infection, not enough exercise, a coronary accident, emotional stress, certain drugs given for high blood pressure.

Of course, if there has ever been diabetes in the family, be on guard. A predisposition to the disease generally is inherited (one out of five persons who have a diabetic relative will develop it).

The usual variety of diabetes is what the doctors call diabetes mellitus: an innate inability of the system to produce enough effective insulin. Once the pancreas' insulin production is impaired, the body can't use the sugar that's present in carbohydrates, and throws it off in the urine. A standard urine test for sugar will spot the disease at this point. And a strict diet-drug regimen is markedly successful in keeping symptoms under control so that most diabetics lead fairly normal lives.

Aside from cutting down on calories, the 40-plus diabetic generally needs only a moderate reduction in carbohydrate consumption. And the development of anti-diabetes tablets in recent years has revolutionized treatment by eliminating the need for daily insulin injections in most cases over age 40. Juvenile diabetics (those who show symptoms before age 20) still need daily shots. The later the disease erupts, incidentally, the milder the case.

Prompt treatment usually can spare the diabetic much discomfort and severe complications. In fact, persons who develop diabetes after age 40 have a life expectancy almost equal to the rest of the population.

One worrisome aspect of the disease can be circulatory complications—which may develop ahead of overt diabetes. Before any sugar imbalance shows up in a urine test, latent diabetes frequently attacks blood vessels—impairing circulation to feet, heart, kidneys, eyes.

Thus, a juvenile diabetic could have the circulatory system of a 60-year-old man by age 30. This explains why cardiovascular and kidney complications are the major cause of death—accounting for 77% of all diabetic deaths. (Diabetic coma, previously the prime cause of death, is now rare and the result only of gross neglect.) This apparent relationship between diabetes and cardiovascular disease points up the importance of detecting the disease early.

Researchers are now concentrating on early diagnostic tests to spot latent diabetes before it causes damage. One hopeful result is the cortisone-glucose tolerance test, which has proved successful in pinpointing borderline cases. Meanwhile, all the evidence points to weight control—especially among those with diabetic relatives—as an effective way of preventing diabetes.

Back trouble: the big brigade

Oh, my aching back! That's the lament of more 50-year-old businessmen than you can shake a heating pad at. This pain-in-the-back brigade suffers an ailment that is among the most difficult to diagnose and to correct.

Deskbound types are prone to the problem. New York's Executive Health Examiners, for instance, reports that nearly 25% of the sedentary middle-agers it examines have some form of back trouble. It's equally certain that you, as a potential sufferer, can do much to head off this painful malaise before it gets you down.

Why is diagnosis hard? Look at the physical causes of lower back pain. Strained ligaments in the spine, made worse by weak back muscles that give poor support, can be the problem. Degeneration (wear and tear) of discs and joints in the spine, especially after age 45, can lead to osteoarthritis and much pain. The misplaced or "slipped" disc is not so frequent a cause as most people think. Finally, among older men, prostate, kidney, and bladder ailments can lie at the root of the trouble.

Your physician will try to eliminate serious causes first, then get down to the prevalent ones: strained ligaments or arthritis. *Note:* Upper back pain—not so frequent—may have similar causes, but also may indicate heart or lung disease, or just poor posture. So, if you're a sufferer, go to the doctor with a spirit of tolerance and a hope—but no demand—for prompt action.

A typical scene: You awake in the morning and find it hard to sit up. You have severe stiffness in the lower back. This is common if you are over 40. It may mean that you sleep on too soft a mattress, have a touch of arthritis, maybe both. But see a doctor—a good rule for all back pains—if the condition lasts over two weeks.

See your regular doctor first and let him screen out and treat the usual causes, or send you on to an orthopedic specialist. *Note:* Don't jump to conclusions if he refers you to a specialist—the general practitioner, faced with problems of diagnosis, may simply be playing it safe.

Types of therapy? It may be as simple as using a heat pad; it could also involve an operation. A firm mattress is commonly prescribed (a soft one can cause severe pain). Raising the heel of one shoe ¼-in. or ½-in. sometimes is helpful. Some specialists prescribe Novocaine or Xylocaine shots to kill the pain. Massage by a physiotherapist is a mainstay.

Most orthopedic specialists will use surgery as a last resort, after lesser methods have failed. About 90% of back troubles remain nonsurgical. If you wind up facing an operation, realize that surgery to correct a slipped disc or defect in a spinal bone is "major". Hospitalization will run one to four weeks, followed by four to six weeks, sometimes longer, at home.

On the positive side, you can rest assured that although there aren't too many claims for 100% cures, the improvement rate is very high. Office people most always are able to resume their normal routines with reasonable if not complete comfort. The fatality rate is negligible. And contrary to a widespread fear, there is rarely any risk of lower-body paralysis.

How to avoid all these problems? Daily exercise is the answer. Stronger back and abdominal muscles that will help support your weight without strain on the spine can be developed by a simple routine of brisk walking (at least 30 minutes), plus about 15 minutes of calisthenics each day. The sitting-up exercises, however, must be planned.

Simple limbering exercises are fine. So are isometrics—muscle tensing and relaxing exercises—because they develop muscle without strenuous contortions. A good one is to lie flat on your back and push your back downward against the bed or floor; or, lie flat and do 45-degree straight-leg raises. Straining to touch toes or the floor without bending the knees can be dangerous. So can sit-ups from a flat position, or pulling knees to the chest.

Golf won't cause back troubles unless you've already some underlying condition. If you have a tendency to back pain, be moderate about tennis.

Vision and the man past 45

The "slowing down" that afflicts many an executive in his later middle years might stem from a score or more different causes. But one thing that's likely to contribute in a good number of cases, say the specialists, is inefficient vision.

Probably 50% of all deskbound men over the age of 45 will find—even if they are wearing glasses—that their vision isn't as good as they would like it to be. *One obvious point*: If you're past 40 and already wear glasses, make it a rule of thumb to have your lenses checked every two years. If you need glasses for the first time—or if you need new lenses—you'll find some new products that weren't available a year or so ago.

Better quality plastic is now going into plastic lenses to make them less subject to scratching. But their prime advantage is that they are also lighter than glass; this can mean much greater wearing comfort in cases where lightness is most important.

Bifocals now come in "no-line" models—they show no line of demarcation between the segments of the lens. This is important to some people who feel that wearing bifocals is a sign of old age. A few wearers, though, complain that it takes a lot of time and trouble to get used to seeing without distortion past the zone of transition between the two areas of the new lenses.

Coming back into favor is the old half-eye lens. It's simply the framed lower half of the lens (the reading segment of a bifocal). It, too, is lightweight. But some wearers are bothered by too often getting the top horizontal rim of the frame in their line of vision. One alternative for those who need reading glasses but no correction for distant sight, is to get a lens with plain glass in the top half.

Tinted lenses for regular wear, incidentally, are overrated. The eye needs tint protection only when there is excessive glare. As for frames, the best advice is: If they're comfortable to wear and correctly center the line of vision, they'll suit your eyes. Quality of frames is best gauged by price. Frames with built-in hearing aids should sit snugly around your temples; there's no denying that these frames are heavy and hard to wear.

Top-quality lenses and frames, with lenses ground for single correction, cost from $22 to $35; the price spread depends mainly on the frames you select. Bifocals will run from $45 to $60. Often less expensive glasses are advertised as being of "first" quality—but in terms of the trade this actually means second line.

If you want to dispose of frames altogether and switch to contact lenses, you'll likely need something more than mere vanity for a motive. A middle-aged man requires, on the average, at least a month of training before he can wear contact lenses comfortably. Some people take three months—and even more—to get used to contacts.

Most contacts correct distant sight only. Usually, you'll still have to wear glasses—in addition to the contacts—to correct your vision for close work.

On the medical side: The two prime threats to your sight are glaucoma (a disease that damages sight by causing an abnormal buildup of pressure inside the eye), and growth of a cataract (which leads to clouding of the eye lens and shutting off images). A thorough, skilled eye examination will show up an incipient cataract—one reason why a yearly exam by an opthalmologist is sometimes recommended. In any case, when you have your regular annual physical exam, insist on a tonometer pressure test for glaucoma.

Hearing, and the available aids

What with 6 million Americans suffering a serious hearing handicap—and 10 million more persons with some hearing loss —the hearing aid business is booming. For you, as a buyer, the trick is to get an aid that suits your condition best—which means, among other things, buying for maximum efficiency, not just appearance. Two points to keep in mind at the outset:

- Businessmen who work under heavy strain often are psychologically prone to subnormal hearing. Tensions aren't the root cause (heredity, infections, allergies, and arterial diseases are)—but given a physical cause, emotional stress can greatly magnify the condition.

- A man who puts off getting professional help is asking for trouble. For one thing, the longer he waits, the longer it will take to learn to use a hearing aid with comfort. The "training" period can jump from, say, six weeks to as much as six months, even longer. You pay for procrastination.

You'll be wise to go first to your family doctor—if you suspect that you may have to shop for a hearing aid. He can give you at least a superficial test and then refer you to an otolaryngologist. The specialist will test your hearing-frequency range, and particularly your ability to hear speech. In some cases, your own doctor will send you to a special hospital or university clinic.

There are, of course, many ways to treat hearing loss. Medication occasionally helps, or surgery. For example, in some cases an operation can restore the mobility of vibratory bones in the middle ear. But the mechanical hearing aid has brought back clear sound to far more people than have all other techniques combined.

Armed with a physician's advice, you can start looking over the market. First, you'll find the conventional type of aid, with a microphone-amplifier unit worn in the pocket and a cord leading to an ear receiver. These are now far less cumbersome than a few years ago—cutting out one big disadvantage. Pocket units are 1 to 2 in. long, weigh 1½ to 2 oz., with the battery built in. Cost is $250 up—for first quality.

The conventional aid is for the person whose hearing problem is moderate to serious. The units have more power than the tiny, sleeker types—and besides this, they require less repair and fussing to keep in adjustment.

Next, there's the eyeglass aid with the hearing units inside the temple bars of the glasses. These can be designed for one or both ears. The double-aid (binaural) can produce what the ads claim: a stereo effect—provided the correction needed is similar in both ears. This aid is light (1 oz. on each side with battery), comfortable to wear, works well with glasses. Appearance is good, too.

The over-the-ear type is another tiny gadget, now only 1½ in. long and weighing ⅓ to ½ oz., with the main unit behind the ear and a tube leading to an earplug. The style is comfortable, easy to use.

But the smaller, stylish hearing aids—such as the eyeglass and over-the-ear models—have drawbacks: Their power is limited (compared with the pocket style), repairs are tricky (and often frequent), and you need a spare (again, $250 and up, for first quality).

Finally, there's the all-in-ear aid, latest on the market. This is a minute, complete unit that fits entirely inside the ear. But it serves only mild conditions, and—pending further research— is apt to give the wearer some trouble with feedback noises. Before considering this type, consult your physician.

Among quality makes: Beltone, Maico, Radioear, Sonotone, and Zenith (all American); Norelco (Dutch), Widex (Danish),

Siemens (German), and Omikron (Swiss). These companies, among others, make all types of aids.

VIP virus: a nasty cold, that is

If you are felled by executive flu—a nasty winter cold, that is— be extra cautious about what you buy to treat it. And read labels carefully. With today's array of non-prescription cold prepara- tions—pills, drops, lozenges, cough sirups, and all the rest— it's tempting to take the doctoring into your own hands. But self-medication can be dangerous.

In fact, it's a good idea to consult your doctor if you're run- ning a fever—especially if a sore throat or chest pains go along. It's also a danger signal if a cold drags on for 10 days without improvement or hoarseness persists three or four days.

The reason for caution is that over-the-counter drugs are potent. To some people, they can also be hazardous. The key is your physical makeup and drug sensitivity, and these vary greatly—even in the same person. Even the dosage recommend- ed on the label as safe can be harmless to one person, risky to another. Again, the "safe" dosage has so little effect on some people that they take too much—and risk severe reactions and side effects. These can result from, say, a seemingly innocuous six squirts instead of three from a nose spray.

There's risk, too, in using cold preparations too long—for more than 48 or 72 hours. They're strictly for temporary use. Be especially wary in cases of chronic illness—hypertension, glaucoma, heart, thyroid, kidney, or circulatory trouble—or when under a doctor's medication for any complaint other than the cold. Ask his advice.

Another potential danger is that self-medication in some cases can mask a serious condition—and allow it to progress. For example, you may be treating a streptococcus infection as a "simple sore throat"—with dire results.

How do the cold preparations work? The nasal decongestants, for instance, contain both vasoconstrictors and antihistamines. Vasoconstrictors give relief against stuffiness by constricting swollen blood vessels. But repeated use can reverse the effect and cause more swelling instead. Vasoconstrictors also act as stimulants; so they can cause nervousness, insomnia, and sometimes with overdosing, heart palpitations and a rise in blood pressure. The antihistamines dry up a cold. But repeated doses can overdo it and even bring on allergies and skin eruptions. They can also make you drowsy.

Even pain-killing aspirin can have side effects—stomach irritation, indigestion, or eventually ulcers. The aspirin substitutes containing phenacetin or acetaminophen relieve pain without irritating the stomach—but kidney injury can result from excessive and prolonged use.

Still, used judiciously, over-the-counter drugs can give welcome and safe relief to most people—especially if they believe the product will help. Doctors claim that faith in a remedy often helps it work—psychologically. But note that cold preparations relieve only the symptoms—not the cold itself, which can stem from one or more of 35 to 40 viruses. An effective cold vaccine is in the future and the wonder drugs, like penicillin and neomycin, have no impact on cold viruses.

Your best attack on a cold is still plenty of rest—preferably in bed. Aspirin or a substitute help muscle aches and pains, and hot gargles soothe a raw throat, as well as troches that anesthetize and stimulate secretions. As for lozenges and troches containing antibiotics and sulfa, they are worthless for a cold—and doctors warn that they may prevent effective use of wonder drugs in a more serious illness by building up resistance or allergy.

For preventing colds, the best prescription seems to be adequate rest and enough moisture in the air. Mounting scientific evidence indicates that low humidity in heated rooms dries the nose and throat, makes them susceptible to infection. A home humidifier might be one answer.

The desert air: in your house

During the winter heating season, the average American home is drier than the Sahara Desert—relative humidity of 13 to 15%

vs. the desert's 25%. And this low humidity draws a lot of the blame for winter colds. It makes the entire respiratory tract more vulnerable to infection, chronic hoarseness, and coughing. The older you are, the more the discomfort and hazard.

One solution is to install a home humidifier—which can raise relative humidity to 35 or 45%. Large 40-lb. console-style humidifiers are equipped with humidistats to give proper moisture control. Cost: $60 to $100. Using about a gallon of water per day per room, they humidify six to eight rooms for 24 hours before needing a refill. Smaller, portable units take two to four gallons of water, weigh 12 to 15 lb., and cost $25 to $50 (plus/an extra $10 to $20 for humidistat).

If you live in an area where the mineral content of the water is high, get the evaporator type rather then the atomizer variety. If you have a hot-air heating system, consider a furnace unit with automatic water refill. The unit costs roughly $100, with installation. A house using 1,000 gallons of oil a year probably would use 11 to 12 gallons of water daily.

Reputable makes of various types include Eaton, Cory, Sunbeam, Wirthington, Aprilair. Be sure to get a unit of copper or stainless steel, which resists rust and corrosion. Incidentally, a humidifier has another important virtue: It helps protect valuable antiques and paintings from drying out and cracking.

Suntan—and sunburn

The noonday sun may be fine for some people, but it can be murder for fair-skinned persons. If you're bent on getting a tan, don't overdo it. Remember, too much sunning can be dangerous. It can lead to heat prostration, sunstroke, and severe burns; it can aggravate some serious diseases. And prolonged overexposure is pinpointed as the leading cause of skin cancer. At least 110,000 cases of this will show up in the U.S. this year.

Light-skinned persons—especially redheads and blonds—are most vulnerable to skin cancer because their skins can't build up protective pigment against the sun's burning rays (strongest from 10 A.M. to 2 P.M.). So if exposure to the sun usually turns you lobster-red, it's wise to cover up. Clothing will absorb virtually all ultraviolet rays.

Note: Modern medicines can play tricks even on experienced sunbathers. If you're taking antibiotics (especially tetracyclines), tranquilizers, diuretics, anti-diabetics, or anti-fungus agents, check with your doctor. Otherwise you may wind up with a severe burn, rash, or hives.

Sunbathers with none of those problems still face a difficulty: selecting a worthwhile suntan lotion from among the hundreds of brands. One of the more effective ones is plain zinc oxide. But you have to apply it heavily in white blotches, so it won't help your appearance. Your best bet is to check lotion labels carefully and pick a bottle that contains one or another of these sun screening agents: para-aminobenzoate (PABA), anthranilate, benzimidazole, benzophenone, cinnamate, or salicylate. These chemicals absorb the harmful ultraviolet rays before they hit the skin.

Researchers at Massachusetts General Hospital recently found that preparations containing PABA or closely related substances that have been dissolved in ethyl alcohol provide the most effective protection.

One new commercial product similar to the Massachusetts General formulas is Block Out. It won't let you get much of a tan, but it won't let you broil yourself, either. You'll get more tan—but still good protection—by using UVAL, RVP, Neo-A-Fil, or Solbar. *Note:* Apply these lotions frequently, especially after swimming or perspiring heavily. Most preparations wash away quickly.

Even if you tan well, spend no more than 15 to 30 minutes in the sun your first day out. Increase the time gradually. But keep shaded the following day if you're still red or your burn will be doubly severe. The best treatment for painful redness is to apply a cool compress (whole milk is soothing) and then dab on mineral oil. You'll probably stop looking like a lobster after three days. If you're overdone to the point of severe burn, chills, fever, blistering, and even infection, you'll need a doctor's care.

Chronically overexposed sunworshippers—particularly those with heavily freckled, leathery skin—should see a doctor if they spot a horny skin growth (keratosis) or notice changes in any existing growths. Skin cancer is the most curable as well as most common form of cancer in this country, with more than 90% of all patients recovering fully if treated reasonably early. Most vulnerable skin areas are those most in the sun: face, ears, back of the neck, arms, and hands.

Sunglasses galore

What's new in sunglasses?—just about every shape, size, color, and quality imaginable. Here's a quick buying guide for the family:

Shapes go from huge 2½-in. circles to tiny triangles. Odd shape alone won't hurt your eyes, say the specialists. But too small a lens means sideglare, little comfort. Also, corrective lenses often won't give the needed result if they've been fitted into oddly shaped frames. *Tip:* Too wide temple bars (a fad) cut side vision; they can be especially dangerous when you're driving.

Vivid offbeat colors (blue, pink, orange) are bad for the eyes. They fail to filter out ultraviolet or infrared rays, and give an uneven screening to the visible spectrum. *And note:* They distort colors and, eventually, color perception. The best color is neutral gray, with tan or pale green rated second.

Quality lenses come in three color tones: light (impractical), medium (best for general use), and dark (best for the beach or water sports).

Top brand names include American Optical, Bausch & Lomb, May, Shuron-Continental, and Titmus; at quality department and sporting goods stores—and sometimes, drug stores—in an $8-to$20 price range. A pair of $2 sunglasses may not hurt; sometimes, though, they're bad.

Morning-after department

Despite all their resolutions, a lot of people will greet next New Year's Day with a king-sized hangover. With all the seasonal celebrations and "open-house" shindigs to trap you, the vital questions are:

- How can you prepare for the night out to cut the risk of a hangover?
- What can you do the next day if your precautions have failed?

There are some scientific (and some not-so-scientific) answers: The obvious thing, of course, is simply not to drink. But if this has no appeal, try to approach the evening in a relaxed mood. Emotional stress intensifies the risk of a hangover. Says Harvard specialist Dr. Morris Chafetz: "Drinking under very tense conditions adds double force to a hangover."

But assume that you're relaxed, serene, and in the holiday spirit. There are some anti-hangover tips worth trying.

First, the experts suggest that you eat an hour or so before the party. Milk, cheese, lean meats—and if you can stand it, some swallows of olive oil—are recommended. The food will coat the stomach and slow the rate of alcohol absorption into the bloodstream. It can work wonders, the experts say. Avoid carbonated drinks before an evening out—they speed the rate of absorption considerably, and the first drinks may sneak up on you.

Try taking a one-hour nap, then a hot and cold shower, and while you're putting in the shirt studs drink 12 oz. of milk and chew a few antacid tablets, advises a Manhattan physician who specializes in treating executives over 40. The milk lines the stomach and the tablets buffer what's to come. *Caution:* Above all, avoid alcohol if you're under medication such as tranquilizers or antihistamines. The mix can hit hard and could be lethal.

Once at the party, you might try the obvious: Limit consumption. Apart from this advice, here are a few ideas for the evening:

Take a good half hour to consume your first drink. This gears your system for what's to come. Also, try to spread your drinks fairly evenly throughout the evening instead of bunching them fast and then "coasting," a popular habit at country club dances.

Two or three tall glasses of ice water during the evening help to keep up the body's "water balance" and thus lessen the possible hangover. Obviously, highballs (best with plain water) serve the same purpose.

There's no proof that mixing drinks will compound a hangover. "But," says one old pro, "sweet cocktails, then a shift to plain whiskey, followed by a champagne breakfast will murder some of my patients this New Year's."

Note: Smoking all evening will likely sharpen a hangover.

Cures for the morning after could fill a book. Here are a few recommended ones:

■ Aspirin (two every four hours) is particularly good if taken with a bit of bicarb to cut the acid effect. Antacid tablets at this stage are optional. It may be too late for them to do much good, according to the experts.

■ Beef bouillon restores lost potassium and helps overcome fatigue.

■ Sucrose taken in the form of orange or cranberry juice replaces lost glycogen, relieves sweating and dizziness.

■ Vitamin B (a hefty dose taken orally) helps ease jangled nerves; some specialists suggest a mild tranquilizer (for example, Compazine).

A morning-after remedy containing alcohol may work wonders—though it only postpones the hour of judgment. "But it's a sure-fire method if you're committed to another party on New Year's Day," says Cornell specialist Dr. Frank Seixas. The best eye-opener drink is milk punch. Use 1½ oz. bourbon, 1 tsp. fine granulated sugar, and 6 oz. milk; shake with ice and strain.

Travelers: to your good health

Planning a global swing? À votre santé. But to keep healthy, be cautious. Montezuma's revenge can curse you even in spick-and-span Scotland and Switzerland; you can even get sick in London (ever try an Indian curry in Soho?). So, for a painless journey, here's the latest on travel health:

First: Get your shots. Smallpox (single shot) is now the only one required; you can't get back into the U.S. without it. But tetanus (three injections) and polio (two oral doses, initially) are strongly recommended. Tetanus, especially, makes sense in view of the surge in auto accidents (ever try driving in Rome?). As for polio: There's no evidence that people over 40 are immune—despite the rumor.

Guarding against typhoid (three shots) and infectious hepatitis (one) is smart if you'll be where the water is questionable. That can mean from Hong Kong (scrub your teeth at the tap and you may be out for a week) to a village cafe on the road to Cannes. To be on the safe side, add yellow fever, typhus, cholera, if you're going to remote areas of Asia, Latin America, or Africa.

Timing: Two visits to a doctor, spread over three weeks, will get you just about every shot on the list and take you safely from Calcutta to Panama City and back. For a European swing, figure on one fast visit.

The more time allowed for a series of shots, the better, because you avoid the possibility of "cross" reactions and sometimes dire side effects. If you're in a hurry, arrange to finish your shots overseas. Listings of recommended physicians abroad are available, and should be carried in any case. Intermedic publishes an up-to-date directory of qualified, English-speaking doctors (777 Third Avenue, New York, N.Y. 10017).

If you travel a lot—and to remote locales—a compact medical kit stored in your gear makes good sense. The latest recommendations:

- Paregoric or Kaopectate for mild diarrhea. If this, plus a bland diet, doesn't fix you in three or four days, you'll need to see an MD.

- An oral antibiotic, like Tetracycline, plus a strong antiseptic ointment, like Mycitracin (both prescription). Drugs like these often are hard to get overseas when you need them. *Note:* Be cautious in buying unfamiliar drugs abroad; many potent, dangerous ones are available over the counter.

- Water purification tablets (Halazone, Abbott, Globaline, Maltbie). Take along an immersion heater for fast boiling of water or coffee if you'll be in really remote areas. Or better yet drink only bottled beer, wine, water (no ice).

■ Motion sickness pills (Marezine, Bonine, Dramamine) for somebody in the family who's especially sensitive. You might also need antihistamines, for colds and for anyone prone to earache or deafness due to flying.

Rule of thumb: Since you'll be confronting a lot of exotic bugs, call a doctor if a fever lasts more than 24 hours. Consult your MD list, or the nearest U.S. embassy or consulate.

If you have any chronic condition—heart, diabetes, and so on —get a Medical Passport for your physician to fill out, detailing your history and treatment (M. P. Foundation, 35 E. 69th Street, New York, N.Y. 10021).

In recent years, more books have been written about the psychology of the businessman than about his techniques of management in a corporate organization. Here are some additional thoughts—on the organization man's psychological make-up.

Fatigue

When an executive hits those "middle years" strange things often begin to happen. He's up near the top of the management ladder; his children are through college and probably raising families of their own; he can still put enough belt into his golf swing to whip some of the youngsters at the country club.

Everything should look rosy. But then he starts feeling tired and listless. His energy begins to ebb too fast each day. Few businessmen in such a position are ready to admit publicly that they're constantly feeling fatigued. But many physicians maintain that fatigue is the No. 1 complaint among middle-aged businessmen.

There is a chance, of course, that tiredness and listlessness may stem from some physical problem. So, obviously, you need to see a doctor to make sure that it isn't caused by anemia, diabetes, or heart trouble. But, say doctors, at least 80% of middle-aged businessmen who complain of fatigue can pass a physical with nothing more serious than an admonition to lose 10 lb. or a suggestion to get new reading glasses.

Most often, the root of the problem is something that may surprise you: It lies in a deep-seated, unrecognized boredom. Typically, the "tired" executive is as far up as he's going in his company or industry. Much of the old challenge is gone. He's working as hard as ever, maybe harder, but he gets a lot less stimulation from his job. The thought of eventual retirement becomes lodged firmly in the back of his mind about this time. That adds to frustration. Inevitably, he begins to slow down a bit physically.

At home, with the children gone, his own marriage often lags in stimulation. His social life has taken on a dull sameness. These are the things that add up to middle-age "executive fatigue"—the physicians' euphemism for boredom.

The problem, then, is what to do about it. Doctors recognize that the solutions they offer to the busy but frustrated executive who comes to them seeking diagnosis and relief from his fatigue all too often sound like a Boy Scout lecture.

"Get a strong hobby interest and get regular daily exercise" are often the nub of the prescription. The businessman will usually snort and say he is much too involved with his work to do that. But, say physicians, following such advice is about the only way to beat the boredom that's at the root of all the trouble. And enough doctors have seen enough good results among executives who have followed that prescription to be sure that there is value in the standard remedies.

But there's more to this line of advice: Take more vacation time, change your pace at the office, do more business traveling, find a new outlet for creative energy. High on the list also is: Don't take your work home, but—if you feel you must—then make it a minimum amount. This, say doctors, definitely will increase your efficiency in the office—especially if you are a top executive who shouldn't be worrying about routine details, anyway.

Getting enough sleep—and getting it without the aid of sleeping pills—is also most important. Fitful or insufficient sleep only adds to boredom and fatigue. At age 50 you probably need eight hours of sleep a day—and certainly no less than seven hours. You can't safely get by with five or six hours on week nights and then try to make it up by sleeping more on Sundays. It nothing else, your efficiency will be impaired.

You have to learn to set aside worries and stresses before you retire. It isn't always easy. Try a bottle of beer followed by a warm (not hot) shower at bedtime. Or unwind by taking an easy 15-minute walk outdoors.

Occasionally "executive fatigue" signals a serious emotional problem that requires some type of psychiatric care. In such cases a person will usually show additional symptoms: irritability, restlessness, too heavy drinking—and in the executive, anxiety about facing the job and a seeming inability to make decisions. Here an emotional check-up is needed.

Tensions

Stress, pressure, and tension are part and parcel of the business executive's job—the price he pays for the involvement and responsibilities of executive life. But they're not necessarily harmful. Indeed, the man of action thrives on them, finds them stimulating. Simply holding a responsible position indicates that you can stand more stresses than the average man and probably that you work best when "tensed."

Both psychiatrists and internists emphasize that stress and tension are a normal part of life. Only the dullard is free of them. And, of course, what is a tension-producing, stressful situation to one person will be almost routine to another.

It boils down to the individual's own tolerance for tension. A man working below his tension tolerance point won't realize his potential or know the satisfaction of full achievement. If he goes too far beyond it, he feels irritable, unhappy, "under pressure."

The point is that tensions that strain a man's tolerance for them are harmful only if they continue without let-up. Even excessive tension won't hurt, so long as it's of short duration (what's short varies with the individual—and the state of his health). However, many executives—keyed up to the daily demands of their jobs—don't realize they have been pushing their tolerance point too hard. There's no specific test for tension, obviously. But certain symptoms are frequently identified with too much of it. One of the first is inability to get to sleep, waking early in the morning or throughout the night. Another telltale sign is fatigue—the kind you feel in the morning as well as at night.

Frequent headaches, indigestion, or tightness around the back of the neck and shoulders round out the symptoms of excessive, destructive tension. At this point, a medical examination is important to determine if an illness is at the root of the trouble. But in most people, these are purely symptoms of too much tension.

When you're tense, your blood pressure and pulse rise slightly, body temperature goes up, digestion slows, and muscles tighten. All this is normal, and provides that extra stamina and alertness needed to cope with a stressful situation.

But when the body can't return to normal because of persistent, continued stress and tension, the system is impaired. Blood pressure remains too high, muscles stay taut. The result will be changes in the body that can set the stage for heart disease, chronic high blood pressure, ulcers, asthma, arthritis. *Note:* Tension is never the sole cause of these disorders. There usually must be a basic weakness or predisposition.

Physical exercise and diversion are the best antidotes for tension buildup. Relaxing in an easy chair with a book or television is no sure way of releasing emotional tension. Rather, experts who have studied the problem in executives feel that sedentary living—which allows little physical release of tension—is one of the major culprits in a tense age.

They suggest an "anti-tension" routine for the desk-bound executive: regular 15-minute walks in the morning, evening, and at lunchtime; 10-minute work breaks every two hours during the day; a hobby or absorbing interest that involves some physical activity, and is totally different from your regular work routine.

Above all, don't look to tranquilizers—drugs or drinks—for relief of tension. Pills have their place and, indeed, are very useful for temporary periods of unusual stress, such as a death in the family. But the person who relies on them to see him through situations that are a regular part of his life—such as responsibilities of the job—is simply admitting that he can't cope.

Sex

How do you feel about the main currents of your life—career, family responsibilities, your marriage? Particularly, how do you feel about the role that sex plays in your life? For a man of, say, 45 to 55, clear-cut answers to these questions are often difficult. Says a leading New York specialist: "The trouble is, too many men push this type of inventory-taking out of their minds."

The executive in this middle age bracket—working under heavy business and domestic pressure—may begin to experience something new: He finds himself tired, listless, too hemmed in by responsibility. He feels run down, and sometimes he notices with alarm that his interest in sex has run down, too. This point he finds dreadfully hard to admit, even to himself. He may even put on blinders, and use pure physical fatigue as the excuse for his weaker sex drive. If he does this, he's kidding himself.

His prime problem is not physical, but emotional. An executive in this spot must take stock of more than his muscle tone and his waistline. First—and most important—there's the wearing thin under the burden of stepped-up emotional pressure. At the office he's likely geared up over everything from possible promotion to a possible merger of the company. Or he may face the rude realization that he has gone as far as he will go in business—and trying to accept this may twist and turn inside him.

On the home front he's pressured by a mix of problems ranging from his teenager's attitude about smoking pot to his frighteningly thin savings in relation to income. His round of social affairs is even getting to be a bore.

There's a second possible cause of his problem—the male climacteric which, to some degree, happens to every man. It usually occurs between 45 and 55, and is a biological-psychological process of aging. The climacteric in some men produces no symptoms at all, but in others it can produce emotions ranging from feelings of futility to dark depression. It may last a few weeks, or as long as a year or so; it varies greatly.

In any case, the danger is that the victim of all these heavy emotional strains and pressures may react quite childishly. Feeling depressed—and with a fear of losing libido—the victim may flirt with real trouble. In rashness he might decide on a quick divorce and remarriage to a woman who better "understands him." This may fail miserably.

Or an otherwise sensible man may put a deep dent in his business career by impulsive, even irrational fits of anger and conflict at the office. Or he may put himself under impossible added burdens, refusing, for instance, to delegate authority. Thus, in trying to prove his worth and shore his sagging confidence, he may push himself deeper into his own miseries.

How does a man win out in this battle of the middle years? If he's smart, he does it largely by learning to understand his own emotions. The first step is some thoughtful self-analysis. If the going gets too rough, the search for understanding needs the aid of a trained person—internist, psychiatrist, or psychologist. One session—or a few—may well do the job.

First, the middle-aged man should understand that a decline in sexual interests is commonplace—and temporary. But the more worry, the worse it gets. He will snap back—on a new but still satisfying level of sex activity—if he gives himself a fair chance. He must know, too, that he's far from alone. His friends in the same age group have similar woes and regrets—even if they won't admit it.

Divorce or a foolish job change aren't the only things to beware. A man shouldn't be fooled into thinking that drugs or health foods or vitamins will put him where he was sexually at age 40—they won't, doctors say. Also, he shouldn't play mathematics with sex. Once a week is about average at age 50.

Sleep

Are business problems keeping you awake nights? If so, you risk joining the one in four Americans now taking sedatives, according to a recent symposium at the University of California School of Medicine.

The best advice, say doctors, is to steer clear of sleeping pills except in such non-recurring situations as a long plane trip. If you are a chronic non-sleeper—and the label may fit if you have had trouble sleeping for more than a week—see a doctor. Your restlessness may have deep physical or psychological roots.

Barbiturates, the most potent sleep producers, and tranquilizers both require a doctor's prescription. Both can become addictive. So avoid prolonged use and increasing amounts—you may wind up with typical drug withdrawal symptoms if you stop. If your prescribed dosage no longer works, see your doctor —don't boost up the dosage on your own. *Caution:* Never mix barbiturates with alcohol. Both depress the central nervous system, and their combined effects can be fatal.

The milder over-the-counter sleeping pills usually contain antihistamines, not barbiturates, which produce drowsiness. They are not usually habit-forming. *Note:* Some people are sensitive to antihistamines, and get allergic side effects, such as rash or hives. Aspirin?—ask your doctor.

Alcoholism

Well over 6 million Americans are alcoholics, and some estimates go a lot higher. This is despite the best efforts of Alcoholics Anonymous. Still, specialists say with more assurance than ever that AA is by far the best hope for retrieving a man from alcoholism. Where many medical men were skeptical of AA's value a few years ago, most now applaud its work. "It's what gets results," says top Harvard psychiatrist Dr. Graham Blaine, Jr.

If you have doubts, the medics point to these figures from a survey: About 40% of those entering AA stop drinking right away; 25% more stop within a year; another 15% eventually manage to quit. Only 20% are hard-core cases who never "make" the AA program.

Not bad odds, say the physicians. So, if you have a close friend with a liquor problem, nudge him into AA if you can. *And note:* There is now a stronger tie between AA and psychiatry. Treatment is vital, say many specialists. But getting sober—the AA part—must come first.

Suppose your friend is in bad shape and you call AA. What happens? Within a few hours, maybe a day, two AA members will show up. One might be a shopkeeper and the other, say, the vice-president of a suburban bank. They'll want to talk to your friend privately (no relatives in the room), and they may call a doctor.

Or, if your friend will go, they may pack him off to a clinic for alcoholics for drying-out treatment that usually takes five days ($100 to $150). In the clinic, he'll get sedation plus contact with visiting AAs who will serve cold ginger ale and push the AA concept. If your friend is away from home—out of town or in a hotel—AA will see that he gets home, unless, of course, he needs hospitalization first.

The big point: If he wants help, AA will get him over the crisis.

Thus AA's long-range program starts as soon as a man is able to navigate. The philosophy boils down to this:

- An admission that with drinking, life has become unmanageable.
- A firm decision to ask for help.
- A self-analysis and practical plan to shape up honestly.
- An attempt to apply AA teachings daily and assist other alcoholics.

Your big mistake could be in pushing your friend. He must make the basic AA decision himself. Suggest it, maybe pointedly, but no more. If your friend wants AA's help, members will soon have him at local group meetings—maybe the same night, if he can make it.

AAs will even drive your friend to evening meetings in their cars. And if he shows a sustained interest, they'll keep it up— even if he has a "slip" and takes a drink. One thing the AAs won't do (and you shouldn't do) is nag him to get sober. It won't work, and may have a reverse effect.

At a typical meeting, 25 to 50 AAs will gather in a church hall, hear some talks, then have coffee and cake. The speakers will be candid. The idea, of course, is that your friend will soon "relate."

The activity builds, month by month. Your man can even join AA luncheon clubs in town, attend meetings in other cities, even abroad, if he travels on business, and work at regional AA offices. During this process, his dependence on alcohol ebbs away.

But one day, the steady coffee-and-cake routine ends. After several years of sobriety, it's now recognized, your friend should be able to lessen his AA participation. He can never drink socially. But he can participate in the normal span of social and career activities.

The growing tie between AA and psychiatry is now widely recognized; a mutual respect has developed. Says Dr. Ruth Fox of New York, a noted specialist on alcoholism: "About 50% of all AAs can make a healthy adjustment with AA alone—it's enough. Another 25% need limited therapy, and the rest need more." But keep in mind: AA itself is a form of group therapy.

Cigarettes

Tobacco isn't alcohol. But tobacco is deadly in its own right— despite the sex-and-smoke ads on TV. There is plenty of research to prove the deadly part. But the trouble with all the research is that while it dramatizes how dangerous the habit can be (at age 50, a pack-a-day man has almost five years cut from life expectancy), it doesn't tell you much about how to quit.

Still, there is some hard information on quitting—some of it solidly scientific, some of it simply inspirational. At the outset, keep in mind two main points—one of them obvious. You must sit down with yourself and make a strong, all-out decision to quit. Anything less is a waste of time.

Then—and this is largely new thinking—realize that how you go about quitting may depend on the type of smoker you are. Most smokers are people who simply seek positive enjoyment from the habit; they will have less trouble quitting than others, and should try tapering off.

But there are "hard-core" smokers, solidly addicted to smoking which they use as an emotional crutch. This group amounts to an estimated 25% to 35% of all smokers; they should quit cold.

You may be able to answer this for yourself, or may want to discuss it with your doctor. Generally—if you're like most smokers—you'll want to first try quitting on your own. One key is to find something else to do whenever you have the urge to light up. Take a lemon drop, a mint, or chew some gum. (But skip rich candy and other foods, or you may wind up with two bad habits instead of one.)

Anything you can do to interrupt the mind and motion pattern associated with lighting up—such as jotting down the time in a notebook—will be helpful. This point is being stressed.

What about drugs? Non-prescription products that contain lobeline (a nicotine substitute) often have little effect, according to some experts.

You can also try switching to cigars or pipes—and not inhale. This type of smoking appears to do little harm. Remember, though, that some of the new cigars are quite small and mild; you may find yourself inhaling.

The object of your exercise—assuming you're not the addictive type—should be to cut down gradually by smoking, say, 20% fewer cigarettes each week over a five-week period. There's no telling how difficult it will be. Many encounter severe withdrawal symptoms: hunger, dizziness, irritability, poor concentration. Don't feel you're exceptional if you try to stop and fail.

If you'd like to read up on a detailed withdrawal program, see Arthur Cain's *The Cigarette Habit—An Easy Cure* (Dolphin). This book, originally in hard cover, is available in some public libraries.

You may decide, after all, to rely on your doctor. If you're a difficult case, with health presently in danger, he may go so far as to suggest a withdrawal clinic (provided there's one in your area). To some people the clinic routine is surprisingly stimulating; others find it difficult. Clinics rely largely on group therapy and mutual assistance, much like Alcoholics Anonymous. Sessions last six to eight weeks.

But since experience with clinics has been mixed, it's more likely that your doctor will put you on a personal schedule. This might include such aids as tranquilizers, appetite-suppressing drugs, and possibly lobeline.

One of the most persuasive arguments for quitting that can confront a smoker is to be told that his habit will in the long run hurt his children. Evidence clearly shows that when parents smoke, their teen-aged children copy them. Apart from stopping yourself, you might point out to your youngster that the death rate per year among men who began smoking after age 25 is about 40% higher than for non-smokers. It is about 125% higher among men who first started smoking before age 15.

Psychiatry

Doing it on your own—facing daily life, that is—may become too much. An executive is foolish to push beyond a certain point without seeking help. Here's one rationale.

A top management man worth his salt will have first-hand knowledge of tension, pressure, and anxiety. The question is, how well does he handle the stress? If he's in his 40s or 50s, and finds that his job and social responsibilities—and his sex life— add up to too much frustration, he might be wise to consider psychiatry.

There are important new trends in psychotherapy:

■ Sex problems faced by middle-aged men are point one— and here there is new information, new understanding that wasn't available a few years ago.

■ Family therapy is coming into its own—and for the troubled

50-year-old executive a program that involves working with his wife, possibly his children, might well spell the difference.

■ Chemotherapy has advanced—for example, better non-addictive drugs are available for the treatment of such symptoms as emotional depression, chronic irritability, and insomnia.

The profile of a candidate for this type of checkup is pretty clear. He's usually about 45 to 55, ambitious, hard-driving—often the type who likes to be independent, doesn't want to seek help if he can avoid it. Typically, he faces this career dilemma: He must either push hard to reach the top—or force himself to face the fact that he isn't going to make it.

Specialists point out that signs of serious trouble appear when a man begins to feel he can't cope, when the zest is gone—and is replaced by nagging worry, unaccountable hostility toward others, depression, and maybe excessive drinking or eating.

The executive, especially, is apt to feel a strange sense of boredom, and an unexplained inability to make sure decisions. He'll tend to consider dramatic solutions—changing careers, changing wives, fleeing to the Caribbean. These may be a symptom, not a solution. In any case, the experts say: A man with brains enough—and courage enough—to recognize his own symptoms has half the battle won.

If a man takes stock, and decides to consult a psychiatrist, then what? First, he should dismiss the notion that it inevitably means years of treatment. This simply isn't true. The initial checkup session, in some cases, may be enough to spark the needed self-understanding—and do the job. This, though, is rare.

More likely, a series of consultations, lasting maybe three to six months (often twice a week), will be recommended by the doctor—though a psychiatrist won't be pinned down to a definition of the term of therapy.

In any case, if a man approaches his problem with an open mind, the time needed for helpful therapy can be far shorter than most people realize. Complete psychoanalysis—two years, or more—rarely will be required.

Open-mindedness is vital, of course—and this means partly a man's ability to speak out without reserve on such subjects as sex relations. What about the business of "slowing down" sexually, so much feared by this age group? The experts say it comes to this:

Many a man, starting usually in his middle or late 40s, begins to experience what he fears is a "natural" decline in sex drive and activity. The best opinion—based on new research—says that this isn't really inevitable. True, it's quite common. But it's more a mark of a general decline in physical health, brought on—not so much by age—but by too much sedentary living, overeating, too little relaxation and exercise.

The executive is especially prone to this cycle because he's at the highest-pitched point of his business life—at the very time when he should be taking better care of himself.

What about the trend toward "family therapy"? In many cases today, both a man and his wife, possibly his teen-agers, will be called in by the psychiatrist for group and separate consultations. In effect, it becomes a highly sophisticated form of marriage counseling. If the parents have problems, these will, of course, be reflected in the children. And they may need help without your knowing it.

Counseling

People who think little of marriage counseling are missing the point. Marriage counseling is more meaningful today than you may imagine.

More effective techniques are giving psychologists, clergymen, and others new skills in the art of counseling. If a middle-aged businessman, for instance, finds that stresses on the home front seem to be taking over, he might want to see a qualified man. He'll find no panacea. But he may get some surprising answers.

If you're the hard-driving executive type, it's possible that you may be a candidate for marriage counseling. "Don't be afraid of it," says Harvard psychologist Dr. George Goethals.

In considering this, note at the outset:

- Preventive medicine is how some leading specialists describe marriage counseling; it can dilute problems before they reach the critical stage.

- Pre-therapy can be another of its functions; counseling can safely screen out the occasional individual who needs psychotherapy.

- Family counseling will involve the problems of teen-agers, as well as the husband and wife; this can be important for many families.

The routine is simple. You go to the counselor—clergyman, social worker, psychologist, psychiatrist—either alone, at first, or with your wife. You talk out your problems. This unwinding, in itself, relieves built-up tensions and frustrations. You'll gain the objective view of the counselor, if nothing more.

Usually a series of sessions is needed. The average: weekly sessions running 45 minutes each for three to four months.

"Husband-wife grievances have a habit of simmering beneath the surface for years," says the head of a suburban New York counseling service. "Then something happens to add pressure— a child leaves home, a parent moves in, a business chance is lost. Counseling can avoid a blow-up."

In most cases the counselor's theme is simple: He tries to get the man and his wife talking—to pick up the lost thread of communication. "Or we help them find it for the first time," says the New York expert.

Problems taken to counselors range wide. Typical is the executive who has "come up the hard way" and can't tolerate his wife's free-spending attitudes and habits. Conversely, there's the man who can't live with his wife's frugality, which may stem from her feelings of insecurity. A skilled counselor will help a couple see their own motivations.

The career crisis that many middle-aged men meet is another cause of tension. A man of 45 to 55 will face a major career decision—and may have to accept the fact that his earlier aims were too ambitious. "Facing this adjustment," says a Westchester County psychiatrist, "can be hard on the husband and hard as hell on his wife and kids."

Obviously, many couples run into marital troubles over sex. For example, at age 45 to 50, say the experts, some executives who battle hard in business will lose a degree of interest in sex, while their wives may have an upswing of interest. "A man should realize that this low point for him is probably just temporary," says the Westchester adviser. Giving such reassurance is a big part of skilled counseling these days.

"The hardest part may be finding your man," says Dr. Morton Miller, director of projects at the National Institute of Mental Health. "You have to do some careful looking at credentials." Clergymen do counseling, but generally limit themselves to what one experienced cleric calls "ordinary domestic tensions." The psychologist with limited training may be fine, but only for basic counseling.

The best qualified counselors—at least, for possible long-term problems—are well-rated psychologists (many of them PhDs) and psychiatrists. It's a case of careful inquiry, starting with your clergyman, family doctor, local hospital, or a member of the Family Service Association of America.

Reading up: *Counseling in Marital Problems,* by Richard H. Klemer, is an excellent general review (Williams & Wilkins). Try your public library.

A sober problem: the nursing home

Are you faced with getting an elderly family member settled in a nursing home? In the past five years countless new homes have sprung up, and the trend has been to big, opulent establishments with everything to meet the eye—from color TV to displays of physiotherapy equipment.

But picking a home takes more than simply looking over the physical plant. "Sympathetic care is more important than the frills," says a Boston expert, "and today the frills build up the prices."

Overall cost at a quality nursing home can run from $6,000 to $12,000 a year. In major cities, it averages around $7,500. Medicare helps post-hospital cases only—and with strictly limited benefits.

Figure a private room at $125 to $200 a week, and two in a room at $100 to $150. Then come the extras. Doctor calls run $10 to $30 a month—but in many cases much more; if you're paying for weekly visits, you may have some double-checking to do. Drugs come high, too. Figure $40 to $50 a month; if the tab is much over $60, something may be amiss. Physiotherapy can run to $100 a month, and lab fees can go to $50.

Small silver lining: Two in a room is less lonely and best for most people.

To pick up some leads on possible homes, your best bet is to talk first with your own physician and then, if you find it's needed, with a specialist in geriatrics. But bear in mind that he may be owner or part-owner of a nursing home.

After you've got a list of four or five homes, check their formal status: A home should be fully licensed by the state, hold membership in the American Nursing Home Association and, ideally, be listed by the Joint Commission on Accreditation of Hospitals, a new group evaluating the homes.

A home should be approved by the federal Medicare office. But if the patient is to get Medicare payments he must be hospitalized for at least three days before going into a nursing home, and his condition must require skilled post-hospital nursing care. Medicare then pays such costs for up to 100 days.

But beyond these formalities, how do you judge the quality of a home? You must see it personally. "Going there is vital," says a Washington expert. "It's something you can't shirk."

Among the bench marks that will help you judge the nursing home: There should be a doctor on call and a registered nurse on hand 24 hours a day, a staff nurse for every six to eight patients in daytime and one for every 12 to 15 at night. Size up the type of people involved—search for compassion as well as efficiency.

A hospital-like 100-bed nursing home may have ample personnel, but a 20-bed home may offer more personalized care. You must be the judge. *Note:* Don't pick a home for its pleasant countryside locale; nurses may be in too short supply, and quality of care may suffer.

There should be a licensed physiotherapist, part-time at least, plus lamps, whirlpools, walkers, and other such equipment. But just getting a patient up on his feet may be the most important kind of therapy. Some homes make little effort to get their patients walking daily—they're easier to manage in bed. Sometimes drugs are used partly to keep patients docile; if tranquilizers are a steady routine, check with the doctor.

There should be supervised entertainment—games, art work —and patients should be encouraged to read newspapers as well as watch television. This can reduce the need for drugs, and greatly influence mental outlook among the elderly.

One clue to the attitude toward patients' activity: the dining routine. Anyone who is able to get there should eat in a dining room, even if they must be wheeled in two or three times a day.

Tax side: If a patient goes into a nursing home or home for the aged because of poor physical condition, and a principal reason for going there is the availability of medical care, then the entire cost is tax-deductible. But the rule is fuzzy; it comes down to the individual case.

Index